Walter Rye

A History of Norfolk

Walter Rye

A History of Norfolk

ISBN/EAN: 9783744778664

Printed in Europe, USA, Canada, Australia, Japan

Cover: Foto ©ninafisch / pixelio.de

More available books at **www.hansebooks.com**

POPULAR COUNTY HISTORIES.

A

HISTORY OF NORFOLK.

BY

WALTER RYE,

EDITOR OF 'THE NORFOLK ANTIQUARIAN MISCELLANY.'

LONDON:
ELLIOT STOCK, 62, PATERNOSTER ROW, E.C.
1887.

CONTENTS.

	PAGE
I. NORFOLK BEFORE THE NORMANS	1
I. THE ABORIGINES	1
II. THE EARLIER DANES	3
III. WHO BROUGHT IN THE TERMINATIONS 'INGHAM' AND 'INGTON'?	11
IV. THE ROMANS	14
V. THE SAXONS	18
VI. THE PIRATE DANES	19
II. THE NORMAN CONQUEST	23
I. THE CHIEF GRANTEES AND HOW THEY DIED OUT	23
II. EXISTING NORMAN NAMES	27
III. FICTITIOUS NORMAN PEDIGREES	28
III. RESULTS OF THE CONQUEST	33
I. CASTLE BUILDING	33
II. THE GROWTH OF THE MONASTERIES	37
III. THE OVERSTOCK OF CHURCHES	43
IV. PERSECUTIONS AND RISINGS	46
V. THE NORFOLK OF ELIZABETH	70
VI. NORFOLK'S PART IN THE 'EASTERN ASSOCIATION'	85
VII. OUR LATER HISTORY	94

Contents.

		PAGE
VIII.	THE OLD PEASANT LIFE	106
IX.	THE GENTLER LIFE	122
X.	THE TOWN LIFE	144
XI.	THE MONKS AND THE FRIARS	164
°XI.	THE PARSONS AND THEIR CHURCHES	180
XII.	THE TOWNS	205
XIII.	THE WATERING PLACES AND COAST LINE	242
XIV.	THE BROADS AND MARSHES	256
XV.	THE SUPERSTITIONS, FOLK-LORE AND DIALECT	287

A HISTORY OF NORFOLK.

I.

NORFOLK BEFORE THE NORMANS.

I.—THE ABORIGINES.

IN attempting to write truthfully of the earlier known history of Norfolk, little indeed can be said of the Aborigines. They are of course supposed to have come to England while it was yet a peninsula, and to have roamed about half-naked, subsisting on such animals as they could kill with flint-headed arrows and celts.

Whether they lived in hollows of the ground, such as Grimes Graves, the Weybourne Pits,* and the Shrieking Pits at Aylmerton, is very doubtful.† Canon Greenwell has demonstrated in 'Norf. Arch.,' vii., p. 359, that Grimes Graves, at all events, were only flint works; and, indeed, it can hardly be seriously

* For a paper on them by H. Harrod, see 'N. A.,' vol. iii., p. 232.
† For alleged Lake dwellings on Wretham Mere, see A. Newton's 'Zoology of Ancient Europe.'

argued that any race of men, however primitive, would deliberately huddle down in holes which would collect all the drainage, and be most inconvenient for cooking, and be literally death-traps if attacked by an enemy. Again, the difficulty which would be experienced by men who had flint instruments only, in felling timber sufficiently large to roof-in pits measuring forty feet across, would seem insuperable,* and the facts that no cemetery and no quantity of animal bones have been found in the neighbourhood are all against the idea.

Probably these people were called Iceni; at least we must trust Ptolemy for the assertion, but what line of demarcation, if any, there was between them and the Cenimagni of Suffolk no one can say.

Of the Druids, and whether they ever existed here or at all, we know as little. Possibly, some of the bunds, or banks, and trackways, faintly traceable here and there, were the works of these Iceni or 'Cenimagni;' but there is no proof whatever of this. All is really a blank. Of cromlechs, and suchlike, we have none: there are celts and hatchets, pottery and beads, and that is all.†

It has been conjectured that a few place-names, such as Lynn ('a lake'), and Brandon, and some rivernames, as Wensum and Yare, are aboriginal, and as far as regards the rivers this may be so; though why the Yare should come from the Celtic 'Garu'=

* The Rev. C. R. Manning argued the 'dwelling-place' theory in 'N. A.,' vol. vii., p. 169.

† The opening of the great barrow at Stow Heath, in 1808, produced many of these articles.

rough,* it would be hard to say. But the early spelling of Lynn was Lenn, a farm, no doubt the same as Løen in Denmark; and Brandon could not have come from 'don,' a hill, for there is not one near, but is more likely the Danish 'Branden,' a still existing village. Breydon water by Yarmouth, for the same reason, cannot come from 'don.'

II.—THE EARLIER DANES.

THE people of whose existence we have the first tangible and undoubted proof in our county are, to my mind, the Danes, whose first, and I think hitherto unsuspected, invasion, I hope to show was *before* that of the Romans, and not after those of the Romans and Saxons.

As I shall prove hereafter, there are—chiefly in the N.E. half of the county—256 places, either identical wholly (78) or in part (53) in name with villages still in Denmark, or provable to be Danish by their prefixes or affixes (125). How many more in the same district were also colonized by the Danes, it is now impossible to say; but it is clear that the colonization—whenever it took place—was in that part of the county almost an exclusive one. That it was anterior to the Romans seems to me clear, for we find the root syllables of

* It flows most placidly through a very level country. The 'don' in Breydon Water seems Celtic at first sight, but there is an entire absence of hill for miles, and I apprehend it is a corruption of the Danish 'Bredeholm,' a village name still occurring in Denmark. Similarly 'Wensum' may be the Danish Vensholm,' and the Bure be traced to the river which gives a name to the Danish Burfjord.

A Popular History of Norfolk.

Brancaster and Tasburgh represented to this day in Denmark ;* and it is absurd to suppose that this enormous and comprehensive invasion was the result of the intermittent rushes of the pirate Danes of the ninth and tenth centuries. As my proposed transference of epochs† is sure to meet with determined opposition, I must be excused if I go into the question of Danish settlements in Norfolk at considerable length.

The importance and extent of the Danish settlement—whenever it took place—may be judged from the fact that no less than six of the Hundreds, viz. Forehoe, Gallow, Holt, Humbleyard, Loddon, and Lopham, are identical in name with Danish villages ; while five more, North and South Greenhoe, Grimshoe, East and West Flegg, are obviously Danish also.

No less than seventy-eight places in Norfolk‡ are practically identical with existent Danish villages, viz.:

Aaker—Acre (2). Branden—Brandon parva.
Aldbjerg—Alburgh. Bregnedal—Bracondale.
Barmer—Barmer. Brunsted—Brunsted.
Bjergholm--Bircham tofts. Darum—Dereham.
Björncholm—Burnham. Delling—Dalling.§

° In the South we find the Danish village named Lunden amplified into the Roman Londinium, and Dovre into Dubræ. Examples of this might easily be multiplied, *e.g.*, Don into Doncaster.

† For correspondence on this subject, see *Athenæum* of Sept.—Oct., 1883.

‡ And yet the writer of Murray's 'Guide' wrote that 'it is remarkable that so few names of places in Norfolk and Suffolk can be assigned to a Danish origin' (!).

§ See also Field Dalling, of which the first part may be Fjeld. There is a Fjeld Dal in Norway.

Dybdale—Burnham
　Deepdale.
Eiersted—Irstead.
Felborg—Felbrigg.
Fœrhoi—Forehoe.
Fielby—Filby.
Galthoe—Gallow.
Gesing—Gissing.
Grœsholm—Gresham.
Grœnhœi—Greenhoe.
Hanning—Honing.*
Hassel fiord—Hassal
　Grove, near Fran-
　sham.
Hedeskov—Haddiscoe.
Helgehave—Helgay.
Helsinge—Elsing.
Holme—Holme Hale.
———— St. Benets.
———— Runcton.
———— next - the -
　　　　Sea.
Holt—Holt.
Horning—Horning.
Horse—Horsey.
Horsted—Horstead.
Humblegaard—Humble-
　yard.
Karhov—Carrow.
Kjelling—Kelling.
Kimmerlve—Kimberley.
Kirkeby—Kirby Cane.

Knappen—Knapton.
Knarreborg—Narburgh.
Kolby—Coleby.
Korrup—Corpusty.†
Krœmmer—Cromer.
Lodne—Loddon.
Laen—Lynn.‡
Lammess—Lammas.
Langholm—Langham.
Luddeholme—Ludham.
Lopholm—Lopham.
Lyng—Lyng.
Marslund—Marshland.
Miels—Meals by Burn-
　ham.
Morten—Merton (?).
Nyland—Nayland.
Orested—Worstead (?).
Polleholm—Pulham.
Risinge—Castle Rising.
Ryborg—Ryburgh.
Sahlhuus—Salhouse.
　　„　　—Salthouse.
Sal—Sall.
Saxtorp—Saxthorp.
Skjernenge—Scarning.
Snorren—Snorring (?).
Soested—Sustead.
Söholm—Saham (?).
Strœden Strelev—Strat-
　ton Strawless.§
Tidsel—Tivetshall.‖

° Originally spelt Haning.
† Pronounced ' Kurrup-stie.'
‡ Originally ' Len.'
§ It is very noteworthy that this place was called Stratton *Streles* in 56 Henry III.—see my Calendar to Norfolk Fines, p. 111.
‖ Pronounced ' Titsel.'

Toft—Toft Monks.
—— Trees.
—— West.
Thorp—Thorp.
—— Abbots.
—— parva.

Thorp—Market.
—— by Haddiscoe.
Vestervik—Westwick.
Vindeholm—Windham.

Among these occur such hard jobs for etymologists as Acre,* Lammas, Corpusty, Sall, Snoring, Cromer, Carrow, Haddiscoe, Humbleyard, and Stratton Strawless, but the difficulty is cleared away at once when we see their prototypes still in Denmark.

The occurrence in pairs or groups† of these reproduced names is very noticeable, *e.g.*:

Lynge and Elsing.
Corpusty and Saxthorpe.
Dereham and Scarning.
Wymondham and Kimberley.
Honing and Brunstead.
Pulham and Tivetshall ['Titsel'].

Lynge and Helsinge.
Korrup [stre] and Saxtorp.
Darum and Skjerninge.
Vindeholm and Kimmerlev.
Hanning and Brunsted.
Polleholm and Tidsel.

Round Norwich (itself with a Danish affix) we get Kes*wick*, Post*wick*, West*wick* ward, Guist*wick*, Cowholm‡ (the site of the Cathedral), *Thorpe*,§ Pock*thorp*, *Bracondale* [Bregnedale] and *Carrow* [Karhou].||

---

* Of course no village could ever have been called after any one acre of land.

† I do not mean that the two Danish villages are necessarily close to one another, but that there are two of the same names as the English pair.

‡ Probably the Danish Karholm, as also Carrow = Karhou.

§ There was a Tol*thorp* Manor in Norwich.

|| May not Ber Street simply have been the Danish Bjerg, and Tombland from Tömmer?

Again, the acceptance of the theory of 'transplantation' of place-names frees us from the absurdity of many of our so-called derivations. We need no longer believe that Scarning was a 'dirty village,' or Dereham so called from its deer, that Burnham Deepdale was so called from a non-existent dale, that Felbrigg was a bridge where there was no water, or that Pulham was a village of wells, or that Ling-wood meant a wood of ling.

Take Braconash. If Bracon = bracken, as we are told it is in Bracondale, this should mean 'Fern-ash,' which is absurd; and, as if to make it clearer, we find a 'Bregnedal' in Denmark, which is of course our present Bracondale, which, as Munford admits, has no dale near it.

Grant that place-names were transplanted in ages ago as they are now-a-days, we may easily understand that the original Danish village may well have been in a dale, while the Norfolk one that took its name from it is on a hill.

Besides these absolute identities, we find there are fifty-three names of places the first and characteristic parts of which are identical with those of Danish villages, viz. :

Barmer—Barford.
  ,,   Barwick.
  ,,   Barney.*
Brakken—Braconash.
Blixtorp—Blickling.

Brandse—Brancaster.
Breining—Briningham.
Braendesgaard—Brandeston.
Ermelund—Irmingland.

° It is noteworthy that these three and Barmer all lie altogether. The old derivation of Barford from 'barley ford' is too absurd to be seriously considered.

Gasse—Gasthorp.
Gimming—Gimmingham.
Hardenberg — Hardingham.
Hassing—Hassingham.
Havre—Haverland.
Helling—Hellington.
Herringe—Herringby.
Hevring—Heveringland.
Holk—Holkham.
Horn—Horningtoft.
Hors—Horsford.
  „ Horsham.
  „ Horstead.
Hun—Hunworth.
Hyllynge—Hillington.
Hove—Hoveton.
Jelling—Illington.
Kaal—Calthorpe.
Kat—Catfield.
  „ Catton.
Kjettinge — Ketteringham.

Klippede—Clippesby.
Koldkjar—Colkirk.
Kong—Congham.
Kringel—Cringleford.
Randers—Randworth.
Ravning—Raveningham.
Ridemanas—Ridlington.
Ringe—Ringland.
  „ Ringstead.
Rolles—Rollesby.
Rude—Rudham.
Sax—Saxlingham.
  „ Saxthorpe.
Skotte—Scottow.
Strade—Stradsett.
Tase—Tasburgh.
Thiele—Thelveton.
Tjele—Tilney.
Tude—Tuddenham.
Tuns—Tunstead.
  „ Tunstall.
Vare—Wareham.
Velling—Wellingham.

It is noticeable that several of these names, as Gas*thorpe*, Herring*by*, Horning*toft*, Ingoldes*thorpe*, Cal*thorpe*, Clippes*by*, Rolles*by*, Sax*thorpe*, Scotto*w*, and Strad*sett*, bear undoubted Danish affixes.

Now, if we look at the map opposite, we shall see that the great bulk of these identities with Danish villages lie in the north and north-east of the county within a quasi-triangle of which the sea-coast is practically the hypothenuse; a line drawn from the sea at Yarmouth to Harleston is the base, and another thence to Hunstanton the perpendicular. The triangle, though only one-half of the whole county contains a vast majority of the examples.

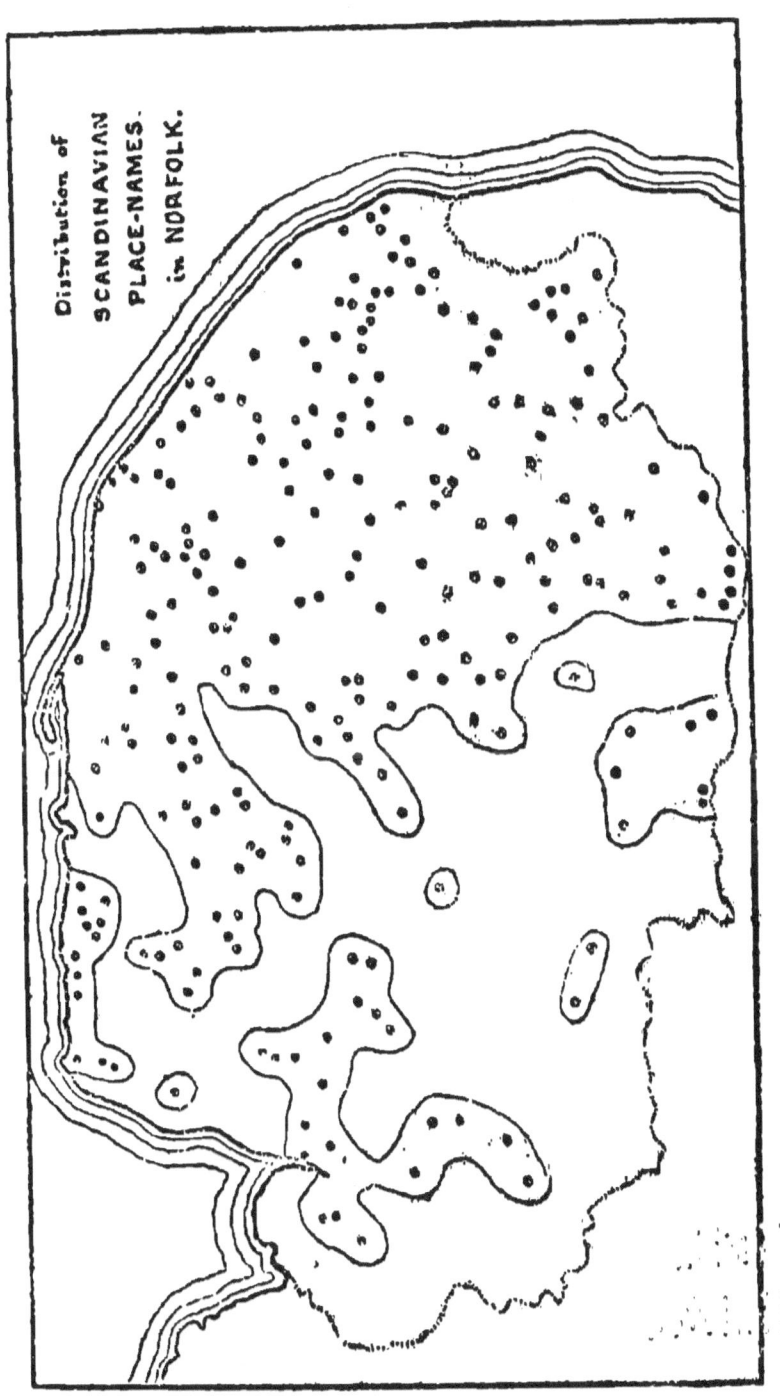

Norfolk before the Normans. 9

A very singular thing occurs here: the Hundreds of East and West Flegg have always been assumed to have been exclusively Danish from their own names, and from their almost invariable termination 'by;' but I cannot find that one of the place-names in it, or the adjoining Hundred of Plumstead (a tract of about 600 square miles), is identical with any place in Denmark. This would seem to point that this district was colonized by another Scandinavian race, possibly Swedes or Norwegians.

The only parts of the county absolutely free from Danish, or indeed any Scandinavian names, are (*a*) a strip of country stretching from the coast north of Lynn for about 20 miles, and extending nearly to Dereham ; and (*b*) a long and wide strip extending from Southery and Thetford up towards the northeast of the county. This is easily to be accounted for from the fact that these districts are, and always were, the most sterile in the county.

Besides the obviously Scandinavian* names mentioned in the foregoing tables there are the following, which may be fairly assumed to be so from their affixes :

° The absolute identities between the Scandinavian place-names in Norfolk and Lincoln, showing the common origin of their settlers, is very interesting. I fancy that few Norfolk men know that there are places named Thetford, Wymondham, Whitwell, Roughton, Reepham, Walcot, Ashby, etc., in Lincoln, while some variorum readings may help us to better understand some other Norfolk places, *e.g.*, Welbourn, Elsham, Scotter, Roxholme, Dunholme, Swayfield and Martin. Potter Hanworth, too, may be compared with our Potter Heigham.

By* - - - - 17
Oe and Hoe - - - 8
Toft - - - - 4
Thorp† - - - 32
Wick - - - - 13
Thwaite - - - 3
Holme - - - 4
Strand - - - 2
Sett - - - - 6
Other obviously Danish names,
   e.g., Sco Ruston, Thur-
   garton, etc. - - <u>36</u>
                                   125

If we add to these the 78 identities, and the 53 places whose first syllables coincide with those of Danish villages, we get a total of 256 places, which we may fairly assume to have been Danish settlements, out of our 740 Norfolk parishes.

How many more originally had Danish terminations such as 'holm,' but which have been corrupted into 'ham,'‡ it is hard to say; but as our maps show us

* These figures only represent the 'bys,' etc., not heretofore noted specially. For 'a fairly complete list see ' Norfolk Antiq. Misc.,' vol. i., p. 186. Subsequent search has furnished me with many other instances of places in Norfolk bearing Scandinavian terminations, but as they are not parish names and would be useless for the purpose of comparative analysis, I do not set them out here.

† Besides those places now bearing the affix, there were formerly many others : *e.g.*, Foston was Fos*thorpe;* Cley was Cly*thorpe;* Wretham was Wretham*thorpe;* and no doubt there were many others (*e.g.*, Applethorp in Mitford Hundred, mentioned in Domesday) which are now lost, especially on the coast. Gronen*howe*, we know, was washed away.—' East Anglian,' vol. iii., p. 270.

‡ *E.g.*, Martham and Runham, which were once Martholm and

that the vast proportion of those names were north of a line drawn between Lynn and Bungay, it may be said that the whole of the county, except the Downham, Swaffham, and Thetford districts, was nearly exclusively Danish.

III.—WHO BROUGHT IN THE TERMINATIONS 'INGHAM' AND 'INGTON'?

ON closely scrutinizing the map of Norfolk, the distribution of these place-names seems to me so peculiar as to be worthy of some special notice and of a map.

Kemble, in his 'Appendix,' gives a long list of places in England bearing these terminations, which he believes to have been named after ancient Saxon 'marks,' and indeed assumes, from the existence of such place-names, the existence of tribal families, whose names he supposes ended in 'ingas.' His theory, in short, is that Æslington means the town of the Æslingas, and so on; and because he finds names like Æslingas in Kent, Æscingas in Surrey, and Anningas in Northampton, occurring in Saxon charters, concludes that such names were necessarily Saxon—the possibility of an earlier invasion by any other race of men having escaped him.

After careful consideration, I have come to the conclusion that place-names like Hannington, Gimmingham, Briningham, and so on, were simply intended to mean 'the town or village of the settlers

---

Runholm. Wroxham was no doubt the same as the Roxholme of Lincoln.

from Hanning, Gimming, or Brining'—places beyond the sea.*

In our county (see p. 7), we find that the first two syllables of Briningham, Gimmingham, Hardingham, Hassingham, Hellington, Herringby, Hillington, Herringland, Raveningham, Ketteringham, and Wellingham, are neither more nor less than the names of existing Danish villages. Is there any pretence to say that they are also family names deducible from any known personal name-root? Is it not reasonable to suppose that their termination 'ing' originally had its natural meaning of meadow, and not its fanciful one of 'a-family-derived-from,' given it by the believers in the mark theory.

We must really give our ancestors credit for not being absolute fools. The absurdity of the old school of etymologists in making (x)ingham mean (x)-marshy-meadow-town, is of course now exploded; but I venture to think the 'mark' theory is often as wrong. In the parallel cases of (y)ham-ton, the absurdity of making the word mean (y)-village-town, was too gross and was never put forward; but really there is little difference between the two.

The way in which the 'inghams' and 'ingtons' are distributed over this county is very peculiar, and will be best understood by a reference to the map opposite this page. It will be seen that they

* On the other hand, I will not commit myself to the theory that these 'inghams' and 'ingtons' are necessarily Danish. I do not find them in Danish maps, though there are plenty of 'inglunds,' 'inggaardes,' and so on.

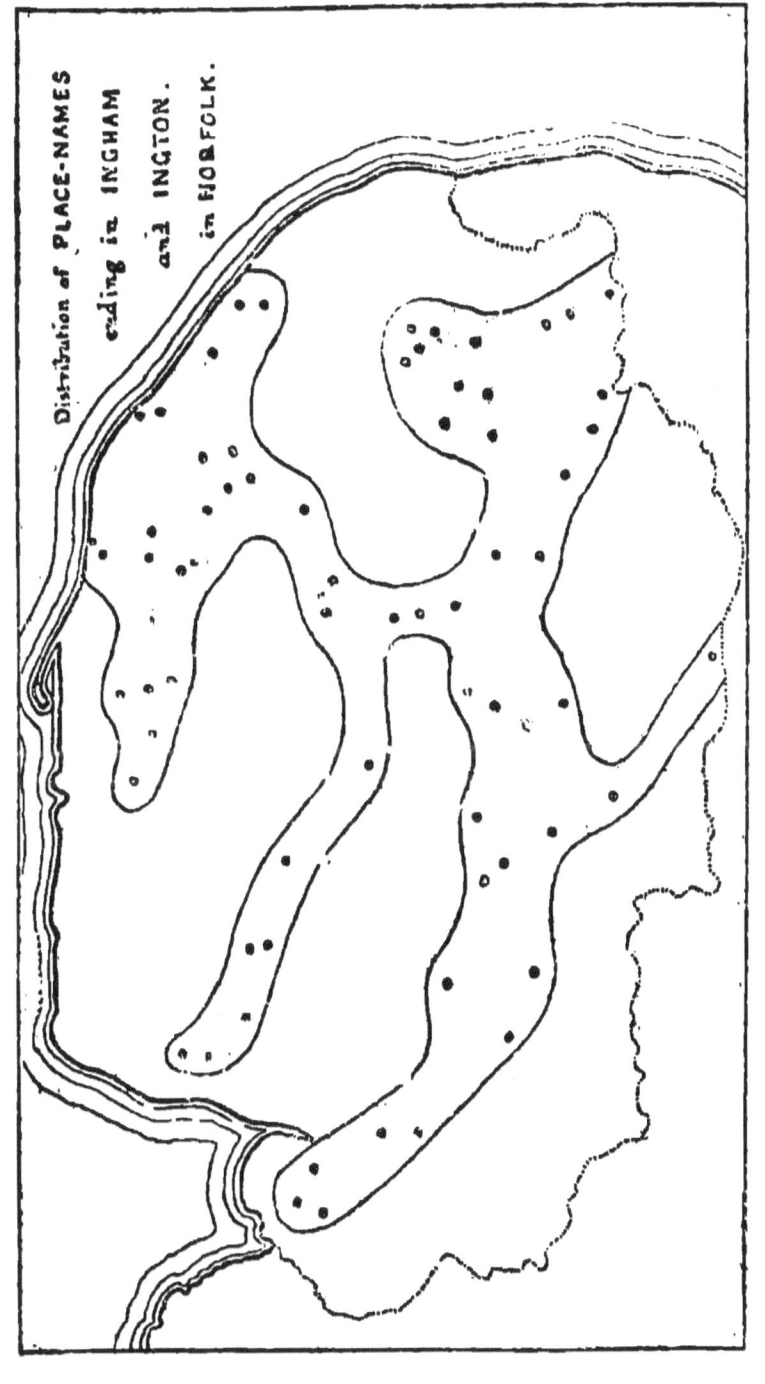

always occur within a few miles of one another, and that there are five great tracts of country which have not one example. Whether these place-names mark the invasion of a race of people who landed at the south-east by Lowestoft, and pushed upwards, chiefly to the fertile land of Holt and North Erpingham, but which also sent out two long feeling expeditions, ending in the one case at Terrington, and in the other at Sandringham, I will not guess. The way in which, as it were, a single file of these names stretches for fifty miles across the country, from Hevingham to Sandringham, is, to say the least, suggestive of such a theory.

Something may be learnt by comparing the relative proportion* of these 'inghams' and 'ingtons' with the well-known Danish endings of 'by,' 'fleet,' 'toft,' etc., in two groups of adjoining counties.

Four North Coast Counties.

	'inghams' and 'ingtons.'	'bys,' etc.
Northumberland	18	23
Durham	8	30
York	47	181
Lincoln	48	198
	121	432 [1 : 3]

* I here use the figures given by Mr. W. R. Browne in his valuable paper on 'The Distribution of English Place Names' (Philological Society), which are near enough, and are the more valuable from not being specially compiled for this purpose, and as more likely to be relatively right.

Five East and South Coast Counties.

	'inghams' and 'ingtons.'	'bys,' etc.
Norfolk	55	56
Suffolk	20	23
Essex	7	9
Kent	16	14
Sussex	16	10
	114	112 [1 : 1]

This result is a very peculiar one. On a coast-line divided nearly equally by the two batches of counties, a people who chose to call some villages 'ingham' and 'ington' settled all along the coast from Northumberland to Sussex, very evenly in proportion to the areas of such counties; but another race, which settled more than thrice as densely in the four northern, barely held their own in the five southern counties. The extraordinary sub-differences of ratios between Lincoln and Norfolk, and Norfolk and Suffolk, are puzzles quite beyond my power to solve.

IV.—THE ROMANS.

WHEN we come to the ROMANS we get to undisputed ground. There is no room for speculation when standing under the walls of Caister by Norwich, and admiring their grand solidity, and the vast area they enclose. This Caister is, however, the only station in Norfolk which has anything to show above ground; for the other Caister by Yarmouth is practically gone.

Norfolk before the Normans.

Perhaps the most striking piece of Roman road is that which enters the county at Scole, where Roman remains have been found.* It then runs straight up by Dickle*burgh*, while a little farther on we have Al*burgh* lying a few miles off to the right. Farther up the road is Long *Stratton*—the town on the 'street'—where Roman urns have also been found; and we soon reach the important station of Tas*burgh* ('Ad Taum')—enclosing twenty-four acres —of which some remains are still visible. Next comes the splendid still-existing walled station of *Caister*, enclosing thirty-five acres, and said to be the largest in England; but whether this or Norwich,† a few miles on, was the Venta Icenorum, who shall decide?

Up the Waveney from Lowestoft there are traces of Roman occupation, for past Beccles remains have been found at Geldeston, near which is also a place called Dun*bury* Hill. From Bungay there seems to have been a second road to Norwich, for urns and coins have been found at Ditchingham and Hedenham, and on the road stands *Burgh* Apton.

From Yarmouth—guarded on the south by the splendid still-existing station at Burgh in Suffolk, from the north by *Caister*‡ (one or other of them being *Garianonum*)—we can trace marks of Roman

---

* Roman remains have been found also at Diss, hard by.

† Polydore Vergil (for what he is worth) talks of Cambridge being founded on a White Hill under the auspices of a King Gurgunt. Had he floating about in his mind ' Caer Gwent' and Blanchefleur of Norwich?

‡ Many Roman coins were found in a field here called East Bloody Burgh Furlong.

occupation, stretching in a directly straight line across country to Weybourne, pottery and coins having been found at *Burgh* St. Mary, Potter Heigham, Small*burgh* (near which is the Devil's Ditch, reputed to be a Roman camp or look-out), Felmingham, Al*borough*, and Baconsthorpe, where a very large find (seven or eight stone weight !) of coins was made in 1878.

Whether the straight road out of Norwich through St. Faith's was a Roman road leading to the coast by Cromer, I cannot say; but the names of *Stratton* occurring at Stratton Strawless,* and of *Burgh* by Aylsham, are suggestive, the more especially as Al*borough** lies due north of them.

I should hardly doubt that the coast road from Happis*burgh* to Bran*caster* (Branodunum), where there is still a camp, was at all events used by the Romans; for not only have Roman remains been found at Weybourne, but I find Incle*borough* Hill, Wal*bury* Hill, Gran*borough* Hill, and War*borough* Hill on its line, and the so-called Danish camp at Burnham may after all be Roman. It is said, on what authority I don't know, that this coast road was called the 'Jews' Way.' Another 'Jews' Way' leads from Burgh Castle, near Yarmouth.

That the Romans had a place of observation somewhere at the corner by Hunstanton seems most probable, as it is hardly likely they would omit to have

° It will be noticed that I mention Alborough, Stratton Strawless, and Ryburgh, as *possibly* Roman, though I have pointed out in Section II. of this chapter that their names are identical with Danish place-names. It is best to be honest and to point out both possibilities.

one on such an unrivalled position. Moreover, the so-called 'Peddars' Way,'* which runs straight as a line from the important station at *Castle Acre*, would, if produced, exactly hit the best situation on the coast for such a look-out.

On the west coast south of Hunstanton we find the great camp at *Castle Rising*, commanding the low-lying land near Lynn, while on the south side of Lynn we have the Roman Bank running south from Sutton Bridge, with Roman remains at Walton, another 'Ingle*borough*' hard by it, and another Ox*burgh* just below Wisbeach.

South of Castle Acre we find Nar*burgh*, Hil*borough*, Ox*burgh*, and Ig*borough* (both of the last two have been thought to be the Icianos of Antoninus), all north of Thetford† (Sitomagus).

From Thetford there was no doubt another Roman way to Norwich, for we have traces of them at Buckenham and Attle*borough*.

Other detached Roman settlements were at *Cas*ton, Whin*burgh*, Matteshall *Burgh*, Ry*burgh*, and *North Elmham*.

Sepulchral urns, coins, and such like have been found in plenty, but no villas or buildings of any importance, and I think not even one tesselated pavement. The urns, etc., found in the Roman cemetery at Brampton were described by Sir Thomas Browne in his 'Hydriotaphia, or Urn Burial.'

* I can't stand the idea that this way was simply to lead to an unimportant chapel like St. Edmund's at Hunstanton.
† Can the 'Brandon' hard by be another 'Branodunum'?

It is possible that in our existing surnames Tuck and Tucker, Dack and Lack, we have traces of the Roman personal names Tuccius, Daccius and Laccius.

V.—THE SAXONS.

IT is very improbable that the coming of the Saxons was the simultaneous preconcerted inroad, under Hengist and Horsa, described by the early history books. The eastern part of England was too handy to the mainland not to tempt its occupants over from early times. Anyhow, even in the third century the east coast was, either from its being settled by Saxons or by its being peculiarly subject to their inroads, known as the 'Saxon Shore,' for the Roman representative here was called the 'Comes Littoris Saxonici.' The greater invasions no doubt took place in or about 449, and in less than a century the Angles, the Jutes, and the Saxons, who in popular parlance have been jumbled together and called 'Saxons,' or 'Anglo-Saxons,' had gained as much of England as they ever gained. That they gained much of Norfolk seems to me extremely doubtful.

Nor is there much that is reliable in their so-called early history in the east of England. Sigebert is said to have founded Bury St. Edmund's Abbey, and to have retired to it in 644; and the kingdom of East Anglia is said to have been added in 792 by Offa to his kingdom of Mercia.

But really until a comparatively late date there is nothing in the history of East Anglia but a string of bare names, which may or may not have been evolved from the inner consciousness of early monkish writers.

In 867 we are told that Hinguar and Hubba, the sons of Lothbroch, came over with a vast army to revenge the death of their father, who is said to have been murdered at Reedham. King Edmund himself was no doubt martyred; but the whole story, from the shipwreck of Lothbroch to the talking, though severed, head of Edmund, is so interwoven with fiction that it is very hard to know what to believe.

Of tangible traces of the Saxons in Norfolk we have few. There are some coins from the Thetford mint, and there are some churches which still show the architecture which has been arbitrarily called 'Saxon,' and that is all. The well-known font at Burnham Deepdale, the massy towers of Tasburgh and South Lopham churches, and the arch on the south side of St. Julian, Norwich, are all said by the Rev. R. Hart, in his very admirable lecture on 'Norfolk Antiquities,' to be examples of Saxon work, and to those may be added the repaired ruin at Runcton.

At South Creak there is a large camp, said to be Saxon, and the way that goes from it was called 'Blood Gate.'

VI.—THE PIRATE DANES.

THE second, or what we may term the PIRATE DANES, came over about 867 under Hinguar and Hubba, and soon became masters of Norfolk, pushing out once more the 'Saxons' from their never strong hold in the county. Stronger proof could hardly be offered of an earlier Danish settlement than that the names of one of those who fought here *against* the recent or pirate Danes were Ulfkettle Snelling— both essentially Danish names.

That the very large proportion of Danish place-names in Norfolk can possibly be accounted for by the intermittent raids of the 9th and 10th centuries seems to me absurd. If the similar raids in France and Normandy have left next to no trace on their maps, why should the invasions on our east coast have left such strong evidences? However, the Danes, whether early or late, left strong enough traces of their occupation in the names of the people, and the old law of the district for the 'Denalagu,' or Danelaw, ran east as well as north of the Watling Street, and the bulk of such of our Norfolk names as we can trace to have been borne at an early date, are Danish. A few will suffice :

Agard.	Craimer.	Harrold.	Nelson.
Abel.	Fisker.	Holm.	Rump.
Algar.	Frey.	Hubbersty.	Skalders.
Bacon.	Frost.	Jermiin.	Skyles.
Bagge.	Garnaes.	Johnson.	Skoyles.
Balle.	Gierling.	Kabell.	Thorold.
Barrett.	Grimbold.	Kemp.	Thurgar.
Balding.	Grimmer.	Knowt.	Thurling.
Baldry.	Hacon.	Marshall.	Thurkettle.
Bennett.	Hagen.	Martin.	Thurtle.
Bugg.	Hammond.	Nekar.	Watling.

It would have been strange if, after the two invasions of the Danes, we had not found strong traces of them in Domesday Book. There are 10,097 'freemen' ('liberi homines') mentioned in it, of whom 4,277 were in Norfolk, 5,344 in Suffolk, 314 in Essex, and only 162 in all the rest of England! In counties known to be colonized by the Saxons we find a preponderance of 'servi' and 'villani'; but here it is obvious the majority of the landowners were small independent freeholders, and there can be little doubt they owed their independence to the fact that they—the North folk and the South folk—occupied nearly all the two counties they had recently re-conquered, and, being a warlike race only just settling down from conquest, were wisely let alone by William and his advisers.

A reference to the admirable shaded Domesday maps of England in Seebohm's early English Community will show very strongly that the Danish counties of Lincolnshire, Norfolk, and Suffolk have far and away the *largest* proportion of 'socmanni' and 'liberi homines,' and the *smallest* proportion of 'servi' in England. Indeed there were *no* 'servi' in

* Though somewhat travelling beyond my province, I may be allowed to suggest that immense light would be thrown on the origin of many of our English surnames if the list of Danish place-names were carefully examined. A very short examination discovered the following: Bennebo (Benbow); Benzon (Benson); Birkebek (Birkbeck); Birket, Bjærkelev (Berkeley); Bonnet, Botten, Braa (Bray); Corselitze (Corsellis); Haarbotle (Harbottle); Hegnet (Hignet); Herskind (Erskine); Kabbel (Cabbell); Karhow (Carew); Kattehöi (Catty); Kolbek (Colbeck); Lyndulse (Lindsay); Lœgard (Legard); Lommelev (Lumley); Loveland, Lovel, Nörris (Norris); Raaby (Raby); and Rasley (Rashleigh).

Lincoln, and only about 4 per cent. in Norfolk and Suffolk. Of 'bordarii' and 'cotarii' we have about the average of the rest of England; but, on the other hand, we have not half the average of 'villani.'

II.

THE NORMAN CONQUEST.

I.—THE CHIEF GRANTEES AND HOW THEY DIED OUT.

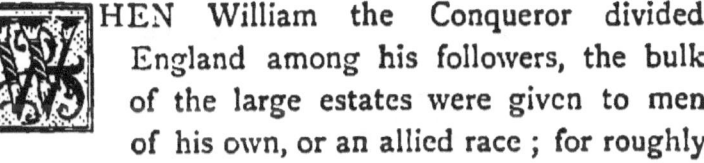HEN William the Conqueror divided England among his followers, the bulk of the large estates were given to men of his own, or an allied race ; for roughly speaking, the 1,300,000 acres which make up our county were parcelled out into 1,392 estates, manors, knights' fees—call them what you will—of which Normans held by far the most, as far as value was concerned. A 'knight's fee' has been variously estimated, but 800 acres is generally thought to have been its average size. This would account for 1,113,600 of these acres, and the difference (together with the large amount of the coast now lost, as at Eccles, Shipden, Keswick, and Whimpwell) was probably either waste water and fen, or the holdings of the small freeholders mentioned above. That such small freeholders were not free tenants of any manor

seems tolerably clear from their dealing with their properties by fine in the King's Court.

The following table will show the number of the manors held by the different lay grantees, and, roughly speaking, what they had done to deserve their grants. It is noticeable, however, that though the King held *fewer* manors than Bigot, Warren, or Beaufoy, his were valued at £1,324 a year as against Beaufoy's £357 ; Warren's £329 ; Bigot's £289.

    Manors

Roger Bigot, or Bigod - - - - - 187

    Suppressed (?) Ralph de Waers (Guader) rebellion in 1074, and founded Thetford Abbey. He was the ancestor of the Roger Bigod who told the King he would send him back the heads of his thrashers if he sent them to Norfolk.

William de Warren - - - - - 145

    Said, though on doubtful authority, to have married Gundreda, the Conqueror's daughter.* He built Castle Acre Castle, and founded the priory there.

William de Beaufoy, Bishop of Thetford - - 98

    Said to have been Chancellor to the King. He gave most of his property to the bishopric, and Hubert de Rye, who would seem to have married his widow, took the rest—*nescio quo warranto.*

The King - - - - - - - 95

* Mr. Chester Waters's recent pamphlet on the subject seems to conclusively settle that he did not.

	Manors
Alan, Earl of Richmond - - - - -	56

He is possibly the Count Alan who married the King's daughter, Constance, but it is very doubtful whether all the manors granted to 'Comes Alanus' were granted to one person, as there were three persons then so called.

Ralph Bainard - - - - - -	52

Lord of Castle Baynard, in London.

Ralph de Bellafago - - - - - -	52

Thought to have been a brother, or kinsman, of William de Beaufoy, the Bishop and Chancellor. His land, also, seems to have gone to the de Ryes.

Godric Dapifer - - - - -	41

The King's Steward for this district, who also held 67 manors for the King. He is said to have been ancestor of the de Calthorpes.

William de Scohies - - - - -	43

A Norman from the town of Escoues, or Escoyes. Nothing is known of him, but that he sold most of his land, A.D. 1102.

Walter Giffart - - - - - -	30

Was one of the Council held at Lillebonne, to decide on the invasion of England. Distinguished himself at the battles of Mortemer and Hastings, where he describes himself as white and bald-headed, weak, and short of breath.

	Manors
Robert Malet - - - - - - -	25

He was son of the William Malet who committed Harold's body to be buried after Hastings, and was made Governor of York Castle. Robert himself fought at Hastings.

Hermer de Ferrariis - - - - -	22

'Conspicuous as being by far the largest unlawful invader on the lands of the freemen of the county, and was probably one of the most violent and tyrannical of the powerful Norman barons' (Munford). Said to be ancestor of the de Wormegay family.

Ralph de Todeni [de Conches] - - -	20

Guessed to have been the 'son, nephew, or other relation' of Roger de Toesny, the standard-bearer and rebel who was killed in 1036. He distinguished himself in the battle of Mortemer, in 1054, and in the 'Roman de Rou,' is said to have declined to carry the standard at Hastings, preferring to join in the active fighting.

Hugh de Montfort - - - - - -	17

He had distinguished himself at the battle of Mortemer, in 1054, when Henry I. of France was defeated, and was 'Master of the Horse' at Hastings.

Peter de Valoines - - - - - -	17

Is said to have been nephew to the Conqueror, and to have married Albreda, sister of Eudo de Rye, the King's Dapifer.

	Manors
Eudo de Rye (Dapifer) - - - - -	9

Son of Hubert de Rye, who saved the Conqueror's life, in 1044, from a conspiracy. The King's Dapifer, or Steward, and Governor of Colchester Castle. His brother, Hubert, was Governor of Norwich Castle, and part founder of the Cathedral.

It is strange to note how soon the disintegration of these fifteen great estates began. Malet's land was taken away from him while he lived; Scohies sold his; Giffart's, Montfort's, and Rye's passed out of their names to their daughters and heiresses. Both the Beaufoys' lands were apparently given away from the male branch of the family to a man who married the widow of its head. Ferrar's and Warren's estates went to heiresses in three, and Valoines's in four generations. The King most unfairly took away Bigot's ancestral property, in the fifth generation, by a piece of very sharp practice, while the Todeni's died out in the male line in 1311, and the Bainards a few years later.

II.—EXISTING NORMAN NAMES.

OF course a few namesakes and possible descendants from collateral branches of some of the tenants *in capite* still remain in the county, *e.g.*, Warren and Rye. I have not included Algar, Almar, Asger, and other personal names, as the present bearers of them may come from any of the sub-tenants and others. Still these may be noticed:

Algarus . . .	Algar.
Almarus . . .	Aylmer.
Bunde (*liber homo*) .	Bunn ?
Coleman (*liber homo*)	Coleman and Colman.
Curcon de . .	Curson.
Durandus . .	Durrant.
Fisc (*liber homo*) .	Fisk.
Fulcherus . .	Fulcher.
Ketel (*liber homo*) .	Ketel.
Malet . . .	Mallet.
Quintinus . .	Quinton.
Rainerus . .	Rayner.
Ramis de . .	Reymes and Rhymes
Stanardes . .	Stannard.
Suetman (*liber homo*)	Swatman.
Toli . . .	Tooley.
Turchetel . .	Thurketel.
Verli de . . .	Varly.
Wimerus . .	Wymer.

Most of the names in the second column occur in the 'New Domesday' of 1873. The place-names introduced by the Normans were few. They nicknamed Norwich Castle 'Blanche-flower,' and called three Priories 'Mountgrace,' 'Mountjoy,' and 'Normansburgh ;' but most of their names were affixes, like Swanton *Morley*, Stow *Bardolph*, Saham *Tony*, and Framingham *Pigot*. Of their language, the word 'largesse,' so dear to harvest-men, is the best known one that remains.

III.—FICTITIOUS NORMAN PEDIGREES.

THE desire of the heads of wealthy and powerful families to trace their pedigrees from some one who 'came over with the Conqueror' has always been strong. We all know how the 'Roll of Battle Abbey' —or rather the various lists that go by this name— have been tampered with by the insertion of various obviously non-Norman names. But the worst concoctions had their origin in the reign of Elizabeth, when Harvey, Glover, and other unscrupulous heralds forged and invented Norman ancestors for well-to-do families all over England.

Recent research has done much to purge the Peerage of these ridiculous fabrications; but a collection of them would be an instructive commentary on the value of the work of the older heralds and of the 'visitations.'

A few of the worst cases in our county are the pedigrees of:

(a) *Howard*, Duke of Norfolk—Premier Peer and Earl Marshal of England. This family descends from Sir William Howard, who was a grown man and on the Bench in 1293, whose real pedigree is very obscure and doubtful, and who invariably spelt his name Haward.

There is great reason to believe that Haward is simply 'Heyward,' defined by Halliwell as the person who guarded the farmyard at night. Two *Coram rege* rolls, referred to by the heralds as mentioning William 'de' Howard and William 'Hauward,' have each been tampered with to make them so read—the 'le,' which was undoubtedly in the first, having been cut out; and the tail of the 'y' in the second having been also removed with a knife, to make 'Hayward' read 'Hauward.'

The pedigree itself was concocted very carelessly, and can deceive no one. It traces the Howards to 'Auber, Earl of Passy, in Normandy,' whose grandson, Roger Fitz Valerine, is said to have owned the Castle of Howarden, or 'Howard's den' (!). Alliances with the Bigods, the St. Meres, the Bardolphs, the Brus, and the Trusbuts are liberally provided, to bring in nice-looking quarterings, while an alternative descent from Hereward the Wake is also put forward.

Unluckily the matches in question are conspicuous by their absence from the very well-known pedigrees of the families in question ; and as to the Bigod match, Maud Bigod was living in 1245, while her alleged *great-great-great-great-grandson*, the judge, was a judge in 1293 ! The whole of this fiction has now been abandoned by the family.

(*b*) *Townshend* (Marquis), of Rainham. The ancestor created for this family was one Lodovic, a 'noble Norman,' who is said to have obtained the manor of Ranham, temp. Hen. I., by marrying Elizabeth de Hauville—the actual fact being that the first Towshend traceable at Rainham was one John *atte* Townshend, who was a sub-tenant there in 1398 !

'John atte Townshend,' as every one knows, simply means 'John who lives at the end of the town '—a very unlikely sobriquet for a Norman who had married the heiress of the manor. As a matter of fact, Hauville's manor did not come to the Townshends till about 1420. I regret to say that this pedigree is still adhered to, and the arms of Hauville quartered by the present marquis.

(c.) *Clere*, of Blickling and Ormesby. This family was traced to one Clere monte, 'assistant to William Duke of Normandy.' Matches with the Earl of Patele, Martell, Amberfield, Molyns, and others were provided, as in the Howard fabrication; but the concoctor fell into just such a muddle with his dates as did he who invented the Townshend pedigree, for he makes a man who was alive in 1316 *great-great-great-grandfather* to a man who levied a fine, and was therefore of age only sixteen years later.

(d) *Hare*, of Stow Bardolph. The early part of this pedigree—tracing the Hares from Jervis, Earl of Harcourt, who came in with the Conqueror—is too ridiculous to need any exposure here.

It is singular to note that very fair presumptive pedigrees, showing descents from old Norfolk families, probably of Norman origin, could have been framed for the last two families, if the heralds had done their duty; for, as early as John, I find the De Cleres at Ormesby (a fact of which the pedigree-forgers were blissfully ignorant); and there can be little doubt that the Hares were a branch of the widespread family of Le Eyr or Le Heyr. The rush for a Norman pedigree at any cost was, however, so great that there was no time for any genuine research. Even the De Greys of Merton, the oldest and best of our Norfolk families —overlooking their obvious descent from Arnolph de Grai, of Grai in Normandy—were induced to begin their pedigree with an imaginary junction with 'Rollo or Fulbert *de Croy*,' of Picardy.

Nothing, in fact, was too wild or too absurd. Quarterings were recklessly appropriated, and remain to this day monuments of the impudent zeal of the fabricators and the credulity of their employers. The Boleyn pedigree, concocted when the Lord Mayor began to get into society, is as rotten as his grand-daughter's character; while the Bulwer family—who I believe to be really descended on the female side from the old family of the De Dallings —actually wanted to make out that their patronymic was not Bull-ward, the man who looked after the manor bull, but Bölver, one of the war-titles of Odin!

III.

RESULTS OF THE CONQUEST.

I.—CASTLE BUILDING.

RIGHT and left, all over Norfolk, directly the Norman grantees came to take up their possessions, rose up their castles. 'New and strong, and cruel in their strength, how the English must have loathed the damp smell of the fresh mortar, and the sight of the heaps of rubble, and the chippings of the stone, and the blurring of the lime upon the green sward ; and how hopeless they must have felt when the great gates opened, and the wains were drawn in, heavily laden with the salted beeves, and the sacks of corn and meal furnished by the royal demesnes, the manors which had belonged to Edward the Confessor, now the spoil of the stranger: and when they looked into the castle court, thronged by the soldiers in bright mail, and heard the carpenters working upon the ordnance—every blow and stroke, even of the hammer or mallet speaking the language of defiance.' So said Palgrave, who, in spite of his alien descent, wrote as forcibly and strongly on the subject as though he had been of kin to the men whose feelings he was so well describing.

Norwich Castle — once called 'Blanchflower'— thought to have been built by Canute on an old site, was of course the most important of all the Norfolk castles. Singularly enough, it was the only one of them which was ever held against the Conqueror, when Ralph de Guaer, or de Guader, the Earl of the East Angles, when he rebelled in 1074, defended it. After he fled it was stoutly defended for him by his wife, and held out for some time against the King's army, capitulating only on honourable terms. Roger Bigod is said to have then had its custody, but whether it was he or another Roger Bigod who built Bigod's Tower and the great keep—one of the largest in England—is not known. For one hundred and fifty years or so its history was a stirring one, for it was held against the Barons for Rufus, seized again in Stephen's interest, reseized by Hugh Bigod in the reign of Henry II. (1174), when Jordan de Fantosme says: 'A Lorraine traitor betrayed it, therefore it was surprised,' and taken by Lewis of France, it is said by treachery, in 1216.

Next in importance to Norwich was, of course, Castle Acre, built by William de Warren, who, we have seen, was the second largest landholder in the county, and who was not, like Bigod, so lucky as to drop into a ready-built castle.

Odo, the warlike Bishop of Bayeux, who was the

King's half-brother, and had a grant of Rising, which commanded the low-lying land by Lynn, no doubt erected a temporary fortress there — on the old Roman mound — and when his lands were taken from him and given to the De Albinis, William de Albini built the present grand castle on its site.

The Beaufoys, or their successors the Ryes, were thought by the late Mr. G. A. Carthew (Hist. of Launditch, iii., p. 417) to have had a castle at Swanton Morley, where there is still a place called the Castle Island, and some traces of walls and a moat.

It is singular that these three castles stretch almost in a line with themselves and Norwich across the centre of the county.

More northerly, up the Aylsham Road, was Horsford Castle, built by Walter de Cadomo, a sub-tenant of the Malets. A circular mound with traces of an outer ditch is all that is now left of the keep that once commanded the northern road. There is no reason to suppose that Thetford Castle mound ever had any Norman fortification on it — indeed, its summit is far too small for one — and the castle which dominated these parts was no doubt that at Old Buckenham, built by De Albini, of which nothing but a ruined building, probably the donjon, and a fragment of wall remain. At Kenninghall, no doubt, De Albini had some sort of a castle on the site of the old works, but I believe I am correct in saying that there is now no trace of it. Again, there is little doubt there was a castle at Gimmingham, for Edward I. stayed there in 1277 and 1285, when inspecting his castles and forts.

How many of the 1150 castles which are said to have been built in England during the reign of Stephen, and to have been destroyed in that of Henry II., were in Norfolk, it is now impossible to state. I, for one, very much doubt the figure at which they were estimated,* and prefer Robert de Torigny's estimate of 375.

The later castles, erected by royal licenses† to crenellate, were at

> Great Hautboys—licensed to Robert Baynard, in 6 Edward II.
>
> Gresham—licensed to Edmund Bacon, in 12 Edward II.
>
> Scoulton—licensed to Constantine de Mortuomari, in 13 Edward II.
>
> Claxton—licensed to William de Kerdeston, in 14 and 50 Edward III.
>
> Lyng—licensed to John de Norwich, in 17 Edward III.
>
> Blakeworth in Stoke—licensed to John de Norwich, in 17 Edward III.
>
> Oxburgh—licensed to Edmund Bedingfeld, in 21 Edward IV.

* Winwall House, in Wereham, though undoubtedly Norman, was too small and too clearly non-fortified to have been a castle. It is said to have been the prison of the Honour of Clare, and is only 35 ft. by 27ft., and 16 ft. high.

† Sometimes the Lords built castles without license, e.g. in 3 Edw. I. Wm. Belet of Shouldham ' built a castle to the King's prejudice, and that of his castle at Norwich.' Mannington is said to have had an embattled castle, which was built by Wm. Sumner by license of the King.

Of these the last-named is fairly perfect, and Gresham has some ruins left standing, though there is not much there. Slight traces are left of Hautboys, Lyng, and Claxton, but of Scoulton and Blakeworth I find nothing. The Bishops of Norwich had licenses to fortify their palaces as under:

    Norwich - - - 1 Edward III.
    Gaywood - - 11 Richard II.
    North Elmham - 11 Richard II.

William Belet built a castle at Marham 'to the prejudice of our Lord the King and his castle of Norwich,' before 1274, when it was presented (Kirkpatrick, p. 254), but nothing seems known of it now.

Caister Castle, by Yarmouth, which was built soon after the year 1415 by Sir John Fastolf, Middleton Tower by Lord Scales, and Baconsthorpe Castle, probably completed in its present form about the same time, are three of the most perfect ruins; while the manor-house of East Barsham, and Beaupré Hall in Outwell, were both practically fortified castles.

Berlinge Castle, Norfolk, is mentioned on the Patent Roll of 3 Richard II., 3rd pt., m. 23, as being confirmed to William Bardolf, and I think this must be a mistake for Lerling, as there is no such place as Berling, while the Bardolphs had to do with Larling, I cannot, however, trace anything about a castle here.

II.—THE GROWTH OF THE MONASTERIES.

Three only of the Norfolk monasteries, viz., East Dereham Nunnery, said to have been built by "Anna

King of the East Angles," in 645; St. Benet's at Holme, said to have been founded by Canute; and Molycourt, were in existence when William I. came over to England. Nothing is now left of the first or the last, while of St. Benet's, once a mitred abbey with enormous possessions, there are but the ruins of a great gateway, and some long and wide foundations above ground.

From the Conquest to the end of the 13th century, the pious of Norfolk built and endowed monastic establishments with great and unallayed vigour, for the rate of building varied very slightly; the figures shown by an analysis I have made as carefully as the information in existence would allow, being as follows:

```
From 1066 to 1100  -  -  -  15
  ,,  1101 to 1200  -  -  -  30
  ,,  1201 to 1300  -  -  -  26
```

But in the next century the falling off was immense, the figures being:

```
From 1301 to 1387* -  -  -  6
```

Nearly every great family founded one monastery or nunnery at least. The De Warrens founded at Castle Acre, Heacham, Thetford (2), Slevesholm, and Wormegay; the Bigods at Pentney, Thetford, and Weybridge; and the De Albinis at Wymondham, Old Buckenham, and Marham. Herbert de Lozinga, the wise and able Bishop of Norwich, has had the credit

---

* The last date I find, viz., Austin Friars at Thetford, by John of Gaunt.

of being the greatest founder. His fair fame has for years been smirched by a ridiculous fable, that '*de* Lozinga' meant '*the* flatterer or liar.' It has been proved to demonstration that his name simply meant 'of Lorraine,' and that there was another bishop—at Hereford—at the same time of the same name. That he is, however, entitled to all the credit of building the priories of Norwich, Yarmouth, and Lynn, and the monastery of North Elmham, seems more doubtful. It has been appositely said (I forget where) that it is more probable he was the energetic collector of the funds for such foundations—in fact, the honorary secretary of an early Church Building Association; for it is idle to suppose that any one man could have been wealthy enough to erect such edifices as those just named, at his own expense.

The impetus given by his example was no doubt immense. Nobles who saw with pleased awe the enormous foundations and beautiful work at Norwich, went away to erect not unworthy companions to the great church: William de Warrenne at Castle Acre, Peter de Valoignes and his wife at Binham, Ralph de Tony at Westacre, and William de Glanville at Bacton or Bromholm; and the ruins of their work remain to this day, to show us how beautiful and how sound it was. If it were possible to tabulate the connections and relationship of all the worthy founders, I think it would be seen that much of this good work was done by groups of certain families and their connections.

Take, for example: Ralph de Cadomo and his wife, Sybilla de Cheyney, founded Horsham. William de

Cheyney, who I take to be her brother, founded Coxford. William de Cheyney, Sybilla's son, founded Sibton; while his daughter Margaret (herself a great benefactor to Carrow) married first Robert Fitz-Roger, who founded Langley, and secondly Roger de Cressy. Roger married Isabel de Rye, who founded Beeston. Her father Hubert and her uncle Henry were great givers to Canterbury, Belvoir, Norwich, and Southwark; while her father Hubert was part founder of Norwich, her uncle Eudo founded St. John's, Colchester, and her aunt founded Binham. Her mother, Agnes de Tony, founded Aldby, and her father Robert founded Belvoir. Here we have sixteen persons, shown in one pedigree, founding *nine* abbeys, etc., between them, while the other six all gave largely to similar work.

Of course, of the earlier foundations those for Benedictines were far most numerous. Out of the first fifteen, the earliest four and eight of the other eleven were of this order. The Austin or Black Canons first effected a settlement here at Walsingham about 1061, and again at Pentney some time in the Conqueror's reign.

William de Warrenne brought the Cluniacs in when he made Castle Acre a cell to his great Lewes Priory in 1085, and from that time they became as numerous as their predecessors.

The three orders had it all their own way till 1139, when the Canons of St. Sepulchre and Holy Cross effected a settlement at Stratford. The nuns of the Order of Fontevrault came in about 1181, the Pre-

Results of the Conquest. 41

monstratensian or White Canons in 1188, the Cistercians sometime in the reign of Henry II., the Gilbertines in that of Richard I., while the Friars Preachers or Black Friars and the Friars Minors or Grey Friars reached Norwich simultaneously in 1226. The Carmelites or White Friars were at Lynn before 1260, while the Austin Friars did not come in till the beginning of the reign of Edward I.

The following table will show the relative numbers of the Norfolk monastic establishments and their total:

Benedictines	27
Austin or Black Canons	18
Cluniacs	8
Carmelites or White Friars	6
Friars Preachers or Black Friars	5
Friars Minors or Grey Friars	4
Austin Friars	3
Premonstratensian or White Canons	3
Cistercians	3
Friars of the Sack	2
Friars of Our Lady	2
Red Friars	1
Canons of St. Augustine	1
Canons of St. Augustine and of Mertune	1
St. Sepulchre or Holy Cross	1
Fontevrault	1
Gilbertines	1
Holy Trinity for the Redemption of Captives	1
	82

Of which sixty-six were regulars and sixteen friars. We are now brought face to face with the question

—What was it that caused, first the gradual and then the total cessation of abbey-building in Norfolk? It may be said that it was because enough had been built to serve the county, but I do not think that was the real reason. Certainly a similar reason cannot be given to account for the enormous number of churches in our county—more than in even Yorkshire, a county three times its size.

I think the real cause was partly the great increase in number of semi-private chantries,*—for men who could not afford to build an abbey could found a chantry ; and it would seem to have become the fashion rather to found a chantry on your own account than be a very small part-founder of an abbey—and more greatly the way in which religious guilds were increasing in number and strength in the reign of Richard II., when we find the building of monasteries coming to a deadlock.

The guild certificates taken in that reign, which are still preserved in the Public Record Office, give in several cases the dates of their foundations. At Norwich the dates are 1307, 1350, 1360, 1364, 1375, 1376, 1380, 1384, 1385, and 1385 ; and at Lynn, 1316, 1329, 1359, 1367, 1368, 1372, 1374, 1376, 1376, and 1383 ; while another (Oxburgh) is dated 1378. The rapid growth of these guilds—which wisely combined a burial club and a convivial club,† with business-like provisions for the safe insurance of their members

* Taylor estimates them at 138 in Norfolk, and the guilds at 909.

† For some notes as to their observances and drinking-bouts, see chap. viii.

through purgatory—it will be noticed took place at the very time when the increase of the monasteries was ceasing.

Of the military orders, the Knights Templars had a small preceptory at Haddiscoe from 1218 to 1312, of which no traces now remain. Nor is there anything left of the Commandery of the Knights Hospitallers, founded in 1173 at Carbrooke; which was of course, while it existed, the only place in the county where excommunication had no terrors, the Hospitallers like the Templars having the peculiar privilege of giving spiritual comfort and Christian burial during an interdict.* With the plunder of this house Henry VIII. partly endowed the 'Poor Knights of Windsor,' five of whom are still kept out of the Carbrooke estate.

III.—THE OVERSTOCK OF CHURCHES.

Perhaps no problem is more troublesome to the Norfolk antiquary than the long-vexed question— Why Norfolk, of all counties in England, should have so extremely large a number of churches? It is not as though its population was enormous in early times, when much of its sterile face was covered up with briar and wood, and much more hidden with water and marsh. How then are we to account for the fact that Norfolk, with its 2,024 square miles, has 730 parishes and churches, 117 more than Yorkshire, with

---

* Another of their privileges was that their tenants and retainers could fix a cross on their houses as a sign of exemption from tithes and other imposts.

nearly treble its area, viz., 5,836 square miles? It is singular that the next greatest numbers are also both for Eastern counties, viz., Lincolnshire (632) and Suffolk (510).*

While Westmoreland has 23·8, Northumberland 22·1, Cumberland 14·6, Durham 13·1, Cheshire 11·9, Lancashire 10·9, Yorkshire 9·5 square miles on an average to a parish, and the average of all the English counties is only 5·1, we are overstocked with a church to every 2·7,† and Suffolk is about the same (2·9). It is very noticeable that not only had each little village its church, but some places had two or more in one churchyard; *e.g.*, St. Mary and St. Margaret of Antingham, where the tradition goes that they were built by two sisters who had quarrelled and would not go to church together. Another story of quarrelling sisters is at Ranworth, where two ladies' are said to have disputed who should take precedence; the unsuccessful one built Panxworth for herself.

Not only were the parish churches so numerous, but I have every reason to believe that the relative proportion of all monastic and conventual foundations was equally high, while the number of guilds was enormous. Taylor counted 909, which is, I fancy, an under-estimate, for there were 75 that we know of in Lynn alone.

Taylor says on this point, 'The Diocese of Norwich

---

* The monastic and conventual foundations in Norfolk were 153, against Suffolk's 94, while Cambridge only had 8 (?).— *Taylor.*

† And yet some few parishes are very large; *e.g.*, Outwell is 16,454 acres, but not all in Norfolk.

contains about one-twentieth of the superficial extent of all England and Wales: its proportion of monastic revenues is about one-sixteenth of the whole. . . And the number of monasteries, colleges, and hospitals included within the same district, is something less than one-eighth of the whole'

IV.

PERSECUTIONS AND RISINGS.

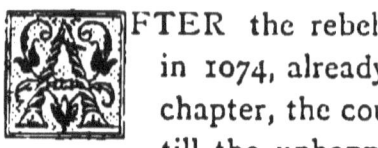FTER the rebellion of Ralph de Guaer, in 1074, already touched on in the third chapter, the county remained fairly quiet till the unhappy occurrence at Richard I.'s coronation began the series of persecutions of the Jews in England, which is so foul a blot on our history.

I say 'began' somewhat doubtfully, because there can be little doubt that when the monstrous charge against the Norwich Jews, of crucifying a little Christian boy—afterwards canonized as St. William, the Boy and Martyr—and burying his body in Thorpe Wood, was made in 1137 or 1144,* it was made the excuse for murder and plunder, as were all subsequent incidents of a similar sort.

To one fact I would draw special attention, and that is that even in the ridiculous account in the 'New Legend,' it is said that the Jews went to the Sheriff and bribed him. If there is one thing more

---

* The Chronicles differ as to the date, but the latter is, I believe, right.

sure than another about all these accusations, it is that the Jews always openly appealed to the civil power at once.

When Richard was crowned in 1189, the tide of persecution which began, it is said, by a scare at his coronation, but which was more probably the result of a pre-arranged plunder-plot, reached Norwich among other towns, and the Jews were attacked and slain in their own houses, except those who managed to escape into the castle, which was then, as on other occasions, their only refuge.

This massacre was followed,* or possibly duplicated, at Lynn, where it was alleged that the Jews were so enraged at the conversion of one of their body to Christianity, that they set upon him in order to kill him, that he took refuge in a church, and that they broke open the doors to get at him. The story goes on to say that the townspeople did not like to interfere because the King had taken the Jews under his protection, but that some pious strangers and foreigners, who were trading there, fell on the Jews, slew several of them, and burnt and pillaged their houses, and, having thus fulfilled their religious duties, gathered up their plunder and sailed away.

This was followed in 1223 by a paltry little persecution by the Bishops, who gave directions that no one should sell victuals to the Jews, or have any communication with them. The King, however, derived too much income from the Israelites to allow them to be starved, so he sent down close letters

* William of Newbury says preceded.

to the Sheriffs of Norwich, ordering that victuals and other necessities should be sold them.*

In 1230 the Norwich Jews were accused of seizing a Christian boy—Odard, the son of Benedict, the physician—as he was playing in the streets of Norwich, and circumcising him, calling him 'Jurnepin,' as a new name. Some historians† have alleged that the Jews proposed to murder him afterwards, but this is obviously incorrect, for a day and a night after the occurrence he was allowed to go away—one can hardly suppose a lad of five could 'escape' from a gang of adult murderers—and was found near the river-bank 'crying and howling' by a woman, who took him home with her. Next day the Jews seem to have come openly to her house claiming him as 'their Jew,' and warning the woman to give him no pig's-flesh to eat, because he was a Jew.

I think I have shown in my account of the affair‡ that it arose from a bold and fanatical attempt on the part of the Norwich Jews to rescue what they thought a brand from the burning, and bring back a lost sheep to the true fold of Israel. 'Benedict,' the boy's father's name, was one well known among the Jews of Norwich (one of those accused of the assault was a 'Benedict' himself), and the profession of a physician was at that time essentially Jewish. Just at this time, too, we know that conversion was going on in Norwich, for a convert, called Hugh de Norwico,

---
° Close Roll of 7 Henry III., m. 29.
† *E.g.*, Holingshed.
‡ Norf. Ant. Misc., i., pp. 312-344.

was sent up in 18 Henry III., from Norwich, to the 'Domus Conversorum,' as we see from an entry in the Close Roll of that year. That the Jews did sometimes make desperate efforts to counteract conversion, seems to be proved from entries occurring in the Close Roll only three years later, in which the Oxford Jews are said to have taken away, or stolen, a converted and baptized child;* and in 18 Edward I. we find, among the petitions to Parliament, one begging the King to revoke the baptism of a Jew boy, which had taken place in St. Clement's Church, London. Be that as it may, the incident of 1230, whatever prompted it, was eventually taken advantage of by the clergy, and after a remarkable interval —four or five years—an indictment was preferred against thirteen of the chief Norwich Jews for having mutilated the boy 'in despite of the Crucifixion and of Christianity,' and ten of the Jews who appeared were sent to prison.

To allay the excitement no doubt caused among the ignorant by the prosecution, the King sent a close letter to the Sheriff of Norfolk and Suffolk, prohibiting any Christian woman from serving the Jews, either by nursing the children or in any other way, an ordinance which was followed the next year (1236) by one which directed that no interest should run during the minority of the heir for a debt due to a Jew from the heir's ancestor. For four years the prisoners were kept in ward. Then they paid the King a fine of £20 to be tried by a mixed jury, but a

* Close Roll, 21 Henry III., m. 22.

month afterwards he broke faith with them, and countermanded the directions for such jury, and directed that his Justices should try them as they should think best.

When and where they were tried I cannot find out, but two at least were hung, and Stow says the others had to pay a fine of 20,000 marks. Here the episode ends, and with it practically the history of the Norwich Jews, though we hear indirectly that their house called 'Thor' was burned down, and that not long after Abraham, the son of Deulecresse, was drawn and burnt for blasphemy. It has been the custom to upbraid the Jews for taking excessive interest, e.g., in one case* 86⅔ per cent. per annum; but if they took it with one hand they had to pay away most of it to the King with the other; e.g., Josce Barlibred had to pay 2,000 marks in 1186 for bare liberty to live in England; Jurnet was fined 5,525½ marks in the same year; and Isaac† of Norwich, in 1218, had to pay the immense sum of 10,000 marks —£6,666 13s. 4d. of *their* money—while in *eight* years Jew fines amounting to £420,000 were collected. Again, it is doubtful whether they ever got or held much of their profits. The King would in very many cases quietly 'pardon' or remit to debtors debts which did not belong to *him*, but to a Jew; and the unhappy lender might whistle, not only for his

---

* Palgrave, ' Rise and Progress,' ii., p. 9.

† I suspect he was the Isaac whom John persuaded, by his skill in dentistry, to pay 10,000 marks and that the terms were modified by his son.

profit but for the actual money he had lent, of which, to use the technical language of the race-course, he was 'welshed.' They were robbed and mulcted at every turn, and even had to pay to help the outfitting of crusades to recover the Sepulchre of Him in whom they disbelieved and whom they despised. Again, was the personal danger they incurred nothing, and not to be paid for in meal or in malt? Was nothing to be allowed for the risk of their trade, the burnings of their houses, and the massacre of themselves and their families? I cannot see that they got so much out of their business after all. They, like their descendants nowadays, liked a speculative business, but I doubt if the Hebrews of the Stock Exchange would have liked the excitement of the twelfth century. Before leaving the early Norwich Jews I may mention a very curious mediæval caricature of them, which occurs on one of the Jews' Rolls, formerly in the Pell Office, and which shows the insults they had to bear even from those who robbed them. Aaron of Norwich is represented as a three-faced man, crowned. To his right is 'Mosse Mokke,'* one of those hung in the Jurnepin business,† face to face with an obvious large-nosed Jewess, 'Avezardon,' while between them a horned demon, called 'Colbie' or 'Colbif,' is in the rudest way touching their noses, one with the forefinger of each hand. A Jew weighing money in scales has a devil behind him, blowing forked flame into his back; while

○ Misread by Mr. Mason as 'Nolle Mokke' (Hist. Norf., p. 50).
† Norf. Ant. Misc., i., p. 318.

on the right hand of the picture the fiend 'Dagon' and a host of others are taking possession of a castle. The only other instance I have ever seen of this sort of early lampoon is on the Forest Roll for Essex,* where Lok, son of Aaron, is presented for an encroachment on the forest of Essex, in 5 Edward I., and the clerk has, in the margin of the roll, carried his pedigree up a step higher by writing, above a rather clever caricature of him, the words, 'Aaron, fil' Diaboli.'

Passing now from the Jews, who were the innocent causes of the most important local disturbances in our early history, we come to the Monks and Citizens' Riot of 1272; but as this was purely a 'town and gown' row, and as I have treated on it at great length in the Norf. Ant. Misc., vol. ii., p. 17-89, I need not discuss it again here. Next we had a branch of Wat Tyler's rebellion of 1381, which was begun in Suffolk by one John Wrawt† (who is said to have received personal instructions from Tyler in London), but which is generally known as Litester's rebellion. Everyone knows the story how the farmers of the poll-tax were opposed—first in Essex, where a judge sent to quell the malcontents barely escaped with his life, and then more vigorously in Kent, where a collector was killed by Wat Tyler. The movement seems to have enlarged into one that 'no tenant should do service or custom to the lords.'

° No. 1, Exch. Treasury of Receipts.
† There is nothing new under the sun, for here we have an early 'Johnny Raw.'

Persecutions and Risings. 53

John the Litester, though stated by Froissart to have been a Staffordshire man, was no doubt, as Walsingham says, a Norwich dyer, and his three chief aiders were named 'Seth, Trunch, and Cubit.' Of these the first was, I apprehend, a man from Setchey, the chronicler's 'Sech' being misread Seth, as Trunch no doubt was a man from that village. As to Cubit, it is a noteworthy thing that we find Roger Cobet accused of various extortions in the reign of Edward I.,* and that Roger Kybit, no doubt the same man, was in 1315 rated on the Subsidy Roll for Worstead, in which roll Ralph *le Litester* and Roger *le Litester* also occur as living in the same parish. It is probable, therefore, that John the Litester and Cubit were both sons of two Worstead neighbours, and this may possibly account for the rebels turning at last to East Norfolk.

Be that as it may, the rising, whatever caused it, was sharply put down. At first the rioters had great success. The Earl of Suffolk was forced to fly in disguise; and Litester, who captured certain of the gentry, made them his tasters and servers in a sort of mock court, in which the chief was called 'King of the Commons.' Meanwhile, however, Henry le Spencer, Bishop of Norwich, grandson of the vile favourite of Edward II., heard of the news while at 'Burleigh House by Stamford town,'† then his mansion house—and having no reason to love the

---

* Rot. Hundred, i., p. 450.
† If, indeed, as I suspect, he had not gone there from Norwich to gather his retainers and take the rebels in their rear.

commons of Norfolk after the corporeal thrashing he had at their hands in Lynn in 1377—gathered eight lances and a handful of archers, attacked and cut up an outlying party of the rebels at Cambridge, seized and beheaded some of the leaders at Ickling- ham, and coming on by Wymondham to Norwich, soon—nothing succeeding like success—had a strong following of the nobles and gentry. Meanwhile the insurgents had retired on North Walsham and Gimmingham, but, on the Bishop's forces moving on to Felmingham, they retreated to Thorpe Market, and then swinging round, entered North Walsham by the Antingham road, having thus to a certain extent turned the Bishop's flank. Here they entrenched themselves, and on the earth thrown out of their trench they piled up windows, shutters, doors, tables, and such like things, to make a barricade; while, as though to make their men fight more desperately, they blocked up their rear with their camp carts.* Of how their camp was stormed we know but little; all we have is a few graphic sentences, in which the Bishop is described as, lance in hand, dashing on horseback over the trench, "grinding his teeth," and leading the forlorn hope over the barricade, seizing Litester, sternly condemning him to death, then piously giving him absolution, and kindly holding up his head as he was dragged to an immediate gibbet; but in spite of all kindness seeing him hanged, very tenderly but very efficaciously. A good bold soldier

* Compare the story of the Normans burning their ships before Hastings.

this Spencer, but hardly our present idea of a Bishop or an honest man—possibly not as honest a man or as good a citizen as the hanged rebel—for afterwards we find him impeached and found guilty in Parliament of accepting bribes from the French, and distinguishing himself by zealous persecution of the Lollards.*

The scene of the massacre, and possibly of Litester's execution, was on the Norwich side of North Walsham, whither, no doubt, most of the rebels were driven out by the Bishop's rush from the Antingham side of the town. The shaft of a stone cross still stands in the crook of the road to mark the spot. 'They dew say a 'mazin' lot of men are buried in that pightle,' as a rustic told me once.

The severe example made of the leaders, and most of the followers, of this rebellion did not deter others from trying again next year; a scheme for rising at St. Faith's Fair, and seizing St. Bennet's Abbey as a rallying-point, only failing through the treachery of some of the conspirators.

In 1442 the old feud between the monks and citizens broke out again—this time on the quarrel of the Abbot of Holm, who, claiming as owner of the Manor of Heigham, objected to the erection of the 'New Mills,' alleging, untruly, that it hindered his waterway to his abbey, though the citizens had the obvious retort that there had been four mills across the river ever since the Conquest. It was said that the

* To this day the people of Ypres commemorate the deliverance of their city, in 1383, from this warrior-prelate.

Mayor of Norwich and others were accused of declaring that they had power enough to stay the Bishop, the Abbot of Holm, and the Prior of Norwich; and that one John Gladman (from whom this insurrection is popularly called 'Gladman's Insurrection') rode about the city with a paper crown on and a sceptre and sword before him. They seem to have rung the bells and attacked the priory in a half-hearted way, for they never got inside its gates. The citizens' version of all this was that Gladman only rode about on a horse with tinfoil trappings, crowned as 'King of Christmas,' with another clad as 'Lent,' with white and red herring-skins, and his horse ornamented with oyster-shells, and that it was only through the malice of the Countess of Suffolk and Sir Thomas Tuddenham that their innocent 'mirth, disport, and plays' were so misrepresented.

It appears that the Countess, disguised as a country housewife, had gone with Sir Thomas and two others, also disguised, to Lakenham Wood, 'to take the air, and disport themselves beholding the city,' when some of the townsfolk, not knowing who they were, were extremely, though not unnaturally, rude to her.

Ten years later (1452) we get the first inkling of the general unsatisfied feeling among the commoners which afterwards led to Kett's rebellion, for there was something of a gathering, though it came to nothing, in Postwick Wood, headed by one Roger Church, who suggested that a good name for their captain would be 'John Amend-all;' but Church seems to have had even more of the thief in him than is usual in patriots, and no head was made.

Again, in 1454, we find twenty men, 'under colour of hunting,' breaking up the gates and closes of Osborn Moundeford at Braydeston, while twelve more, with bows bent and arrows ready in their hands, kept between the manor-house and the church from 7 a.m. and 3 p.m., apparently lying in wait for the servants, to prevent their interference.

There was something brewing, too, in 1477, when John atte Wode promoted certain 'horrible treasons and conspiracies,' unluckily for him with the privity of one Robert Tomelynson, who informed, and was paid £10 for his treachery. The Pilgrimage of Grace, in 1536, led to a small rising here in the following year, the Sub-Prior of Walsingham and others planning to fire the beacons and journey north at the rate of twenty miles a day; but this, too, was spoilt by informers, and five of the conspirators were executed.

The temper was rising year by year. In 1540, one John Walker, of Griston, said, ' If three or four good fellows would ride in the night, with every man a bell, and cry in every town they passed through, ' To Swaffham! To Swaffham!' by the morning there would be ten thousand assembled at the least.' This intended rising was avowedly against the gentlemen. ' It would be a good thing,' said he, ' if there were only as many gentlemen in Norfolk as there were white bulls.' From after-results it is clear that

Walker was perilously near the truth as to the readiness to rise.

For some time before 1549 the country was filled with strange rumours and quaint prophecies. Labourers whispered to one another that better times were coming for their class, and that

> 'The country gnoffes, Hob, Dick, and Hick,
> With clubbs and clouted shoon,
> Shall fill the vale of Dussin's Dale
> With slaughtered bodies soon,'

never thinking that this was a two-edged prophecy, which was in effect fulfilled by their filling the vale with their own bodies.

Lingard, as of late Professor Rogers, has said that Kett's Rebellion had a religious origin; the former so writing from religious bias, the latter, from ignorance. If ever there were a rising for purely personal grievances, this was one. The petition of the rebels to the King is extant, and it says no word about religion, except to ask that the priests may be resident in their parishes, and not living away as chaplains; and Princess Mary herself, writing from the spot, says that the rising was 'touching no part of religion.'

The real reasons for the insurrection, which did not originate with the very poor, for Kett, the moving spirit, was a man of substance and a landowner, are clearly enough to be gathered from the petition sent up to the King when the rebellion was at its height—a petition reasonable in nearly every particular, and couched in language of studied moderation.

Besides various clauses against enclosures, it asks redress against lords of manors who tried to make their freehold tenants pay their own 'fee,' or head-rent, and castle-guard rent, or blanche-farm, which were obviously outgoings properly payable by the lords and not by the tenants. Again, it asks that all 'bondmen' may be made free, 'for God made all free with His precious blood-shedding;' that all rivers may be free and common to all men for fishing and passage; that parsons shall be resident, and all having a benefice worth more than £10 a year shall, by himself or deputy, teach the poor parish children the catechism and the primer; and, in the interests of their crops, that no one under a certain degree shall keep rabbits unless he 'paled' them in, and that no new dove-houses should be allowed. Nothing could be more reasonable than all this, and the only unfair proposition seems to be that lords of manors should not be allowed to common upon the wastes of their own manors.

The sting of the whole thing was the demand for throwing open enclosures, made by lords of manors, of waste land* over which their tenants had commonable rights. When we remember how London commons, like Wimbledon and Wandsworth, have, in the nineteenth century, in face of determined op-

---

* The late Mr. Carthew thought the rising was caused by the enclosure of open fields over which the manor tenants had grazing and shackage rights during certain times of year: but this theory is untenable, for if any one tenant enclosed his land he lost his shackage rights over the rest of the land—which of course rose in value, being burdened by less cattle.

position, melted almost away under the liberal interpretation the lord took of his rights, we can hardly doubt how wholesale were the enclosures made by mediæval lords, who had a hall-full of armed retainers, and a most profound contempt for their villeins and tenants.

The story of the rising itself is soon told. The fences by which one Green of Wilby had enclosed part of Attleborough Common, were thrown down on the 20th June, 1549.

Nothing more was done for more than a fortnight, when the commoners met at Wymondham, nominally to a 'play,' held there in commemoration of the translation of St. Thomas à Becket, and pulled down some more hedges at Morley, and soon afterwards some more at Hethersett, belonging to Serjeant Flowerdew. Now it happened that he was at feud with the Ketts,* who had also enclosed, and, irate at his hedges being destroyed, bribed the insurgents to destroy Kett's only. Those he had bribed seem to have gone off straight to Kett, who not only agreed to his own enclosures being levelled, but joined heartily in the levelling himself, and then—it is amusing to see how the personal spite comes in again—led them again to Flowerdew's, and ruined all the rest of his hedges, to his intense annoyance,

---

* The Ketts were an old and fairly wealthy Wyndham family. What little is known of them is not altogether in their favour. Thomas Kett, in 1570, betrayed the conspiracy against the Norwich Strangers, and Francis Kett was burnt, in the Armada year, for blaspheming Christ.

he breaking out into violent abuse of Kett and his friends.

Kett then led his men on *via* Cringleford to Bowthorpe, where the High Sheriff boldly rode up to them, proclaimed them rebels, and commanded them to go home, but had to ride for his life, for they tried to seize him.

They pulled down the hedge of the 'Town Close,'* belonging to the poor freemen of Norwich, and began to look out for a place to pitch their camp in. Eaton Wood was found unsuitable, so they determined to make for the high ground of Mousehold Heath, on the other or north side of the city. They asked the Mayor for leave to march through the city peaceably, and, on their being refused, widened Hellisdon Bridge, and took up a temporary position on the high ground at Drayton, moving thence to Mousehold Heath next day, and there pitched their camp. Simultaneously, or nearly so, lesser camps were formed at Rising Chase and at Downham, near which latter place was lately an oak, called Kett's Oak; but these gatherings came to nothing, and need not be mentioned further.

Much has been made of Kett giving licenses to his followers to provide and bring in cattle and victuals to his camp; but it is obvious that if his rising was excusable, his men had to be fed somehow. Sixteen thousand men were now entrenched on Mousehold, ordnance and provisions were being brought in from Paston Hall, Yarmouth, and even Lynn; and as days

* Up the Newmarket Road.

wore on it looked as though the King's Council—who certainly had enough already on their hands with half-a-dozen minor risings—did not care to try to crush this important one.

The insurgents blockaded the city, though they did not actually take possession of it, and levied black-mail right and left. On the 21st July, the King sent a herald offering pardon to all who laid down their arms and went home, an offer which was met by Kett fiercely replying that 'Kings were wont to pardon wicked persons, not innocent and just men;' and the herald had to make sharp shift to get back to the city, accompanied by the Mayor and one Aldrich, who had been constrained hitherto to countenance the rebels in the hopes of keeping them within bounds. That night the Mayor and citizens seem to have fully expected an assault from the country rebels. They 'rampired' Bishop's Gate, by which I expect is meant that they filled up the arch of the gate, which once stood on Bishop's Bridge, with earth. A piece of ordnance was mounted on the old common staith-yard, and was watched by the two Appleyards, while two great pieces, and some iron pieces belonging to Sir William Paston, were sent to the castle.

The next day the rebels came trooping down the hill from 'Kett's Castle' to Bishop's Bridge, and though suffering severely from arrows shot from within, took to the river and drove the unskilled gunners from their posts, and seized the city at considerable loss to themselves, but little to the defenders. The 'ordnance' seemed singularly poor, the powder being either so scarce or so weak that 'the shot followed not.'

Kett then seized the Mayor (Codd) and other of the chief citizens, and kept them prisoners in the camp; and the grim joke was soon put about that anyone coming to Mousehold would soon get a Cod's head for a penny; but after all, at Aldrich's intercession he was let out again.

At last the King's army, under the Marquis of Northampton, and numbering about 2,500 men—many of whom were Italian mercenaries, under one Mala Testa—arrived at St. Stephen's Gate, and were warmly welcomed by the loyal citizens. Skirmishing at once, some of the Italians got the worst of it, and one of them was captured, stripped of his costly armour, and hung upon an oak, though as much as £100 was offered for his ransom.

In the night the rebels made another and very determined rush at the city. On the one side they destroyed Pockthorpe and Magdalen Gates, while on the other they burnt St. Stephen's; but though they fought like fiends, as even their enemies admitted, they met different men this time, and were driven back with great loss. Early in the morning they tried again, this time through the Hospital Meadows; and there in the plain, by the Palace Gates, they met the King's men again, but with better luck, for overpowering them by numbers, they slew Lord Sheffield on the spot—where there still stands a stone with 'S' on it—and fairly drove the troops out of the city. This was on the 1st August. On the 3rd the bad news had reached London, and the Council at once wrote to the Earl of Shrewsbury to be ready to march on Norwich instantly. Then on the 10th the Duke of Somerset was named commander; and lastly, on the 16th, the Earl of Warwick.

It was not till the 23rd, so cautious were the King's troops after the bitter lesson they had had, that they reached the vicinity of Norwich. Terms were again offered to the rebels, and at one time Kett seemed disposed to accept them and chance the royal mercy, but was apparently over-persuaded by his own men, and the fight began by the King's troops breaking into the city by 'Brazen Gates' and St. Stephen's. A curious mistake of Warwick's men (who were not the first, and probably will not be the last, to be confused by the intricacies of Norwich streets) gave the rebels a great advantage, for the drivers of some of his ammunition waggons lost their way, and instead of turning up into the Market Place, blundered straight on by Tombland and St. Martin's Palace plain over Bishop's Bridge, right into the very hands of the rebels, who received them with thanks. One Captain Drury, who seems to have been the capable man, or 'only general,' of the day, cut in upon them and saved something, but with loss of some of his men.

Next day the rebels made head in Tombland, and sent out parties to various points of vantage, such as the corner of Elm Hill and the corner of St. Andrew's Hall, and got the best of a slight skirmish;

upon which Warwick, whose headquarters were in the Market Place, came down in full force by St. John Maddermarket, only to be met by a 'mighty force of arrows as flakes of snow in a tempest.' But the capable Captain Drury coming up with his trained arquebusiers, repaid their 'flakes of snow' with 'a storm of hayle,' shot so low and so true that it turned the fortune of the skirmish. One is apt to think little of the execution of the murder-weapons of our ancestors, but in this short affair, which took place in perhaps an acre of ground, three hundred and twenty men were killed, and many others, 'found creeping in the churchyards and under the walls,' were knocked on the head afterwards.

Intending to follow up his advantage on the following day, Warwick sent ordnance and stores outside the city walls ready for use against Mousehold, but, with incredible carelessness, left them guarded by some Welshmen only. The chief rebel gunner, seeing his opportunity, laid a gun so truly that he shot the King's master-gunner, who, I suppose, was left in charge of his cannon, and then, with some of his followers, came running fast down the hill to secure their plunder, but did not run as fast as the Welsh—a disgrace to the inhabitants of the Principality, which they felt so strongly that the authorities mutilated nearly every known copy of Neville's 'De Furoribus Norf.,' by cutting out the four pages (131-134) which told the story of their disgrace. Once more Captain Drury appeared on the scene, and saved some of the cannon.

The ordnance thus gained was mounted above the city on the hill above Bishop's Bridge (a modern ten-pounder there now would bring the city to its senses in ten minutes), and was served so well that it practically commanded Bishop's Bridge, and battered down a great part of the Cow Tower hard by, as we see it to this day.

The next day was Sunday—and the sorest Sunday Norwich ever saw. By this time all ideas of right or wrong—of grievance or redress—had been lost sight of. The two sides had been fighting long enough to hate one another, and the rebels were getting into the city on every side except Bishop's Bridge. King Street was on fire, and the citizens were begging Warwick to go away lest a worst thing should befall them, and the White Friars Bridge had to be broken down to keep the rebels out.

On the Monday, however, came in a reinforcement of 1,100 Landknechts—a different variety of mercenaries—who fired volleys to announce their coming. The rebels struck their camp on Mousehold, and moved to ' Dussin's Dale,' apparently believing it was the place named in the prophecy cited before. This change being notified to Warwick by the watchman on the cathedral spire, he sallied with his thousand ' Almaines ' and all his horse, Captain Drury, of course, charging in the van.

At the onset, Myles, the same rebel gunner who had shot so straight before, knocked over the King's standard-bearer and his horse with one shot, but he was but one against a thousand, and a thousand trained arquebusiers sent in a withering volley — and the whole thing was over.

It was the old story of untrained men fighting gallantly and well in narrow streets and lanes, and over-appalled when they found themselves butchered wholesale in the open. They ran away, and small blame to them; but if the affair had taken place on the slope, between Ber Street and King Street and the river, I fancy more mercenaries' bodies would have been found in the water than Norwichers. As it was, about 3,500 of them were simply murdered, and the cruelty and the carnage was so great that at last they stood together in confused groups, and picking up their dead companions' weapons determined to die fighting. So bold a front they made, that Warwick rode up to them himself and personally promised them safety. Kett, with five or six men, rode away, but was caught, hung, drawn, and quartered.* He had played for too high a stake —probably he had been forced into doing so—but one cannot sympathize with him, for he was an 'encloser' himself, who sought to make capital out of sudden ratting. He has been called a coward for running away from the fight when it was lost, but he simply took the slight chance left him of saving his life; and, at all events, he did not grovel for mercy just before execution, as Warwick himself did four years later.

* It is curious that the precept to bring him up for trial was signed by Sir Richard *Lyster*, possibly a descendant of his predecessor in rebellion.

Warwick was hailed as a deliverer by the citizens, who never having had much sympathy with the county men, now hated them for their city ruined and their houses despoiled. Everywhere the Warwick badge—the 'ragged staff'—was set up at doors. Its retention outside Bacon's house, in Colegate Street, gave offence to men smarting under the suppression;* but it was in Norwich quite recently, for the sign of the 'Bear and the Ragged Staff' hung out in Fisher's Lane only the other day.

Captain Drury, however—the real competent man on the King's side—mercenary though he was, who lost 60 out of his little band of 180, had to wait for his money; and was ultimately only paid £272 for the services of himself and his 120 living and 60 dead men! They did things cheaper and better then than we do nowadays in the East.

It was long before Kett was forgotten. He had cost the country £28,122 7s. 7d. of the then money to put down, besides all the waste and spoil during the rebellion; and when Warwick came down east four years later, as Duke of Northumberland, in Lady Jane's interest, it was the hatred with which he was hated by the commoners that made it so easy a job for the Catholic gentry to put Mary on the throne. It is a singular coincidence that Kett held Wyndham Manor of the very man who defeated him.

There was a rumour of a rebellion brewing in 1553, when 5,000 men were said to be about to rise

* Blom Norf., iii., p. 257.

and rendezvous at Wisbeach, intending to camp at Tylney Smeath, capture the gentlemen and hold them hostages till the Queen gave them redress; but nothing came of it.

The Harleston rising of 1570, sometimes called Redman's Conspiracy, was really a trade-union riot, aimed against the 'strangers,' viz., the industrious Dutch and Walloons, whose skill and industry afterwards revivified the city; but it was betrayed by Thomas Kett, a kinsman to the late rebel, and three of the conspirators were hung, and no harm done, luckily, to our visitors. With this practically ends our intestine troubles. There were little risings at Aylsham and Norwich during the Civil War, but these I shall touch in my sixth chapter.

V.

THE NORFOLK OF ELIZABETH.

IN dramatic contrast to Elizabeth's first visit to Norfolk was her second, when she made her stately progress through the county in 1578. When Sir Henry Bedingfield brought her prisoner to Oxburgh, he kept her under the closest and most offensive supervision, for when on the journey she wanted to see a game at chess played out, he would not let her do so; and when her hood blew off he made her put it on under a hedgerow, refusing to let her go into a house to adjust her finery. Well might she tell him afterwards with grim humour that whenever she wanted to have a state prisoner hardly handled and strictly kept, she would send for him.

We have the fullest account of Elizabeth's reception in Norwich, and of the stilted addresses which were made to her, in a rare little contemporary work, 'Queen Elizabeth's Progress in Norwich,' by B. G [oldingham] and T. C [hurchyard]. Everything was cleared up and beautified regardless of expense.

The narrow way down St. John's Maddermarket—then the chief thoroughfare from the market-place to the Duke of Norfolk's house—was widened, by cutting away a great piece of the churchyard, which accounts for the church now literally abutting on the street. No tallow was to be melted, no scourer was to use wash, the muck-hills at Brazendoors were cleared away, and St. Giles's Gate was widened. Two thousand five hundred horsemen rendezvoused apparently at the Earl of Surrey's house, at Kenninghall, to do her honour, while sixty of the 'most comely bachelors' of the city—compulsorily taxed for their comeliness—being dressed in black satin doublets (at their own expense by order of the city), met her at Hartford Bridge, where they made her the first oration of welcome. At the Town Close another of the band, dressed up as King Gurguntius, the fabled founder of Norwich and builder of 'Blancheflower,' was ready for her with oration No. 2. The city waits were 'waiting' at St. Stephen's Gate for her with oration or poem No. 3, while further down a turbaned boy on a platform orated her for the fourth time; and some delicate music was being performed, when some lusty ringers—can one doubt they were under St. Peter's bell sollar?—crashed in so loudly with a joy-peal that they drowned the music. In connection with the 'Artizan Strangers Pageant' in St. Stephen's, it is needless to say there was another oration (No. 5); but the show itself must have been rather an interesting one, for perched on a large platform there were representatives of all the different manufactures of the city, with eight little girls busy spinning worsted on one side, and eight more knitting it on the other. In the market-place there was pageant No. 2 and oration No. 6 (over 200 lines this time!), and then a song; after which the wearied Queen escaped to her lodgings in the Bishop's Palace, and to deserved rest.

It is not to be wondered at that she did not come out of doors all day Sunday. On the Monday a gilded coach came tearing up to the Bishop's gates, drawn by galloping horses with their hides painted over, and with artificial wings stuck on their backs, carrying a 'trumpet' sounding, and a boy dressed up as Mercury, who jumped out and inflicted on her an unmercifully long speech. It must have been a relief for her to go out, after the rain, into the fresh air on the Tuesday to Cossey, for some of the tame-deer shooting of which she was so fond, though she was intercepted by some pseudo-heathen tomfoolery in the streets. The Dutch Church gave her a £50 cup and a Latin oration, and so the thing went on day by day. It would be useless to try to describe all the grovelling rubbish that was put before her, and one reads with some little satisfaction how a lot of the mummers were caught in a deluge of rain, and were drenched and their finery spoiled. Who can tell, says the chronicler, what the city lost in velvets, silks, tinsel, and cloth of gold on that occasion! They were going to orate her once more as she was leaving, but she apparently thought this was a little too much, for when Mr. Mayor brake [it gently] to the Lord Chamberlain that he was to utter to her

Majesty another oration, he 'was willed to forbear the utterance of the same his oration,' the Queen graciously accepting the MS. instead, which no doubt was put to some laudable culinary, or other, use, later in the day.

From Norwich she went to the Woodhouses' at Kimberley; then to the Cleres' at Woodrising; then to Blickling, her ancestral home on her mother's side; and then back into Suffolk, and I do not think ever re-visited the county.

Among the places at which she had been entertained in Norwich, was at the Earl of Surrey's house —'Mount Surrey,' at Mousehold Heath—a place which she must have viewed with extreme interest, on account of the tragedy of nearly thirty years before. From the walls of this very house, it will be remembered, one of the foreign mercenaries had been hung, after having been uncased of his costly armour. I expect the reason she was entertained at Mount Surrey, instead of the old Duke's Palace, was that the latter was not then grand enough for the purpose. It was not till 1602 that *the* Duke's Palace was begun, when for fifty years and more the masons were kept at work on it, till it became probably one of the most magnificent buildings in England. Everything was of the most expensive character (the very fire-shovels being of silver); and as it had great dancing-rooms to fill, three 'coaches,' the prototype of our present busses—for they held fourteen—were sent out every afternoon to fetch the ladies of the neighbourhood. Out by Conisford Gates, at the end of King Street, were outlying gardens, belonging to the palace, of great magnificence and extent, stretching along the river, with walks forty feet wide. No wonder its owner, when he was here in his tennis-court, thought himself, as he boasted when he defended his possible match with Mary of Scots, as good as a Scotch King—a boast which availed him, by the way, as little as that of his predecessor Bigod, when he talked of not caring for the King of Cokenay when he was in his castle of Bungay.

Reverting, however, to Queen Elizabeth, her feelings, when in Norfolk in 1578, must have been somewhat mixed. On her mother's side she was herself of Norfolk descent, through the Boleyns, a family inferior as far as blood was concerned to probably every squire who did her homage; for the Boleyns were *nouveaux riches* only, her ancestor being but a London merchant, and the older pedigree usually ascribed to them a fabrication.* When she revisited Blickling, the memory of the shameful deaths of her mother and uncle must have haunted her. While at 'Mount Surrey,' her host and she cannot but have thought of their common kinswoman,

---

* Hepworth Dixon, in his 'History of Two Queens,' vol. i., p. 362, says that the Boleyns were 'a family of French descent, who came to London for the sake of trade.' I should have liked a better authority than this writer, whose inaccuracy is notorious; but on this occasion I think he was right. The Boleyns and the Cleres (both of Blickling) were intermarrying just about the time the ridiculous forged coats of Clere of Cleremount were put up in Blickling Church. This is suspicious.

Catherine Howard, and her end; and it would have been strange if the appearance, at the local Court, of some Appleyard or Robsart did not bring back to her startled mind her share in the murder of Amy Robsart, the unlucky Norfolk girl who stood between her and Leicester.

The brightest page in our local history during this reign is undoubtedly that which records the unswerving and statesmanlike support Elizabeth's councillors gave to the 'strangers,' or foreign settlers, whose pageant to welcome her I have just mentioned.

It has been conjectured* that this was not the first time that foreigners had settled in Norfolk, and taught us the way to use our wool; but I have as yet discovered no evidence in support of the guesses to the effect that they settled at Worstead about 1336, or that they discovered fuller's-earth here The subsidy-rolls of 1 and 6 Edw. III., a few years only before this, show no signs of foreign names. As to the friendly invasion of 1565 there can, however, be no doubt; for many—of whom the most were Dutch, though some were Walloons or French, all of whom had been driven out of the Low Countries by the Duke of Alva—settled here, and introduced the making of 'bayes, sayes, arras, mockades, and such like,' to the great advantage of the city and the encouragement of its trade. The

* Blom. Norf., iii., p. 83.
† Blomefield says 3,000, but there were only 1,132 in 1569.

Dutch had the choir of the Friars Preachers, now St. Andrew's Hall, and the French or Walloons the decayed church of St. Mary-the-Less, on Tombland, assigned to them as places of worship. The Dutch congregation still hangs together nominally, for it has a little property, and one sermon a year is preached to it by the chaplain to the Netherlands Embassy, but the Walloon congregation became extinct in 1836. Both the Dutch and the Walloon settlers were supported by the mayors and by the Duke of Norfolk for some time, and seem to have lived at peace with the townsfolk, till there was an attempt on the part of Thomas Whalle, the Mayor in 1567, to have them ejected. He did contrive to put them under several irksome rules—such as that they should lodge no stranger for more than one night, nor walk in the streets after St. Peter Mancroft's bell had sounded; and, two years later, he reported to the Privy Council that there were continual disputes between the strangers—then numbering 1,132—and the townspeople. On this, the Council prohibited any more settling there; and in 1570 there was a conspiracy, usually called Appleyard's Conspiracy, to expel all the strangers from the country; but this being sharply put down, the *animus* against them seems to have gradually passed away, and the industrious settlers waxed wealthy and important, till at last one of them—Elisha Phillippo—was made Sheriff of Norfolk in 1674, though even as late as 1682 fresh immigrations provoked fresh riots.

In 1571, the strangers numbered 3,925 all told; and ten years after their first coming, they received a very good character * for industry, and especially for that 'they live wholly of themselves without our charge, and do beg of no man, and do sustain all their own people.' In 1582 their numbers had risen to 4,679, and in a very few generations they had practically amalgamated with the townsfolk. Among other benefits they conferred on the city was the introduction of printing, the first Norwich book being printed by 'Anthony Solen, prynter,' in 1570. His real name was Anthonius de la Solemne, 'Tipographus,' and he came from Brabant in 1567 with his wife and two children.

We may make an easy guess, and suppose that he was not unknown to 'Anthonius Rabat bibliopola cum uxore et pueris in Anglia natis [qui] huc ex Flandria venit 1567;' or to Cornelius Van Hille, 'bibliopola,' who came in the same year; or Petrus Jass, 'bibliopola,' who came from Zealand in 1562.

It is, of course, difficult to say what proportion of the present population of Norwich is descended from those Dutch and Walloon strangers of three centuries ago. Their names slid easily into English equivalents—De Witt becomes White, and Le Brun, Browne, as in the case of H. K. Browne's ancestor. Of the French-Walloons we know, of course, of the Martineaus, and there is little difficulty in identifying the names of De Carle, De Caux, Le Fevere (de)

* Dom. S. P. Eliz., vol. xx, No. 49.

Lawn, Goddard (Godart), Fremault, Orfeur, Phillipo, and Philoe.

There are many more of the Dutch recognisable. Of course one could not expect that the descendants of Gerardus *Gallus* would consent to be held up to perpetual derision by adhering to their patronymic; but those of Boos *Gallant* would naturally cling to what was a complimentary epithet in their adopted land. Some, of course, were more tenacious, and Cornelius Vander Goez and Cristianus Rumpf were happy in being the progenitors of the Norwich printers who are not ashamed to worthily bear to this day the unpleasant surnames of Goose and Rump. Such corruptions as Muskett, from Mosquaert, are obvious enough; but one can only guess at what foreign names supplied the extraordinary forms of Hipgame and Copperwheat.

Of the identities of the following there can be little doubt. Those in the second column are names of persons now living in Norwich, and nearly all are to be found in White's Directory of the year 1883.

Aelman	Allman	Deynser, Van	Daynes
Aert	Hart	Firmin	Firman
Allardi	Allard	Gallant	Gallant
Bateman	Bateman	Godardus	Goddard
Becque	Beck	Godscale	Godsall
Bois du	Boyes	Goez	Goose
Brasell	Brazell	Gomerspach	Gomer
Busche	Bush	Gros	Gross
Case	Case	Grouterius	Grout
Crucius	Du Croz	Heyden	Hayden
Denijs	Dennes	Keerle	Curl
Dente, Le	Dent	Lambrecht	Lambert

Los . . .	Loose	Rabat	Raby (?)
Meys . .	Mays	Ram de .	Ramm
Mins . .	Minns	Raet . .	Ray
Moes . .	Morse (?)	Reiner	Rayner
Mol . .	Moll	Rey, Van .	Ray
Monemonte	Monemente	Ryckewaert	Rickwood (?)
Mosquaert	Muskett	Roiler . .	Roll
Mote . .	Mott	Roode, De	Rudd
Pedue . .	Peed	Roosee .	Rose (?)
Poullois .	Poll	Testardus .	Tester
Pres . .	Press	Thornius .	Thorns
Quene . .	Quinney	Turcus .	Tuck (?)

It has only just struck me, as I was writing the above, that it is very probable that the great heartiness with which the Norwich people joined in preparing to meet the Spanish Armada may have been due in some measure to their having among them so many of those who had personally suffered from Spanish persecution. They would hardly be at all backward with money, or trouble to help to repel those under whose hands they had already smarted.

In 1571 the Spaniards had been invited to invade Scotland, and when—directly after the massacre of St. Bartholomew—in the following year it seemed as though England was to be threatened by a Catholic combination, orders were sent down to each county for a return to be immediately made of all the 'able and chosen men' who could be ready upon 'a se'nnighte's warninge,' and what armour was available for them. Norfolk's return was a prompt and satisfactory one, viz., 7,600 men—without reckoning Norwich, and probably Lynn—440 'harquibutters,' 1,260 archers, 1,300 pikemen, and 4,600 billmen.

There was plenty of munitions for them too, viz., 700 'harquebutts, qualyvers, and curriors,' 1,500 long-bows, 530 corslets, and 2,200 almayn rivets, brigandynes, and coats of plate. The force was divided into companies, under the charge of certain captains, some of whom had 300, some 200, and some 100 men.

Early next year other returns were ordered of all men over sixteen, able to bear and use arms, and of horses available for war. The reply shows 8,215 footmen, 28 demi-lances, and 184 light horse or geldings. By 1577 the numbers had grown greatly with the growing need. There were then 12,032 'able men' available, of whom 123 were wheelwrights, 308 were smiths, and 2,453 pioneers and labourers, leaving 9,148 fighting men. The long-bow men had increased in number to 2,045, and there were 1,961 sheaves of arrows for them; while 500 'shott' or marksmen with harquebusse, etc., were being specially trained and exercised, and most of them were found 'very apt and handsome for that purpose,' and all unlawful games were stopped so as to give more time for archery-practice.

Norwich had its separate train-bands, and in 1578 found eighty 'calyver' men, who had two days' firing-practice at a 'hoffe' (butt) of boards on Mousehold Heath;* and during this course of musketry instruction they were paid 8d. a day, and their captain 40s. In 1580 the county return shows its force kept up, there being 9,260 horse and foot, and the subsequent replies

* Where the Norwich volunteers still practise.

are equally satisfactory. By 1584 it would seem that the danger was getting so near that 2,000 men were to be levied and reduced into bands, apparently to be always ready, and not only at a week's notice, and each Hundred had to collect money for powder, match, and lead. Some directions given in the September of this year to the Norwich men are curious.

The demi-lances and light horse were to muster near Magdalen Chapel on Mousehold Heath, on the 5th October, at eight a.m. Each demi-lance was to bring an entire trotting horse or long-trotting gelding, with a strong leather harness, and either a steel or a very strong bolstered saddle; and himself to be armed with demi-lance, armour, staff, sword and dagger, and battle-axe : while each light-horseman was to have a staff, a case of pistols, sword and dagger, jack or coat of plate, skull-cap with covered checks, or burgonet with a corselet. His doublet-sleeves were to be struck down with some small chain or plate—no doubt to prevent his bridle-arm being disabled—and his gelding was to be ridden with a snaffle, and to have a light saddle, 'after the manner of the longest Northern light-horsemen'—the Border-riders—with a case of daggers at it.

As we get on the interest increases, and the entries grow more numerous. A fortress is to be built at a place called Crotche, near Lynn, and fortifications were ordered also at Weybourne Hoop, Sherringham Hithe, Mundesly, Bromholm, Winterton, and Yarmouth. The county watched the beacons nightly, and begged thirty pieces of ordnance from the Council.

Weybourne had always been thought a weak spot on the English coast, for its shore shelves so rapidly that ships of war could ride almost up to it. The old prophecies of a previous reign talked of how a king should land on the north coast at Weybourne Stone, and fight such a battle between Weybourne and Branksbrim, that blood should run from there to Crome Bridge. There was, too, the old rhyme,

> ' He who would Old England win,
> Must at Weybourne Hoop begin.'

In March, 1588, three ships were seen taking soundings off Yarmouth; and in April, Lynn wrote up to the Council that it was fitting out the *Mayflower*, 150 tons, and a pinnace of 40 tons. Is it not within the bounds of possibility that the *Mayflower*, which did its part in defending England from its enemies, may, thirty-two years later, have carried the Pilgrim Fathers to America? Ships were stoutly built in those days; Boston is only just across the water from Lynn, and the old ship may easily have changed hands from one port to another.*

To come back, however, to the spring of 1588. In April the ' Queen's General ' came down to Norwich to judge how we were getting on, and was heartily welcomed, a gilt cup being given him, and great ordnance shot off in his honour in the Castle Yard; and there was ' skirmishing ' on Mousehold, no doubt under his supervision, and a second muster. The armourer and his men were paid for working thirty-

---

* The tonnage of the celebrated *Mayflower* is said to have been 180; but I do not suppose tonnage was very accurately measured in those days.

two days and *nights* (suggestive, this), repairing, amending, and fitting armour. From the 12th to 20th May armour and arms were bought as quick as might be. Two loads of pikes and halberds sent from London to Yarmouth were brought up river to Norwich. A special messenger was sent to the Council, sitting at Greenwich, to beg for powder and great ordnance—Norwich voted £100 for gunpowder, some is stored in the hospital (the bane and the antidote together), and everything is ready.

At last—in July—the Armada came, but it was beaten long before some of its remnants sailed along our coast in ruinous flight to the Orkneys in August. Possibly by way of precaution, on the 24th, 300 soldiers were sent from Norwich to Yarmouth in three keels.* A Lynn man, who brought the good news to Norwich of the 'meeting of the Spaniards on the seas by the Queen's fleet,' was paid 5s.; and the ringers of St. Peter Mancroft had 3s. for 'ringing on the tryumfing day had of the Spanyards,' by the Mayor's command, and 2s. 4d. for ringing on the 'victory day that the Lord gave us over the Spanyards,' as appointed by the Queen—and that was all we had to do with the great scare of the sixteenth century. But I venture to think that the 'country gnoffes,' who had fought so desperately against trained soldiers in Kett's rebellion, would, side by side with the persecuted 'strangers' they had harboured, have rendered as good an account of any

* 'Keels' were the precursors of our present wherries, from which they differed in their rig. See Chapter XIV

reasonable number of Spaniards who might have landed on the Yarmouth denes, as they did of the mercenaries in Norwich streets in 1549.

Three years later the danger was practically over, and the county muster was allowed to fall from the 9,260 of the last return, to 4,574, and gradually fell away to next to nothing till the Civil War trouble, mentioned in the next chapter, began.

A curious side of home life in this reign was the way in which pirates seem to have always been 'hanging' about the coast, though perhaps not in the way those they robbed would have wished. In 1577, a Scotch trader from Aberdeen was taken in 'Laystoft' Roads by one Captain Phibson; and soon after a regular Commission had to be sent down as to piracy, who made a formal return as to the offences and names of the pirates and their aiders in this county. The next year the bailiffs of Yarmouth caught the pirate named Thomas Hitchcock, and he was examined there as to his spoiling two Scottish ships in 1574. Another—Arthur Michelson—was caught at Lynn the same year, and in 1579 one Captain Bellingham seems to have been busy; and we catch another glance at Captain Phibson; and we hear of cloths, stolen on the seas, being landed and fraudulently concealed in the house of Mr. Debdin, at Somerton. This last man's name was sometimes spelt Dibden, and in 1579 he himself is called a pirate.*
It is not a Norfolk name, so perhaps he was an ancestor of Dibden, whose love of the sea and a roving life may have been hereditary.

* Dom. S. P., cxxxi., No. 36.

VI.

NORFOLK'S PART IN THE 'EASTERN ASSOCIATION.'

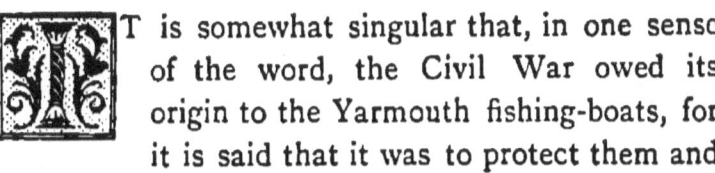T is somewhat singular that, in one sense of the word, the Civil War owed its origin to the Yarmouth fishing-boats, for it is said that it was to protect them and the coast trade generally that the expedient of levying 'ship-money' was hit upon. The Dunkirkers had been scouring the coast for some years. Before 1628 they had actually landed in Tunstead, and the North Sea fishing fleet did not dare to sail without an armed convoy. When the fish was caught it could not be sent down to London, nor could the corn, or the butter, or the cheese. Even when the Commonwealth was in full force, it was said that 'the Dunkirkers and Ostenders know the Norfolk coast so well that they chase and plunder and take us in our own bay.'

It was, therefore, no mere excuse to say that ships of war were urgently needed; and if there had been any certainty that the money raised ostensibly for their supply would have been truly spent in providing them, few Englishmen would have grudged the payment, the more especially as there was plenty of precedent for it. That there was some genuine shipbuilding done is clear, for we find the Justices of Norfolk directed, in May, 1638, to convey 800 loads of timber for the frame of the ship called the *Prince*.

In Norfolk, however, as everywhere else, the difficulty of levying the rate was immense. Constables of Hundreds refused to distrain for arrears, and excuses on excuses were made to the Sheriffs—one of whom wrote pitifully to the Privy Council that he 'has become the most odious, despicable man in the county.'

When the storm broke, probably no county was warmer in favour of the Commonwealth than Norfolk. Hardly a hand was held up for the King. The same sturdy, independent blood that had fought so stoutly for its rights under Litester and Kett, had long chafed under the growing arbitrariness of the Government; and some of those in whose veins it ran had already emigrated, notably many from Hingham, whose colony of the same name is now well known. It was a Norfolk member (Sir Miles Hobart) who shut and locked the door of the House when the King sent the Captain of his Guard to force it and bring away the mace; and so strong was the Parliamentarian majority in the east, that in 1642 it constituted itself into an 'Association,' which comprised Norfolk, Suffolk, Essex, Cambridge, and Herts, which was joined next year by Hunting.

don and Lincoln, with the result of not only keeping the war almost wholly out of its boundaries, but of getting together an army which, 'as soon as their harvest was over,' marched out—in the strange, intermittent way in which the Civil War was conducted throughout—under the command of the Earl of Leicester.

Of their personal conduct, how they were raised and how paid, we know little; and it was to supply this want that an impudent local forger concocted the 'Squire Papers,' which fairly took in Carlyle, who printed them as an appendix to his 'Cromwell's Letters and Speeches.' In my ' Norfolk Antiquarian Miscellany,'* I dissected these papers at some length, but it is hardly worth while going over the ground again here. It will suffice, perhaps, to any one acquainted with the subject, to point out that at a time when double Christian names were so extremely rare that a single example can hardly be found, one list only of a hundred and forty-nine names has *four* examples. The proportion of very unusual and Scriptural Christian names, too, is ridiculously large; but the letters glorified Cromwell and gave plenty of detail, and that was enough for Carlyle, that very-much-overrated-for-historical-accuracy writer.† Since the above was written, Prof. Gairdner has finally burst the bubble in a letter to the *Academy* of March, 1885.

* Vol. ii., p. 16.
† The forged pedigree of Cromwell from the royal family of Stuart also took him in. (See *Genealogist*, Jan. 1885.)

At each extremity of the county there was a little stir. In October, 1642, a King's ship with 140 officers and men, and 300 barrels of gunpowder, and some of the Queen's letters, was captured, without a blow, by the Yarmouth volunteers, who were publicly thanked by the House for their good service; while a year later—September, 1643—Lynn, which had declared for the King, was captured by the Eastern Association army, under the Earl of Manchester. Its royalism was no doubt due to the Le Stranges of Hunstanton, who were powerful neighbouring squires. Sir Hamo Le Strange was chosen Governor, and promised £1,000 of his own money towards the defence, and the garrison had 50 pieces of ordnance, 1,200 muskets, 500 barrels of powder, and three or four troops of horse.

At first the Royalists had a little the best of the skirmishes, but Cromwell, coming up, occupied West Lynn, and began to shoot over the river right into the town—one cannon-ball slapping right into St. Margaret's church during Sunday morning service, smashing one of the pillars, but hurting no one. The maids of Norwich raised a troop, afterwards called the 'Virgin Troop,' and the bachelors were to have got together another, to send to help reduce their sister city—a curious survival of the old joinings together to raise the 'Maiden's Light,' and the 'Bachelor's Light,' in Catholic times. This 'Maiden Troop,' by the way, afterwards had a tradition manufactured for it that it was composed of virtuous maidens who, incensed at the outrages committed on their sex by the Cavaliers, banded together to fight for themselves! However—whether by the maidens or Cromwell—the town was reduced with little bloodshed, in spite of some boasting that ' Manchester might as soon raise his father from the dead as get into Lynn,' and ' that he might as soon get into heaven as into Lynn.'

Sir Hamo Le Strange seems to have professed to be reconciled to the Parliament; but whether this was only a blind must be matter of conjecture, for the next year his son Roger ('Strange Lying Roger,' the pamphleteer) got up a plot for surprising Lynn, and obtained the King's commission at Oxford; but rashly trusting two men named Lemon and Haggard, was betrayed by them, and sentenced to death as a spy, though he contended that what he had done was fair and open warfare. He was remanded, and afterwards escaped, living to be a most virulent writer against the party who intended to hang him.

The King's side never raised its head again in Norfolk after this. There was a commotion in Norwich in 1648, when the Mayor, being a loyal subject, was removed by order of the Parliament. Some of his friends plotted to rescue him by force, and not allow him to be taken up to London by the messenger of the House of Commons, who was staying at the ' Royal,' then the King's Head; and if it had not been for some of the more sensible of the citizens, the freemen—many of whom openly avowed they were for the King— would have killed the messenger, who had to fly for his life without his prisoner. As it was, there was a tumultuous rising and breaking-in of shops, and robbery of arms and powder, and all the makings of a bloodthirsty riot. But Fleetwood's troop, billeted out not far away, came galloping in about five o'clock in the evening, and made short work of the undisciplined mob. Some were holding the 'Committee House,' in Bethlehem Yard, where the Hospital now stands. Everything was in confusion; the troopers were hammering at the gate; gunpowder was lying about loose all over the place—one man afterwards swore that he swept up a hatful from the stairs; and it would have been a miracle if the ninety-eight barrels of gunpowder had *not* blown up, as they did in due course. How many were killed in the 'crack,' as the old writers called it, is not known; but it effectually took all the fight out of the survivors, who scattered and fled. The churches of St. Peter Mancroft and of St. Stephen both suffered from the explosion—especially the former, which, from its churchwardens' accounts, seems to have had its east window blown in; and its bells were rung shortly after, to celebrate its great deliverance from the 'Blowe.' General Fairfax came down in person to see the mischief; and, soon after, the 'mutineers,' 108 in number, were tried, and seven executed in the Castle Ditches. It is hard to say whether there is any truth in the rumour that King Charles hid for four days at Downham, and stayed at the Castle Inn there, though some say he was concealed at Snore Hall, near Ryston.

Of the story so often told by local writers—that

the execution of Charles I. was determined on at a Council held at No. 4, South Quay, Yarmouth, which then belonged to John Carter, whose son married Ireton's daughter—it is hardly necessary to say much by way of criticism. It is a pity we cannot believe the picturesque fabrication—the regicides consulting for hours together in strict privacy, with a servant at the door; the putting off dinner from hour to hour, from four till past eleven at night; and the then sudden dispersal of the conspirators—some for London, some for the army—after a hasty meal. But, except a letter written in 1773, there is not the least foundation for the story; and it is in the highest degree unlikely that those who held the strings in their hands in London should have taken so unnecessary a step as to have rendezvoused at Yarmouth to talk the matter over.

By the way, it is noticeable that Cromwell, like Queen Elizabeth, was from East English blood on his mother's side—being descended from a family named Styward, of Swaffham, for whom a descent from the royal family of Stuart was concocted in the reign of Elizabeth. This fiction, I think I may say, was exposed by me in the *Genealogist* of January, 1885.

It cannot be supposed that when the Royalists at last got the upper hand again, they did not vilify those who had been riding roughshod over them. Miles Corbet, for example—who was probably the most active of the Norfolk regicides, and afterwards executed—was said to have been 'at the beginning of the Parliament £5,000 in debt—more than he was worth. Now one of the Registrars of Chancery, worth £700 a year; besides chairman for scandalous ministers (sic), worth £1,000 per ann., and hath money in his purse.'

A list of the Royalist party in the county, and an account of their properties, and what fines they had to pay, will be found at p. 315 et seq. of Mason's 'History of Norfolk.' Corbett of Sprowston was first a Royalist, but then deserted to the Parliament —the only renegade of the county. De Gray of Merton, Fountaine, Heydon, Jermyn, Le Neve, Paston, and Yelverton were more staunch, and no doubt were rewarded in one way or another by the Merry Monarch; and if the proposed order of 'Knighthood of the Royal Oak' had been instituted, twenty Norfolk men were to have had it.

Some of the outbursts of loyalty under difficulties were amusing. One man got into trouble for saying out at Fersfield:

> 'Heigh-ho for a twopenny halter!
> When you are hanged you shall have good quarter.
> Oh it would be—a brave sight to see
> All the Roundheads—hung on a tree.
> [*Spoken*] O ye rogues, ye must all come to it!'

The little joke as to 'quarter' and 'quartering' is not so bad.

We know that many of the regular clergy suffered much by their ejectment; and when they were at length reinstated, one can fancy the glee and satisfaction with which they reached down the parish registers and, as at Edingthorpe, wrote under the name of the ousted minister some such lines as: 'This Knave Michel, of detestable and most odious memory, was Holder-forth;' and 'When ye Knave Michel held forth, who in effect turn'd the Temple of God into a Tabernacle of Robbers.'

So, then, all was well that ended well; and the ringers of St. Peter Mancroft, who had been pulling away merrily in 1657, 'on the day the Lord Protector was proclaimed,' exercised their professional skill just as heartily in 1660, 'ringinge when the King's armes were sett up.' Perhaps, indeed, it may be doubted if they cared two straws as to what they were ringing about, if their beloved bells swung truly and their 'gotches' of ale were duly replenished.

VII.

OUR LATER HISTORY.

OF James I. the Norfolk people saw a good deal, though nothing much to their edification. Coke (son of the Chief Justice) speaks of his drinking Greek wine so strong that, tasting it out of curiosity, it upset him for three days afterwards; and gives a graphic picture of how the King was 'trussed' or fastened on to his horse's back when he was hunting, and how he rode as he was set, without trying to poise himself in his saddle, and how if his hat were put on awry he let it stop so. Thetford, no doubt for its position for hunting and hawking and its flocks of bustards, was his favourite place in Norfolk. Here, we are told, he had a long-continued cold, which he kept renewing from time to time by getting hot with hunting and then drinking immoderately. Here, too, his timorous mind was grievously offended by the loyal subjects joining too closely in his hunting, and Sir William Woodhouse had to forbid people to come to him on those occasions. From Thetford he sent word to Dame Catherine Corbet, of Woodbastwick, to preserve an eyrie of laniers (hawks) breeding in her woods there. A warren of hares was enclosed for him, in 1606, between Newmarket and Thetford. The 'King's House,' at the latter place, is still one of the most interesting buildings in the town (see *post*, Chapter XII.). More westerly he made his celebrated joke: when on a marshland man boasting that the fertility of West Norfolk marshes was so great that if you placed a stick over-night on the ground you could not see it next morning [for the rapid growth of grass], the King retaliated that he knew meadows in Scotland where, if you put a *horse* over-night you would not see it next day.

But, apart from the stirring times of the Civil War, on which I touched in the last chapter, the history of Norfolk for the last three centuries is really the history of its elections and of its trade. Of the trade I will treat slightly in my ninth chapter; so in this I will say something about the most noticeable of the old-world elections.

Of the very early elections little need be said. The serving the county or city was done with reluctance by the members, who grudged the time and trouble it cost them, and who were in most cases only the nominees of the preponderating parties in the country. It is not till the latter half of the fifteenth century that one gets any details of interest about the elections, and then, as usual, only through the Paston Letters

In 1455, the Duchess of Norfolk writes to John

Paston that it was necessary 'that my lord should have at this time in Parliament such persons as long with him and be of his menial servants,' (!) and asks for Paston's support for John Howard and Sir Roger Chamberlin. There was some faint-hearted opposition to this. Some said that it was 'an evil precedent for the shire that a strange man should be chosen. . . . And that if the gentlemen of the shire will suffer such inconvenience, the shire shall not be called of such worship as it hath been.'

But it all came to nothing—the Under-Sheriff seemed frightened of opposing the great man, and so his two nominees were returned as usual. Half-a-dozen years later (1461) John Paston himself was elected, with his wife's cousin, John Berney, but not so peacefully; for the same Sir John Howard, who was then Sheriff of the county, had a great dispute with Paston in the shire-house, and one of his men struck Paston twice with a dagger—the stroke, however, being luckily stopped by a well-padded doublet.

In 1586 there was a double return for knights of the shire under curious circumstances, *two* writs having been sent down to the Sheriff,—one on the 15th September and the other on the 11th October. The reason for the second return has puzzled Mr. Mason,* but the reason seems clear enough to me, viz., that the first writ was not received in time to be proclaimed, and the freeholders notified—so the Chancery sent down a second writ, which was properly executed. However, the House considered

* Hist. of Norf., vol. i., p. 162.

it would be a perilous precedent for a second writ to have been sent down without its sanction, and so decided in favour of the first return.

The way in which the election of 1614 was conducted by the authorities seems to have given great dissatisfaction, for a petition was presented by many thousands of the freeholders about it—which petition is now preserved among the House of Lords Records. From Additional MS. 27,402, f. 192, it would seem that 'one Mr. Hurne' appeared on behalf of Sir John Hobart, for whom not above twenty votes were given, 'though money was given to procure several,' and raised a disturbance, assaulting a grave divine, knocking down the Sheriff, and breaking his staff of office. There are no returns extant for this election, which, as it will be remembered, was that rendered so noteworthy by the Court candidates being rejected nearly everywhere. It has been assumed, however,[*] that Calthorp and Catelin were duly elected on the strength of the MS. just quoted, referring to their having a majority of 500 and more over Hobart. But our earliest election squib, 'The Dead March,' which is ascribed to 1616, mentions Sir Hamond Le Strange and Sir Henry Bedingfield as being then M.P.'s for the county. Another Hobart (Sir Miles) was one of the members in 1629, and, as before mentioned, was the man who was bold enough to lock the door of the House in the face of the Captain of the King's Guard, and to put the key in his pocket.

[*] Mason's Norfolk, p. 255.

To the Long Parliament of 1640 Sir Thomas Wodehouse and Framingham Gawdy were sent up from Norfolk in the Parliamentary interest. A man called Tobias Fryar (Frere)* stood as a zealot, and of him the following story is preserved in the L'Estrange anecdotes, printed by the Camden Society in 1839:

'Tobias Fryar, a pretended zelote but true ringleader and head of all factions and schismaticall spiritts in the County, puft up with the pride and strength of his party, must needs stand to be Kt. (or rather K[nave]) of the shire for Norff, but fell most shamefully short, and lost it with many squibs and disgraces; only for his comfort a true disciple of his sayd: "However, I am sure Mr. Fryar stood for Christ Jesus, for none but reprobates and prophane wretches went against him"' (No. 553).

Of the election of 1675 some amusing particulars are preserved among the Ingilby MSS.† Sir Robert Kemp was the Government, and Sir Nevill Catlyn the Independent, candidate. Catlyn's party 'used' the 'Royal' (then the King's Head), and the other side, using a stratagem—singularly enough repeated at the same house last election, two or three years ago—ordered a great dinner there, on the pretence that they might 'friendly meet and dine' with the other party, and ultimately secured the whole house

---

* He was more successful in the Short or Barebones Parliament of 1653, and in Cromwell's Second Parliament in 1654.
† 6th Rep. Hist. MSS. Com., p. 371 a.

as their election quarters; Catlyn, who was brought into town by 4,000 horsemen, having to put up with the White Swan, 'at the back side of the butchers' shambles.' Loud complaints were made that the Sheriff and Lord Lieutenant greatly favoured Kemp's side, and that the poll was prematurely closed, and, in effect, that the militia 'governed their poor countrymen.' 'It's much observed here that many of those persons that came to the poll for Sir Robert Kemp cried out that they came for the Lord Lieutenant's sake, and others for this Colonel, Captain, or Justice, but rarely any man said he came for Sir Robert Kemp's sake.'

In 1677, there was a strange election for the city, William Paston—afterwards Earl of Yarmouth—being unwillingly opposed by Captain Augustine Briggs, who was put forward by the 'sectaries, notwithstanding the Captain utterly refused to sign.' This election was also noticeable for the wholesale creation of freemen for the express purpose of voting at it.

The Paston interest in 1678 was thrown in with Calthorp and Catlyn, who are said to have won easily, their supporters voting very evenly, the numbers being 2,243 and 2,242, Sir John (Hobart ?), the favourite of the 'rabble,' only polling 1,733. On the other hand, the return in Ewing's 'Norfolk Lists' gives Hobart and Catlyn as the sitting members, so I suppose Calthorp was thrown out on petition.

Of course, in all Norfolk elections about this time

the figure of Sir Robert Walpole—Squire of Houghton long before he was Prime Minister of England— looms large before us; and we may guess how his influence and his money—or rather the money he handled—were brought to bear on the local politics of his native county. In the first year of the eighteenth century he was married to the daughter of a Lord Mayor of London, and entered Parliament as member for the rotten borough of Castle Rising. So fast did he rise, that he was governing the House in 1708 as Whig Prime Minister. When the Tories came in again, he was impeached for corruption; and in 1712 a majority of the House resolved that he had been guilty of a high breach of trust and notorious corruption while Secretary at War, and he was committed to the Tower and expelled the House. At the dissolution in 1713, he was sent back as member for Lynn, and, when George I. came to the throne, was in the next Ministry, and soon had an opportunity of showing that two could play at impeaching. The rest of his life is matter of public history, and does not affect the county, to which he returned to die, just before the '45. His alleged peculations have some interest for the local historian, for out of them he is thought to have built Houghton Hall, at a fabulous expense, and to have stocked it with pictures so valuable that the Empress of Russia afterwards bought some of them for over £40,000. The house is a hideous one—heavy and dark—built to the designs of Campbell by one Ripley, of whom Pope wrote:

'So Ripley, till his destined space is filled,
Heaps bricks on bricks, and fancies 'tis to build.'

What it cost—building and furnishing—will probably never be known; but it is impossible it could have been erected with honest money, for Walpole's patrimony was little over £2,000 a year.

Any one wanting to read the accusations and insinuations against him and his honesty, cannot do better than read the satirically so-styled 'Robin's Panegyrick, or the Norfolk Miscellany,' which, I think, must contain everything that can possibly be said against him, his family, and his relations. Some of the poetry is amusing; *e.g.*, the ballad styled 'Leheup at Hanover,' affecting to describe how the statesman's son, Horace, and Isaac Leheup—a connection of the family by marriage—grossly misbehaved themselves at Hanover. It begins:

'When Robin ruled the British land
  With gold and silver bright,
To put his kindred all in place
  He ever took delight.
Forth from the venal band he call'd,
  Horace and Isaac came.
He bid 'em go to foreign Courts
  And raise immortal fame.
Two Taylor's daughters, rich and fair,
  Exactly match each brother;
Horace *made suit* and gain'd the one,
  And Isaac *stitch'd* the other.'

This, of course, refers to Horace Walpole's marrying one of the daughters of Peter Lombard, a wellknown tailor, and to the insinuation that Leheup was unduly familiar with another.

In the county, the minister seems to have been popular for his hearty good-temper. An amusing tale is told how, delighted at hearing that the Dereham people meant to pave their town—then, as now, a dirty hole—he invited some of the principal inhabitants to Houghton, and gave them a good dinner, and twenty guineas towards the expense of the work; and that they then rather ungratefully got a trifle too jovial on his liquor, and sang a Jacobite song, 'All joys to Great Cæsar,' under his astonished roof-tree.

It was about this time that the scandal about Castle Rising was at its worst. It shared with Old Sarum the disreputable notoriety of being the rottenest of rotten boroughs.* It is hard to say why it ever returned two members, or one, indeed, for the matter of that. There were formerly fifty burgesses, which number the proprietors of the soil, the Earl of Orford and Countess of Suffolk, judiciously reduced to *two*—each voter therefore sending a representative to Parliament. The whole election was carried out in the chancel of the parish church; and, after it was over, the burgesses 'were carried up to the Castle, where the Treat is provided.' It will be remembered that Castle Rising once sent a waiter as one of its representatives!

The county election of 1714 was one of the most stubborn ever fought in the county, Astley and De Grey winning with 3,059 and 3,183, against Hare and Earle with 2,840 and 2,635.

* It first sent members in 1558, when it was an absolutely insignificant place.

It is curious how some villages voted like a stone wall: *e.g.*, Cromer not giving a vote to Hare and Earle; while, singularly enough, Watton—hard by the De Greys' seat at Merton—gave their adversaries twice as many votes as it did its neighbour. Singularly enough, too, at Dalling—which one would have thought a stronghold of the Earles—they only had a majority of one vote.

Still closer and harder was the fight of 1734, when Bacon and Wodehouse, with 3,224 and 3,153, beat Coke and Morden with 3,081 and 3,147. When it comes to half a dozen votes in three thousand, one trembles to think what frightful bribery must have been going on. This election is said to have cost Sir Robert Walpole £60,000.

The election of 1768, when Astley and Coke beat De Grey and Wodehouse, was closer still, there being again only half a dozen between third and fourth, the numbers being: 1,869, 1,657, 1,651, and 1,565.

Later on, Coke and Astley, when they beat Wodehouse in 1802, only got rid of him by less than 100; but Wodehouse's party began to fall away in 1806, when Coke and Windham beat him anyhow.

To describe the election squibs would take a chapter by itself, which would not be a very edifying or interesting one; for the raciness of the chaff and the abuse is gone when one has to painfully dig out and translate the meaning.

Of course, some things are obvious enough. For

example: if a baronet named Bacon stands for a county, he must expect—though his name comes from an early Danish settler—to be called every variety of hog and pig, and to have a pig's head put to his caricatures.

The history of Norfolk electioneering would be incomplete without a passing reference to Richard Gardiner—better known by his *nom de plume* of 'Dick Merryfellow'—who was born in 1723, long lived at Swaffham, and died at Ingoldisthorpe in 1781. Early in life he had been disappointed in love by being rejected by Miss Sotherton of Taverham, and vented his spleen, in 1754, by publishing a work called 'The History of Pudica, a Lady of Norfolk; with an Account of her Five Lovers—Dick Merryfellow; Count Antiquary; Young Squire Fog, of Dumpling Hall [Edward Hare, Esq., of Sale]; Jack Shadwill, of the Lodge [John Buxton, Esq.]; and Miles Dinglebob, of Popgun Hall, Esq. [Miles Branthwayt, Esq., of Gunthorp].' From the notoriety—one might say popularity—this work obtained, it would seem to have hit the public taste, though to this generation it appears full of dull vulgarities and offensive personalities. Encouraged by its success, he seems to have been afflicted by the *cacoëthes scribendi* for the rest of his life, and dashed into the county electioneering contests with never-ending vigour. Direct brutal personal attacks seem to have been his *forte;* and though I have waded through nearly all the stuff he wrote, I can find nothing to make one even smile, unless it be a solemn letter to John [Buxton, of?] Shadwell, Esq., assuring him solemnly that he need be under no apprehensions about coming to Norwich to serve on the Grand Jury, as the writer had no intention whatever ' of taking you by the nose, or caneing you, or giving you the discipline of the horsewhip ' — an ingenious way of insulting and annoying an adversary, without giving him any legal claim to redress. In 1768 he was a constant writer of squibs and lampoons on the popular side, especially denouncing the ' General Warrants.' A sample of his style at Lynn will suffice :

' Hogge ! that mean wretch whose dirt-collected bags
   Arose from gaping cockles sold in rags,
   Down to thy dunghill, muckworm ! and be dumb,
   Thou son of infamy, though worth a plumb !'

He supported Astley and Coke against Wodehouse and De Grey; but afterwards, having a pecuniary difference with Coke, apparently devoted the rest of his life to vilifying him in prose and rhyme.

Of course, at Norwich nowadays every one knows that the Conservative colours are orange and purple, and the Radical blue and white; but it is not generally known that the great families used to have their own colours—*e.g.*, Coke, orange ; Windham, white ; Wodehouse, pink and purple ; and Astley, green. It is strange that the present Conservative colours would seem to be a combination of the colours of two opposite parties.

VIII.

THE OLD PEASANT LIFE.

N looking at the early history of the tillers of the soil, we have to remember that in old days they were divided into: (1) 'Bondsmen in blood,' who had, practically speaking, to do what the lord of the manor to which they were annexed told them to do; and (2) Free tenants, who were bound by the tenure of their lands to do certain work annually—a survival of whose duties may still be seen in county leases, where the lessee often covenants to do so many days' work with his horses and carts, carrying coal to the 'Hall.' Free labourers were very scarce indeed—one may almost say unknown; so, if the lord wanted more work than his bondsmen could do, or his free tenants would do, he had to make terms with this latter class to do so for a money or other consideration.

The 'bondsmen' were attached to the manor, and their lords could grant them with it, or apparently with any portion of it. Henry de Rye (*ante*, 1162)

granted the mill of Worthing, near Dereham, with Turstan the miller, his mother and brothers, and all their land and substance, to the monks of Castle Acre, and afterwards gave them Philip and Adewald, and all their services and tenures. But I have not met with a case in which the lord granted villeins away from his manor ;* and indeed the essence of the slavery seems to have been its locality ; for I find that when John de Clavering, in 1312, sued eighteen villeins of his manor of Cossey for withdrawing themselves from his manor, six of them successfully pleaded they had obtained their freedom by living in the city of Norwich without paying 'chevage' for a year and a day; and two others, that they had been born in the city, and were so free. This 'chevage' was a fine paid by the villein to his lord for liberty to live outside his manor, and of course operated as an admission of his villeinage while paid. Later on, in some manors, those who paid it were called 'aulepimen,' a word the derivation of which has long puzzled wiser heads than mine. The villeins also paid fines if they married without the lord's license. Occasionally the lord urged by the priest, gave his bondsmen their liberty for the good of his soul, and sometimes they bought it. A villein could not take Holy Orders without his lord's license, and even when this was granted it did not necessarily include a grant of his freedom, as may be seen by two

* Except occasionally when he gave the villeins to some religious house, when by a pleasing fiction they were supposed to be serving God, not man.

licenses I printed in the 'East Anglian' (N. S.), vol. i., p. 5. I have seen fines levied of a man's freedom; and deeds granting it are not uncommon;* but all manors were not so lucky as that of Coltishall, where the King, who was lord, freed all his tenants.

The condition of a bondsman by blood could never have been pleasant; but that they were ever so loutish, or lived in such abject submission, as described by the anonymous Monk of Peterborough, in his 'Descriptio Norfolciensium,' written somewhere about 1300, is absurd. He makes out that they 'gnaw and chew bread made of tares;' do not know an ear of wheat when they see one; live at night in their lord's sheep-fold, to create manure, or pay a money fine if they did not; mistake toads for birds, and so on.

There is no reason to suppose that the alleged lord's right to a first night ever existed in Norfolk; and the idea probably arose from the fact mentioned above, that a tenant marrying out of the homage paid a fine to the lord for doing so. At Gatesthorpe, the fine was the appropriate one of a bed, bolster, sheet, and pillow; and so it was at West Herling, but in the latter place certain tenants called 'molmen' were exempt.

It must not be supposed that the tenants were entirely neglected. Some were no doubt 'house carles,' and had food and fire found them; and we find that at Gimmingham the lord's hall was sup-

* An amusing story of how some peasants bought their freedom, but unluckily used the wax seal on the charter to make a candle, and so spoiled the efficacy of the release, is told by the Monk of Peterborough, mentioned above.

ported by pillars, and the custom and rule was that no tenant socman should go beyond that pillar which was appointed for his station and degree. This would imply a participation in the meals; and we know that at Honingham the lord kept a common oven for the use of his tenants. And I expect the poorer labourers fed better in the thirteenth than in the eighteenth and part of the nineteenth centuries; for I have myself seen a man who told me he had never tasted 'butcher's meat '—pork not being so called.

Manor notices were given out to the tenants in the church, as at Bacton, when they were warned openly on the Sunday to come to the lord's court on the next Friday.*

A mud hut, thatched with fern or brushwood, was probably the best home a villein could expect. There are some cottages now in use near Smallburgh, for cart-sheds and such like, which give one the best possible idea of how the very poor must have lived six centuries ago, with clay floors, no glazed windows, and only a shutter. No doubt cosy and comfortable enough if only kept clean, for mud walls are warm; but, from the fearful head that leprosy (commonly said to have been introduced by the Crusaders) and all sorts of pestilences, such as the Black Death, made, I fear cleanliness was the exception to the rule. From the custom of Hemesby Manor, which gives a list of the articles which the lord could claim on his villein's death, we get a very good idea of the furniture of this same mud hut. Outside was a cart

* Paston 'Letters,' p. 823.

and plough; and inside, 'a table with its cloth, a ladder, a bason and washing vessel, dishes and plates, a cinum (ash-pan?), a tinum (a large vessel), as well as a bed-mattress, a grindstone, a spade and a fork.'

Of course, one could not expect much refinement with these surroundings, and we may remember with shame that it was in respect of a Norfolk manor (Kirkstead) that Baldwin le Pettour did his dirty service each coronation-day. On the other hand, *malgré* the fines on marriage, there was no doubt much connubial felicity; and we may refer with pride to the fact that it was a Norfolk couple who first won the Dunmow Flitch; and probably the 'big goose green,' as Norfolk was once called, had many a pleasant little family, who lived happily ignorant of future school boards and sanitation.

There is not much doubt that when at field-work the 'servi' were subject to some sort of physical restraint; for the reapers were supervised by a man with a rod or wand, as is told in a suit 11 John, Belet *v.* Thorpe, in Shouldham Thorpe. Even the better class of tenants, such as the 'lanceti' (a 'lancetagium' contained eight acres), were subject to many curious and irksome restrictions. They had at Hindringham, in John's time, to keep their sheep in the lord's fold from Martinmas to Candlemas, and then to take their ewes out of fold, and pay foldage; but the other sheep remained all the year in the lord's fold.

Some idea of how the 'work-services' were

arranged may be gleaned from the old customaries. In Brissingham, in 1341, the quit-rents and free-rents were, *inter alia*—212 days' work in autumn (workmen to be fed by the lord); 174 afternoons' work in autumn (no food); 25 days' work with their own carts and horses (no food); 183 'journeys' at plough; and 125 'ale beves,' *i.e.*, carting-days, on which they went or not, as they pleased—the lord treating them, if they came, to ale and food. 'Beeves'? Was this the derivation of the American 'bees'—where men and women give voluntary help, but expect a free feed afterwards? It is curious that a 'bever' is still the harvest-man's snack between breakfast and dinner—otherwise 'noonings.'

Perhaps the best record we have of the routine of duties of a manor is contained in the 'Computus' of Newton, in the marsh-land county, dated 1395. We find, first:

1. The lord's *Demesne Lands* specially accounted for—some as being in his own cultivation, sown with wheat, oats, etc., and some as being let out for a term of years—which proves that farmers were not necessarily yearly tenants in old days.

2. The *Escheated Lands*—*i.e.*, lands which formerly belonged to copyholders, but which had, by some default or another, got into the lord's hands again—the word possibly supplying an irritated copyholder with an origin for the modern word 'cheat.'

3. The *Customary Lands*—under which heading each free tenant accounts for his rent, services, and 'customs' or customary services.

This same 'Compotus' shows us that the 'customs' were often commuted for cash payments. There was here a 'sedyk-sylver'*—payable instead of doing work on the sea-dyke, this being a maritime manor; as well as a 'mowin-silver' and a 'hay-make.' The custom of giving the free tenants *something* for their customary day's labour is clear here. For autumn work they got a penny a day, while the hired labourers got fourpence. Five shillings was paid for food and beer bought for labourers carrying corn according to custom; but I find no trace of refreshments for the hired men.

The various rights of various lords, and the quaint names under which they went, are hardly as well known as they might be. At Eccles, the lord had 'heweshift, reveshift, and ingel,' to be paid by tenants; 'herdershift,' whereby the homage was to choose a shepherd to keep the lord's sheep; 'ingeld;' 'felsine,' paid by the tenants for the common aid; and 'bedgilt.' He also claimed 'resting-geld' for the beasts of strangers resting one night in the common or stock-house, and also 'resting-geld' of all goods coming to land by sea. It is curious that the sea has itself come to land so much in this parish, that there is little of it left, and the church-tower stands up solitary, like a post in a waste of sands.

It is hard to find any distinct evidence whether the poor suffered much by the maladministration of the law; but I fear they must have done so, for in

* Sea dyke silver.

one Gaol Delivery (1332) the two constables of Humbleyard were fined for extortion and fraud; and in 1276 three sheriffs were punished for extortion, while the Earl Warren's bailiff had to pay the King no less than £100 to cover his misdeeds this same year.

The claims and rights of the landlords were often enforced in a way which would astonish modern law-reformers. For example, we see by the Paston Letters that in 1477 Lynstede, the bailiff, is to distrain the crop after it is cut, while it lies on the ground—in plain English, to allow the wretched tenant to be at the expense of reaping before the distraint was to be made; while at Oxnead the farmer is to be allowed to 'in' his crop, and then the bailiff is to seal up the barn-door.

The Norfolk love for litigation, of which Tusser complains so feelingly—which drove the legislature to limit the number of attorneys in the county, and which, it is said, would make one Norfolk farmer sue another for trespass if a cow so much as looked over a hedge—was rife as much among the peasants as among their betters. An amusing entry occurs in a Government return of Crown leases, in which, after mentioning that certain parcels of saltmarsh, at Thornham and elsewhere, had been let to one Bentley, it goes on to say that he could never get possession of them, 'the Country, who had possession of them, being too hard for him at law.'

Small offences were no doubt chiefly dealt with by the manor courts in the olden times. The court really acted as a sanitary board ; for men were often prosecuted for letting their trees overhang the King's highway, for fouling springs, for not repairing roads; for keeping unrung pigs, or savage dogs or bulls, and so forth.

The Burnham Rolls give some very amusing entries of these and other sorts of offences. In the 28 Edw. I., John Doget is fined sixpence for that he slandered ('vilipendulat') a pig belonging to Martin de Southmore, while he was selling it, whereby he lost the sale—probably by calling it measly. Assaults are frequently noticed and punished; and from the frequency of such double-barrelled entries as 'John Aubrey drew blood of Henry Strabald, and Henry Strabald drew blood of John Aubrey' (28 Edw. I.), I am inclined to think that the rustics were more quarrelsome than they are now. All blood-drawing seems to have been noticed—*e.g.*, 'Martin Kutt drew blood of Richard Togood, but accidentally only, and not feloniously; therefore it is condoned.' Perhaps the most amusing of these mediæval misdemeanours is eavesdropping, or skulking, which I find first in these Burnham Rolls in the 26 Hen. VI., when Robert, son of Edmund Palle, was fined sixpence ' for standing at night under the windows of John Gasele, to hear the secrets of the said John.' A dozen years later, John Bourdye and Simon Bourdon were presented as being common skulkers under the windows of their neighbours, and in the church and elsewhere, to hear the secrets of their said neighbours, to the bad example of others. A woman was sometimes prosecuted as a 'common seminatrix discordiæ'—as was the wife of the Rev. F. Richman in 25 Eliz.—or a 'rixatrix.' Some of the quarrels were amusing. At Freethorpe, in 31 Eliz., John Buttyvant assaulted John Curtyes, 'quodam le petchforke.' Curtyes, however, was equal to the occasion; for he arranged that he should be the only man sworn on the next leet: and, expatiating pitifully on the soundness of the drubbing he had received, and how his opponent 'verberavit, percussit, et male tractavit' him, got him fined.

Poaching, of course, went on to a great extent, and, curiously enough, was indulged in by people of a better class than at present. At Burnham, the inhabitants of North Creake Abbey were the chief sinners—possibly preferring to break the monotony of religious exercises by a little excitement, such as 'trespassing in pursuit of conies with furretts, hooks, nets, and other engines,' for which they were fined £10. Other ecclesiastical retainers seem to have used the Burnham warrens without leave. In 24 Hen. VI., the servant of the Canon and the farmer of the Priory of Walsingham were presented for taking and carrying away rabbits with dogs and snares called 'Harepypes,' which I presume were long pipes of canvas, or other material, fitted to the mouth of the burrow. At Merton the 'mere' was poached with a broad net and three bow nets; and in 1403, Edward Howard and William Rokele were presented for hare-hunting in the lord's warren. Before this, Robert, Lord Morley—for poaching on Bishop

Bateman's manor, and shooting his deer—had to walk over the cruel stones of Norwich barefoot and bareheaded, to offer a 6 lb. candle at the cathedral. Again, in 1447, the servants of Sir Robert Conyers and of Master Richard Mounteney were fined for poaching rabbits; but the most impudent case was in 1359, when six men 'arrayed in a riotous manner . . . assaulted with their sticks William, the son of Thomas (de) Grey, clerk, lord of the manor, and beat, wounded, and ill-treated him, and then went on hunting hares with harehounds.'

Another man kept a dog called a 'tumbler' to kill rabbits; which was a dog trained to feign it was lame, and tumble about in a helpless way, till it had lulled the suspicions of its prey, when it recovered its speed in a wonderful way.

The later life could not have been very interesting, being hemmed in by many restrictions. In 1624, it was mooted that all the alehouses should be suppressed;* and in one town, at least (Methwold), tobacco-smoking was absolutely prohibited—at all events in the streets—in 1695. Women who had illegitimate children were publicly whipped in 1634; and for a small theft a man was whipped, 'till his body be Bloody,' as late as 1799.

The poor were however, I think, better looked after, on the whole, then than they are now. As they grew old, they were medically attended at the expense of the parish—as we find from such entries as: 'Paid mother Mason for the leechcraft of her

---
* Tanner MS. 288, folio 265.

eye' (1560); 'Paid to the collectors of Pulham Mary for the leachcraft of John Barnes' (1563); and there are plenty of entries for nursing and watching, and so on. Nor were the poor denied the last rites; for we find the parish paying for 'ringing of the soul bell,' 'for making of her grave,' 'for carrying her to church,' and 'for making her ready to the ground.'

For those a little above the class of labourers, I think I can find traces of a general arrangement by which the aged members of the family and the unmarried daughters were allowed house-room, at all events, by their better-off relations : *e.g.*, in the will of William Thaxter, of Bassingham—a blacksmith, who died 1607—he gives to one of his daughters the use of a chamber in his house till she married, with liberty 'freely to come and go to and from the fire of my said wife.' By the way, it is curious to note how some families stick to one trade. These Thaxters—ancestors of my own, by the way—though originally of course 'thatchers,' seem to have been blacksmiths and ploughwrights for generations.

Of remunerative indoor occupation for the women there seems to have been none—except, of course, spinning and knitting for home consumption—till about 1700, when, for a few years, the country people prospered extremely, through nearly every cottage having a hand-loom for weaving; and the industry kept on till the introduction of machinery.

Once a year the labourers and their wives had a brief respite from labour, and a happy day or two, as they got the harvest in. To this hour, you cannot go through a Norfolk corn-field, as the corn is falling, without being asked for largesse; but the money given now goes to the public-house, or to Norwich, instead of being clubbed together for a genuine jollification in the squire's big barn — more's the pity! In a few years the old songs and jokes will have died out, and live only in the pages of a few collectors. While one can remember them, it is just as well to put one or two on record.

A favourite one was 'The Pye upon the Pear-tree Top:'

'The pye upon the pear-tree top,
  (*Singer holds up a glass of ale.*)
'The pear-tree top—the pear-tree top,
I hold you a crown she is coming down.
  (*Brings it down slowly.*)
She is coming down, she *is* coming down,
I hold you a crown she *is* come down.
  (*Offers it to his right-hand neighbour.*)
She *is* come down—she IS come down,
So lift up your elbow and hold up your chin
And let your next neighbour joggle it in.'

The drinker then tries to drink, while his neighbour tries to stop him by fidgeting his elbow.

We have few apples, and therefore miss the familiar 'Apple Harvest Song,' and the banging off guns into the apple-trees, but 'The Barley-mow Song' we have thus:

'Here's a health to the barley-mow,
Here's a health to the man,
Who [something] well can
  Plough, harrow, and sow.

> 'And when it's well sown,
> Well grown, and well mown,
> Heaped, and well carried in;
> Here's a health to the man,
> Who [something] well can
> > Thresh it and fan it out clean.'

The 'three-out glass' toast of the 'Duke of Norfolk' was in vogue in the beginning of the present century,[*] but I have never heard it myself. The singer came in with a staff in his hand and a soft cushion on his head for a coronet, and advancing to the table, sang thus:

> 'I am the Duke of Norfolk,
> Lately come from Suffolk,
> Am I not to be attended now, now, now?
> > (*The company stand up and sing.*)
>
> Noble duke, be not offended,
> For you shall be attended
> With all the respect that we owe, owe, owe.

DUKE. If I am not attended,
> This company is ended,
> And parted I know not how, how, how.

ALL. Noble duke, be not offended,
> For you shall be attended,
> So toss off your liquor *you* know how, how, how.
> > (*Offer the duke a glass of ale, which he drinks.*)
>
> And if it is all out
> (Let us see, let us see.)
> > (*Look into the glass.*)

DUKE. And if it *is* all out,
> We will drink another bout,
> So here, my fine fellow, here's to thee, thee, thee.
> > (*Duke drinks second glass.*)

[*] E. A., iii., p. 264.

ALL. The reaper and the binder,
The binder and the reaper,
The reaper and the binder of corn, corn, corn ;
So valiant Cupid bend your bow,
And shoot away your arrow, O !
And huntsman, come wind away your horn, horn, horn.'

(*Duke drinks third glass, the harvest horn is blown, and the staff and cushion passed on to the next man, and so the toast goes round the table.*)

There was also 'The Woodcutter's Song':

'Here's a health to the jolly woodcutter,
Who takes his work at his ease ;
He takes it, and he does it,
And he leaves off when he please.°

'He takes his wythe† and winds it,
And he lays it on the ground,
And round the faggot he binds it,
Drink round, drink round, drink round.

'Drink round, drink round, drink round, boys,
Until it comes to me,
For the longer we sit here and drink,
The thirstier we shall be.'

Hone, in his 'Every Day Book,' ii., col. 1166, describes a Norfolk harvest-home, and the following health, which varies but little from one still in use:

'Here's a health unto our master,
He's the founder of the feast ;
God bless his endeavours,
And send him increase,
And send him increase, boys,
All in another year.

° One can fancy the master's doleful assent to this statement.
† Willow rod.

'Here's your master's good health,
　　So drink off your beer,
I wish all things may prosper,
　　Whate'er he takes in hand.
We are all his servants,
　　And are all at his command.
So drink, boys, drink,
And see you do not spill,
　　　　For if you do,
　　　　You shall drink two,
For 'tis your master's will.'

IX.

THE GENTLER LIFE.

T is hard to conceive with any degree of exactitude what the home-life of the nobles and gentlemen was five or six hundred years ago. The very details which would have most interested us were so trite and commonplace to the writers of the day that they passed them by unnoticed, and we have to gather them from incidental mention only.

Our task is harder in Norfolk than elsewhere, for from its being hemmed in by the fen-land on the west, and being almost uninhabitable on its east on account of the spreading 'Broads,' it was usually thought an *ultima thule*, as may be guessed from 'Piers Plowman' writing that he knew no French but of the farthest end of Norfolk—as though this were the place of all places most remote from the gentler education of the Court.

That some, however, on the other hand, did not think so, is clear, for we have the Chronicler Jordan Fantosme writing thus pleasantly of the Norfolk people:

The Gentler Life.

'Jordan Fantosme first wanted to give himself up,
On all the reliques an oath to swear,
There is no clerk in all the world ever so clever in recording
His lesson in his book or in speaking of any art,
Who could tell me, or who can mention
A land which, from hence to Montpellier,
Is worth that of Norfolk, of which you hear me speak;
More honoured knights, or more hospitable,
Or merrier dames to give largely,
Except the town of London, of which nobody knows its peer.'

Of the castles, in which the feudal lords lived, I have said something in my third chapter; and it may be worth noting here, that we have or had in Norfolk some of the most interesting manor-houses in England.

The names of Oxburgh, Beaupré Hall at E. Barsham, Wallington, Arminghall, Stiffkey, Caister, and of many others, will occur to my readers. In all, the comfort and health of the occupants was studied to a degree for which our ancestors do not usually get credit, and a house built now on the strict lines of an old manor-house or castle—not on the mock Gothic of which Shadwell Court is so painful an example—would be far from uncomfortable. They had not, of course, the advantages of recent sanitary discoveries, but the precautions they took to secure pure water and to carry away the sewage were remarkable. Half the mythical stories of subterranean passages—one of which at least is told of every old house—have arisen from the accidental discovery of the great old arched sewers, which were wisely made so large that there was never any chance of their being choked up. The rooms and passages, if they were a little chilly in the winter, through their size and loftiness, must have been always free from that stuffiness and want of ventilation which spoil so many modern mansions.

No better idea of the great personal luxury of some of the squires can be given, than by reproducing a summary of an inventory of Sir John Fastolf's goods, taken in 1459. From the description of 'my master's chamber,' we can almost see the room as it stood, over 400 years ago. There is the bedstead with its mattress (donge) of fine blue, and a feather-bed, and a bolster on it as well as a pair of blankets, a pair of sheets and a counterpane. Over it is the hanging bed, the tester, and the canopy, and a covering. At the windows are three green worsted curtains. On a form is a 'banker,' or covering of tapestry; on the walls are four more green worsted hangings, no doubt to match the curtains, as would the 'cupboard-cloth' hiding the cupboard door. By the fireplace are two standing 'andirons,' a latten chafing-dish, a pair of tongs, a pair of bellows, and what the copyist calls a 'feddefflok,' but which, I suspect, is a misreading for a 'feed-hook' or instrument for making up the fire. On a little pallet, probably for his attendant, are two blankets, a pair of sheets, and a coverlet, while on a folding-table are two little bells to summon attendants; a long (easy) chair and six white cushions, and a green chair, the room being lit by a hanging candlestick of latten.

The sideboard and cupboards of plate are simply astonishing. His gold plate weighed 121 oz., the silver 17,848 oz.! One can hardly fancy a squire with half a ton avoirdupois of plate. Nor is the description of his immense wardrobe much less curious, and the details of the cloths of arras and tapestry are especially interesting—showing how they depicted gentlemen with hawks on wrist; giants with bears' legs in their hands; three archers shooting a duck in the water with a cross-bow; gentlewomen harping by a castle; men drawing water from a well, and so on. The personal luxury must, in this case at all events, have been very great, for pillows of down and pillows of lavender were all over the house, as were feather-beds even in the cook's chamber and the porter's chamber, and it was only the stablemen who had to put up with mattresses. Possibly the weather was colder then than now, and men had to lie warmer, and certainly, with the great abundance of fowl, feathers were cheaper.

That there were, however, many houses furnished like this, I doubt. Certainly, the 'town' houses or private inns at Norwich and Lynn were not; indeed, they seem to have been only caravansaries, for in 1477 provision had to be sent in to one at Norwich —a dozen of ale and bread being brewed and baked against the master's coming from the country.*

The custom of sending out cooked food was not unusual, but it certainly does seem strange to modern ears to read of how the Mayor and Mayoress of

---

* Nearly every Norfolk family of note, by the way, had its 'town' house at Norwich, for the inns were not large enough or good enough to accommodate their trains of retainers.

Norwich, when they came out to Hellesdon to dine with Margaret Paston in 1460, sent their dinner before them.

I can add little to what is actually known about the usual mediæval potables. No doubt men chiefly drank a strong red wine, something between port and claret, and the only entry of note I have come across is one in which Friar Brackley writes in 1460 of having 'malvesey' and 'tyre,' which latter is said to have been a bitter drink, and of giving a man a 'potel of swete wyne.' The fountains running wine, of which we read so much in chronicles, were apparently reproduced in miniature on the table, for we find 'a fountain of latten to set in pots of wine' mentioned in John Fastolf's inventory just cited. By the way, I found an old drinking proverb embedded in one of the Paston Letters, dated 1473. 'Bear the cup even as what-call-ye-him said to Aslak.'

Whilst on odd sayings, I may point out that they swore 'by Blackbeard or Whitebeard'—said to mean by God or by Devil, and talked of a thing being 'nec Dacok nec Facok,' which I do not understand.

The routine of the dinner-table, and the rough hospitality shown at it, the profusion of fresh fish and meat and fowl at one time of the year, and the dreary reiteration of salt-fish and salt-beef—broken only by a little coarse kale and herbs—at the other, are too well known to need repetition here; though anyone curious in such matters can find all he wants in the L'Estrange household books. Some few notes of out-of-the-way viands and zests may, however, be amusing—I need hardly say that they occur in the 'Paston Letters'—practically our only storehouse of such material. In 1452, Margaret Paston wrote to London for a 'booke with chardeqweyns' (which Mr. Gairdner interprets 'quince preserve'), that she may have them in the mornings, as the air was not wholesome. By the same letter, by the way, she bespoke twenty-four trenchers, as she could get none in Norwich, which seems strange. Oranges were sent her in 1470, by the carrier. Next year she wrote to her London correspondent for the prices per pound of pepper, cloves, 'masis' (mace), ginger, cinnamon, almonds, raisens, 'ganyngal,'* saffron, 'raisons of Corons' and 'grenys' (grains of paradise). Later on, two pots of treacle of 'genoré' (Genoa?) are sent for.

Of the hospitality itself there can be no doubt. It obtains now, and hearty and sincere have been its praises from strangers; as, for example, when Stothard in his memoirs says that when he was sketching the monuments in Ingham Church, 'the gentlemen farmers were extremely eager to serve me ... With one or the other I might have dined every day.' But this very hospitality often proved a tax on its recipient, for the system of giving 'vails' grew to such an extent that it is recorded that at an entertainment in 1800, 'the whole household from the butler to the scullion stood in two ranks in the hall

* Ganyngal (?) = Galingale.

to receive the parting present.' The system is said to have been knocked on the head by a poor Cromer parson bluntly telling the squire at Felbrigg that he was obliged to decline his invitation to dinner because he could not afford to pay for one dinner what would provide housekeeping at home for a whole month. This, however, is rather a digression.

One frequently stumbles across passages in old records which make one doubt whether the chivalrous deference and tenderness to the fair sex we read so much about was not more theoretical than real. For example, the conduct of Sir Henry de Seagrave, *Knight*, and his followers, who came in 1312 to the manor-house at Barningham parva, and pricked the mother of William de Barningham with swords, and cut her with knives, to make her tell them of her jewels, money, and plate, does not exactly accord with the knightly duties to woman of which we read in works of chivalry. The King, however, does not seem to have thought very much about the matter, for when the discourteous knight was indicted he was able to produce the royal pardon.

Nor was it exactly polite for Sir John Felbrigg to drag Dame Margery Wymondham out of Felbrigg Hall by the hair of her head, because they differed as to who was entitled to its possession; and we must not forget the fact that Elizabeth Paston, when a grown-up girl, about the year 1449, was beaten once or twice a week, and sometimes twice in one day, and had her head broken in two or three places by her loving parent. Later on we shall see how thieves of lower degree beat old women over eighty on the head so that they caused them wounds to the death.

Possibly it was some such proofs of affection that caused Margery Paston to brave the terrors of a *mésalliance* and pluckily marry the family steward, and so cause her brother to write in high dudgeon that the man 'never should have my goodwill for to make my sister to sell candle and mustard at Framlingham.'

The marrying and giving in marriage of the upper classes was in the earlier middle ages so much a matter of pure business, in which the lady was hardly ever consulted, that such *escapades* were rare indeed, and one must not wonder at the excessively business-like way in which a matrimonial alliance was negotiated even by those who were free to choose for themselves. Mr. Hewlett in the *Antiquary*, some time ago, pointed out the gruesome fact that a young lady of property, who on her death was found to have been *fatua et idiota* from her birth, was married to an unhappy lad, and actually had two children by him.

What, again, can be more unsentimental than the following letter from one brother to another, written in 1481? The writer, it will be seen, goes straight to his subject: 'I heartily recommend myself to you. There is lately become a widow in Worstead who was wife to one Bolt, a worstead merchant, and worth £1000, and gave, to his wife 100 marks in money, stuff of household, and plate to the value of 100 marks, and £10 by the year in land. She is called a fair gentlewoman. She is about 30 years, and has only two children, which shall be at the dead's charge (!). She was his wife but five years.' One can almost fancy 'one Bolt' turning in his grave as this letter was penned.

Five years earlier a strange love-letter was written by John Paston to a girl he had never seen, but of whose charms he had heard from his 'right trusty friend,' R. Stratton (clerk to his kitchen!), in which he beseeches her to ease the poor heart which was sometime at *his* rule, but which is now at hers—not so bad to a person he had never even seen; and the curious part of it is that she reciprocates her unseen lover's passion, and replies just as warmly, possibly glad of a chance to get rid of her pent-up sentiment, and escape in thought from a hum-drum life. That the women then were as artful as they are now is clear enough, *teste* the neat subterfuge which Condona Reynforth suggests to her lover, whom she loved not wisely but too well, in 1478, asking him to write a fictitious letter to the cousin in whose charge she was, calling her away on an imaginary errand.

Of the literary tastes of the early gentry and squires we know little but what is told us in their wills. A testator who died in 1482 had 'La Belle Dame saunce mercye,' 'The Death of Arthur,' a book on the blazoning of arms, Tully 'de Senectute,' and—oh that it were rightly so now!—'A Boke in preente off the Playe of the Chess.'

The squires were great tillers and flock-holders; their 'farmers' were more stewards than leaseholders, and the lords collected most of their rent in kind. It must have been a patriarchal life; for example, Sir Christopher Heydon used to give a Christmas dinner to thirty master shepherds of his own flocks at Baconsthorpe.

Norfolk is well enough known even now for its sport and its game, but it must in early times have simply been the sportsman's paradise. Sandy warrens alive with rabbits and peopled with bustards on the south, great impassable fresh-water marshes on the west, salt-water marshes and cliff on the north, and the great inland water system of the 'Broads,' with their herons, ruffs and reeves, and wild-duck on the east, must have combined to have supplied fish, flesh, and fowl enough for everyone. It was close to these Broads—at Waxham—where Sir William Wodehouse, of that place, who was then James I.'s jester, introduced the 'decoy' system for wild-fowl into England. There were great coursing-meetings in early days, that at Swaffham being perhaps the best known then, as Martham is now.

A 'Norfolk tumbler' was a dog specially trained to affect lameness, and so get within catching-distance of his quarry. Coke sent one to Salisbury to 'play on Salisbury warren,' as we see in the Domestic State Papers of James I.

Otters, of course, were very plentiful, with so much undrained land and so many pools and rivers. Each fresh-water fisherman between the town of Conisford and Hardley Cross was ordered, in 1557, to keep a dog to hunt the otter, and all the fishermen were 'to make a general hunt twice or thrice a year or more at time or times convenient.' In 1729, six residents at Palsgrave, over the Suffolk border, killed *seventeen brace* of otters between March and May, which will give some idea of how plentiful they must have been. Quite recently there used to be some otter-hunting near Norwich; but they are getting scarcer every year, and it is now only by Reedham, and in a few other places, that the early and late oarsman is startled by the heavy plunge of the handsome beast, or sees the evidence of his mischief on the bank.

Of the 'Norfolk trotters' we find early mention; Margaret Paston writing to her husband, in 1460, that three horses had been bought for him at St. Faith's Fair, and that they 'all be Trotters, right fair horses, God save them, and they be well kept.' Norfolk horse-lovers do not, however, seem above improving their breed, for in 1477 John Pimpe writes to a friend at Calais begging him to look at all the good horses there for a prick horse, well trotting of his own courage without force of spurs— if a stirring horse so much the better—somewhat large, though not the largest—but no small horse. He says he does not like a heavy horse in labour, but a heavy horse in flesh and light in courage he loves well; for he loves no horses that will always be lean and slender like greyhounds.

Norfolk seems always to have been a sporting county. There were many race-meetings in old times here; for example, on Mousehold Heath, in the park at Blickling, at Winterton, at Swaffham (where a gold cup was given for three-year-olds at a mile in one heat), and at Thetford, the articles and subscriptions for which, in 1698, 1699, and 1700 are still preserved in the Bodleian Library. Lord Vernon is said to have trained his famous horse 'Florizel' on Ringstead Downs, and Mr. Angerstein's unfortunate experiences with Arabs is familiar to the present generation.

In Attleburgh Church lies 'the famous Captain Gibbs,' who was a great gamester and horseracer in Charles II.'s time, and of whom the greatest exploit recorded was how he 'laid a wager of £500 that he drove his light chaise and four horses up and down the deepest part of the Devil's Ditch on Newmarket Heath; which he performed by making a very light chaise with a jointed perch and without any pole, to the surprise of all the spectators.' That he was not the only 'clever' sportsman of his day will be seen from the following anecdote of Sir Thos. Jermyn, from the L'Estrange Collection, known as the 'Anecdotes and Traditions' (Cam. Soc.):

'Sir Thos. Jermin, meaning to make himself merry and gull the Cockers, sends his man into the Pitt in Shoo Lane with an £100 and a dunghill cocke, neatly trimmed and cutt for the battell. The plot being well layd, the fellow gets another to throw him in and fyte him in Sir Thos. Jermin's name. The fellow beates the £100 against him. The cocke was match't, and bearing Sir Thos. Jermin's name, had many beates on his head; but after three or four good brushes he shewe a faire payre of heeles. Every one wond'red to see Sir Thomas his streine cry craven; and away came his man with his money doubled.'

Another good local sporting story from the same collection is that about the Puritan chaplain and the bowls, viz. :

'My Lord Brookes used to be much resorted to by the preciser sort, who had made good a powerful hand over him; yet they would allow him Christian libertie for his recreations; but being at bowles one day, in much company, and following his caste with much eagernesse, he cried, " Rubbe, rubbe, rubbe, rubbe, rubbe !" His chaplain (a very strict mann) runns presently to him, and in the hearing of diverse, " O good my Lord, leave that to God—you must leave that to God," sayes he.'

William Windham, the statesman and the darling of the county, was a thorough sportsman. When at Eton he was leader of the school at all games. He seems to have been a man of great pluck and personal strength, for he quelled a mutiny in the W Battalion of the local militia by his personal prowess —seizing the leader and thrashing two of his followers. In 1794, too, when he was stoned at Norwich during the election, he jumped out of his carriage and collared his assailant. Bibliomaniacs will remember him kindly when they hear that he lost his life trying to save a friend's library which was being burned.

Stone-throwing at elections seems to have been the

The Gentler Life: 135

regular thing, for when another well-known Norfolk politician and athlete—the Hon. E. Harbord—was being stoned at Norwich, he, being a great cricketer, pleased everyone by the address with which he caught the stones flung at his head.

Talking of cricket, by the way, it may startle lovers of the game to be told that in 1797 Norfolk was strong enough to be backed against 'All England' for £500!

Of eccentric sportsmen of late years we have had plenty of the Windham type, but the strangest of all was the half-mad Walpole of a generation or two back—'Lord George'—who used to drive red-deer four in hand, and on one occasion only just got home in time in front of a pack of hounds which had run his strange team to sight.

He had his good qualities, and they are set out at page 211 of the first volume of 'Pratt's Gleanings; but his eccentricities culminated when he declined to allow the body of his dead mistress to be buried, but hid it away in a dark cupboard under some old boots, fearing it would be taken from him.

I have hitherto touched on the home-life and its pleasures and amusements only, but there must have been a very seamy side to the country gentleman's existence, caused by what would now be called the 'rough' element, and by the bands of thieves. About 23 Edward I., for example, Lessingham Hall was broken into, a servant killed, and goods to the value of £200 stolen by the same gang, who robbed the house of Roger Herman and carried away £400 in silver, and who killed and robbed a man between Henstead and Eccles. The Crown Plea and Gaol Delivery Rolls for Norfolk simply teem with similar examples. Possibly the great quantity of 'brueria,' or land grown over with briars and furze and thereby almost impassable, favoured the thieves by giving them cover in which to hide. About 1332, especially, the time must have been lawless indeed, for at one gaol delivery twenty-seven persons were sentenced to be hung—though, thanks to the King's pardon (no doubt purchased as usual), and to the intervention of the ordinary, five only of them were executed. Sixteen were convicted for murder, but not one was hung, the King and their book-learning saving the rest. A grimmer commentary on the sanctity of property could not be imagined than the fact that those who suffered did so for theft, and not murder. That many of the murderers, however, were not of the common classes, but of the gentry, is clear: for example, *Magister* Richard de Blomvile and others killed Patrick de Burghwode, in Newton Flotman, and his goods were worth 100s.; and Sir Thomas de Nerford, *knight*, slew Harvey de Saham; again, Sir John de Cove, *knight*, actually assaulted Robert de Halle in the presence of the bailiff of Norwich. There is little doubt that some villages must have been little better than the place described in 'Westward Ho' as the rendezvous of the King of the Gubbins; as, for example, Garboldisham, no less than five of the inhabitants of which were tried at one Gaol Delivery for distinct crimes and robberies.

Vindictive attacks on private individuals were not infrequent. Blood's idea was anticipated in 1423, when John Grys of Wighton was attacked in his own house, after wassail, and carried, with his son and his servant, to a gallows to be hung; but as the murderers could find no ropes they cruelly butchered them another way. A few years later (1461) the parson of Snoring fetched Thomas Denys, then Coroner for Norfolk, out of his own house, and he was cruelly murdered; all that was done to the villain-priest being that he was put in the stocks— a singular punishment for being accessory to a murder.

Just before this, in 1452, a band of blackguards under one Charles Nowell infested the east part of Norfolk, and went out marauding six, twelve, and even thirty or more strong. They tried to kill two servants of the Bishop of Norwich in Burlingham Church while mass was being sung there; they tried to break into the White Friars at Norwich, avowedly to get out, dead or alive, some citizens against whom they had a grudge; they attacked John Paston at the door of Norwich Cathedral, and his wife's uncle, Philip Berney, on the same day in Thorpe Wood, and, what is more astonishing, Roger Church, one of the gang, was actually appointed bailiff of Blofield Hundred. Then they broke the parson of Hassingham's head in his own chancel; beat John Wilton in Plumstead churchyard to the danger of his life; and broke into the house of John Coke, of Witton, at 11 p.m., and gave him seven sword wounds; and beat his old mother, a woman of eighty, over the head, 'wheche wownde was never hol to the daye of her deth.'

So far of 'strong thieves.' The resident in the manor-house might at all events raise the hue-and-cry against *them*, and be sure of his neighbours' eager co-operation; but what could he do when it was the neighbour himself who battered at his gate? On the raids on Barningham and Felbrigg I have touched already; but the most lively idea of the woes of a family from intestine war is gained, as most information of this period is gained, from the 'Paston Letters.' The Pastons were besieged in three of their houses—Gresham, Hellesdon, and Caister. In 1450, Lord Molynes came to Paston's moated house at Gresham (Paston not being at home) with a thousand armed men, broke open the outer gates, forcibly carried out the lady of the house, rifled it of £200, cut the door-posts through, and left, remarking that if they had found Paston's friend, John Damme, they would have killed the said John. Their manor-house at Hellesdon by Norwich was raided in 1465 by the Duke of Suffolk, who made the tenants pull it down themselves; and not satisfied with that, ransacked the church, evicted the parson, and spoiled the images. Next, the same duke, in 1469, besieged Caister with 3,000 men, and reduced it by starvation, two men only being killed. In 1478 he looked in again at Hellesdon, but apparently only to annoy Paston, for he only 'drew a stew and took great plenty of fish.' The irate retainer, who described the scene to Paston, wrote that no man could play the part of Herod better than the duke; and tells how, in the hot summer afternoon, he was so feeble that his feet could not bear him, so two men held him up; and when some of his men said Paston should be slain and others that he should be put in prison only, the duke wanted no better than to meet him with a spear and have his heart's blood with his own hands—a pleasant sentiment no doubt reciprocated by Paston.

After all, these violent aggressions on the Pastons may have had a reason for them. We only hear the Paston side of the story.

That the principals did not think it beneath them to commission men to assassinate their opponents, is evident from the *naïve* way in which a servant writes to a master (1451) that 'Gonnor was watched at Felbrigg Hall with forty of the lady's tenants and more *that night that I lay in wait for him*,' and that he durst not go home on the next day till they 'brought him home' safe.

As civilization went on, the 'duello' proved a useful modification of the feud and the assassination, and was decidedly a step in the right direction. A history of Norfolk duels and their causes would be interesting reading, though in many cases we should probably get to know nothing more of them than what the parish register tells us, as where at Downham we read: '1601.—Richard Guibon, of Stow Brinke, slain in fight, within the parish of Downham, by one Clarke of Fincham, was buried the 4th of July.' Of the celebrated duel, fought in November, 1599, between Sir Robert Mansfield and Sir John Heydon, just outside Ber Street, however, we have a full account. The former received two rapier-wounds in the breast and two dagger-stabs in the arm, but had much the better of the fight; for he not only wounded his antagonist in the face and in the thigh, but forced him to sign a paper of submission. They seem, however, to have met again afterwards, and Heydon had still worse luck, for he lost one of his hands, which is said to be still kept in the museum at Canterbury, where it was placed by a descendant of the victor. The full account is printed at pp. 166-7 of Mason's 'History of Norfolk,' where will also be found a challenge from Thomas Lovell to Sir Richard Bacon, dated 1600.

The example seems to have been contagious, for in 1603 John Townshend died of wounds received in a duel with Sir Matthew Brown; and his son, Stanhope Townshend, was also killed in a duel in the Low Countries. In 1634, Sir William Whittipole fought Sir A. Gorge at Calais, but I do not know with what result, and it is rather doubtful if they can be called Norfolk men.

In 1700, Sir Sewster Peyton killed one King, of Bury, and was tried at Norfolk assizes, but he too was hardly a Norfolk man; and in 1708, Sir

Edmund Bacon ran Sir Robert Rich through the body.

A fatal duel took place in 1698, in which Captain Le Neve killed Sir Henry Hobart. The latter accused the former of spreading a report that he was a coward, and behaved himself so in Ireland, by which it is said he lost his Cornish election. Le Neve denied having said so, but Hobart would fight, and was killed. A stone in a plantation on the road leading from Norwich to Holt marks where the unsuccessful politician and duellist fell.

Of course, one cannot hope now to recover the reasons for all the bygone quarrels, but I think it very likely that many of them arose from disputes between the old and the new gentry as to pedigree and position. The early knights made by James I. were not thought much of, and we hear that Sir Edmund Thimblethorp (who was said to have been knighted in 1603 for £7 10s.!) was usually called 'Nimblechoppes.' One dispute, though it did not lead to a duel, was nearly as serious a matter for one of the contestants; for in 1541, Mr. Clere and Sir Edmund Knevet happening to quarrel in the King's tennis-court at Greenwich, the latter foolishly struck the former within the Palace precincts, for which he was adjudged to have his right hand struck off with a chopper. Just before the sentence was carried out, however, he asked as a special favour to have his left hand cut off instead, so that he might still do the King some service with his right, upon which he was pardoned altogether.

Singularly enough, the same story is also told of Edmund Windham and Clere; and it is said that Windham afterwards did do good service in suppressing Kett's rebellion, and that his descendant was practically the discoverer of the Gunpowder plot.

Of the earlier duels there is not much known. Some of them were of course only gentle and more or less joyous passages of arms, as when Sir Thomas 'Harpurgun' (Erpingham) fought Sir John de Barres, in the way told by Froissart, or when Sir John Astley fought two Frenchmen in 1438 and 1442, in one of which he was lucky enough to 'smite Pierre de Massie through the head with a spear;' but some must have been uncommonly like murder, for in 9th John we read of Hugh Patesle being sued by John the brother of Drugo Camerarius for the death of the latter, and of his compromising the matter by arranging to go to Jerusalem for seven years (including going and coming), to serve God for the 'slain man's soul,' while Thomas de Ingoldesthorpe, who seems to have had something to do with the affair, had to find a monk to pray for the soul of the dead man, and to pay his parents forty marks.

It is sad to think of the lives that must have been lost in the olden time through the leeches' want of skill. I cannot help thinking the patients and their friends were grimly conscious of it, and in case of real illness, prepared for death as a matter of course, or only appealed to spiritual help. When John Paston fell ill away from home, his worthy mother sent an image of wax of the patient's weight ('a nodyr ymmage of wax of the weytte of yow') to our Lady of Walsingham, and a noble apiece to the four orders of Friars at Norwich to pray for him, while his anxious wife posted off on pilgrimage herself to Walsingham and the Priory of St. Leonard at Norwich. The language of some of the wills is so earnest, that I cannot help thinking it was the dying man's own, dictated on his death-bed. Sir Thomas Wyndham, in 1521, after committing his soul to God, goes on in a way that makes one fancy he must have held views then almost dangerous, to 'trust that by the special grace and mercy of thy mother, ever virgin, our Lady Mary, in whom, *after thee*, in this mortal life, hath been my most singular trust and confidence,' and so on.

After the death comes the mourning, and, as one might expect, it was punctilious. When Margaret Paston was bereaved, a precedent had to be sought; and Lady Morley and Lady Stapleton, who had themselves recently lost their husbands, were asked what was the right thing to do in 'places of worship,' and decided that at Christmas-tide, after the death, there should be no diceings, nor harpings, nor luting, nor singing, nor loud disports, but only playing at the tables, chess, and cards.

X.

THE TOWN LIFE.

THE life of the rich burghers, when the worsted trade was at its best, must have been one of considerable luxury. An amusing instance, showing how they sometimes defied sumptuary laws and aped the gentry, is in the old story how Sir Philip Calthorp* 'purged John Drakes the shoomaker of Norwich in the time of King Henry the Eighth of the proud humour which our people have to bee of the gentleman's cut':

'This Knight bought on a time as much fine French tawney cloth as should make him a gowne, and sent it to the taylors to bee made. John Drakes, a shoomaker of that town, coming to the sayd taylours, and seeing the Knights gowne-cloth lying there, liking it well, caused the taylour to buy him as much of the same cloth and price to the same intent, and further bade him of the same fashion that the Knight would have his made of. Not long

* Bl. N. iii., p. 217.

after, the Knight, coming to the taylours to take measure of his gowne, perceiving the like gowne-cloth lying there, asked the taylour whose it was. Quoth the taylor, "It is John Drakes's, who will have it made of the selfsame fashion that yours is made of." "Well" (sayd the Knight), "in good time be it. I will" (sayd hee) "have mine made as full of cutts as thy shears can make it." "It shall be done," said the taylor. Whereupon, because the time drew near, he made haste of both their garments. John Drake had no time to go to the taylors till Christmass Day for serving of customers, when he had hoped to have worn his gowne. Perceiving the same to be full of cutts, began to sweare with the taylor for making his gowne after that sort. "I have done nothing" (quoth the taylor) "but that you bade me to do; for as Sir Philip Calthorp's is, even so have I made yours." "By my latchet" (quoth John Drake), "I will never weare gentleman's fashion again!"'

The inner life of the townsman was so bound up with his guilds, trade, and religion, that probably no more striking picture of the manners and customs of the town can be obtained than by a careful inspection of the guild certificates, which were taken in the 12th Richard II. by order of the Government. Some years ago I carefully analyzed* the certificates of Lynn Regis, with the following results, which may serve to illustrate my meaning:

* N. A. M. i., p. 141. (Privately printed.)

The guilds were originated, no doubt, by the small chaplains and minor priests in much the same way, and for much the same objects, as the present Benefit and Friendly Societies are by enterprising publicans, viz., to bring grist to the mill. A flourishing guild, which maintained a chaplain and kept a light ever burning before an image or a shrine, and which buried its dead with pomp and paid for many masses annually, was no bad customer to the church.

Sometimes, possibly, a layman originated it, and this would no doubt be the case in the merchants' or trade guilds, in which religion played a less important part.

Such founder was, it is thought, relieved from payment of all subscriptions, etc., in return for the trouble he had taken.

As far as possible, the framers of the guild rules seem to have desired to keep their members independent of the common law, and some of their rules were very salutary.

Disputes among members were, as much as might be, to be settled by agreement or reference; and no member could bring a suit at law against another without obtaining leave from the alderman, and no brother was allowed to become a pledge or surety for another in any plea or suit without similar leave (Shipman's). In another guild, any quarrel was to be settled, if possible, by the alderman, and if not, the parties might proceed to the law where they listed.

Any brother or sister bearing another any falsehood or wrong had to pay half-a-pound of wax to the light (St. Peter). In another case, anyone guilty of any falsehood, theft, or wrong, was to leave the fraternity for ever.

Anyone rebelling against the laws of Holy Church to lose the benefits of the guild until amendment (St. Leonard); and a similar penalty overtook him who was rebel against the King and unbuxom against the Church.

He who was 'rebel or unbuxom' against the alderman in time of drink or of morwspeche, paid four pounds of wax. But a far heavier penalty, viz., two stone of wax, was incurred by the man who disclosed the secrets of the guild to any strange man or woman.

Other guilds visited the sin of betraying secrets far more lightly, imposing a penalty of one pound only; but another guild had a rule 'that no brother or sister shall discuse the conseil of his fraternity to ne strangere' on pain of forfeiture of his fraternity for evermore.

Besides the religious meetings referred to hereafter, there were generally three or four mornspeches, morwspeches, or speakings, or business meetings, when, as the certificate of the Guild of Young Scholars tells us, it was the duty of the master of the guild to see that the guild goods had been properly spent and accounted for.

The meetings were held at the Guild Hall, and were fixed for certain days, generally named in the ordinances of each guild, though in one case the alderman had power to fix their date.

In any case the dean had to give notice or remind the members of these meetings, and if he failed to do so was fined for each case.

Every member who, being in Lynn on the day of meeting, did not attend, was fined, as was anyone who did not come punctually to the trysting hour, after prime struck, or after prime thrice struck.

If, annoyed at being fined for being a few minutes late, he should 'set him down and grucche' (grumble), he was doubly fined or turned out of the fraternity.

Business then began.

The skevyns, or stewards, first put in written accounts for the past year and vouched them, and statements were made how the guild goods had been expended. The remaining guild chattels or goods were sometimes, it seems, produced before the alderman at the general meeting, and the skevyns who were chosen for the following year had to give security for the guild property.

The election of officers for the ensuing year then commenced. The officers were an alderman, one or two skevyns, and a dean, and sometimes a clerk.

Such officers were not, it seems, chosen by the general body of members, though why not, it would be difficult to say; but the general method was for the outgoing alderman to call up four or more brethren whose business it was to choose them In one case the four chosen by the alderman called up four more, and the eight chose the officials—a far more sensible way.

When elected, the new aldermen and other officials made oath before the old aldermen to keep the ordinances of the guild.

The offices of aldermen and skevyns seem to have been entirely honorary, and no salary, nor, as far as I can make out, any emolument, save an extra allowance of ale, attached to them.

The dean and clerk were, however, paid servants, their annual salaries being generally sixpence and eightpence respectively, yearly, and upon them, probably, the real management of the business fell.

Anyone chosen to fill any one of the guild offices, but refusing to act, was fined according to the dignity of the office he renounced:—an alderman, say, two pounds, a skevyn one pound, and a dean half-a-pound of wax, which no doubt went in aid of the guild light.

The *alderman* was to be . . . 'wise and witty . . . able and cunning to rule and govern the company in the worship of God.'

The *skevyns* were to be 'trust men, and true to keep and receive the goods and chattels of the guild;' half of them in St. Francis's guilds were to be friars, this guild being kept in the convent of Friars Minor.

The *dean* was to 'warn the guild brethren as is the custom in the town of Lynn,' or to warn them to come together when the alderman sent for them, or on any other occasion which might be to the honour and worship of the guild.

The *clerk* was to write and enter the names and necessaries of the guild.

After the election of officials, it is probable that a yearly election of ordinary members took place. In two guilds we know that it is so, for the rules state that new members shall be admitted only at general meetings, except by the assent of all.

A candidate for election in some cases had to be introduced by two brethren, who testified that he was a good man and able, and of good conversation. A countryman might be elected at any time, if known to be of good conversation.

On being admitted, the new member was sworn by the alderman to keep the statutes.

On entrance, the new member paid a certain sum towards the guild stock, varying according to the importance of the guild, and also fees ('the rights of the house') to the alderman, dean, and clerk, and a contribution to the wax stock.

When all the elections were over, no doubt the annual subscriptions were got in, and the charitable contributions, which each member was bound to make for the benefit of the poor brethren, were collected. The guild statutes were to be read out at each meeting by the alderman, who was fined if he did not do so.

This done, we can imagine the table would be spread for the guild feast, and from the great stress all the certificates lay on the quantums of ale, and from the penalties attached on anyone who improperly entered the ale chamber, which no doubt adjoined the Guild Hall, I cannot but think that originally there was a great deal of drinking to very little eating.

Before drinking, however, the light belonging to the guild was lit, and the clerk stood up and bade silence while he prayed or said the bedes for the peace and state of Holy Church and the peace and state of the land. And anyone making a noise or jangling during prayer-time was fined.

The alderman's allowance of ale, 'while it lasteth,' was generally two gallons, the skevyns a gallon, the dean a pottle, and the clerk a pottle.

'While it lasteth' sounds much as if the carouse were kept on *de die in diem* till the liquor was spent, and in fact this is borne out by one certificate, which refers to prayers offered 'every night while drink lasteth.'

Absent friends, however, were not forgotten, and the brethren decidedly drank fair whatever they did, for any brother or sister absent at drinking-time, whether from illness or from being on pilgrimage had a gallon of ale set by for him.

Members were expected to be on their best behaviour during both business and convivial meetings.

Anyone jangling in time of drink or mornspeche, or making any other noise to annoy the company, after the dean had called him to order by commanding him to be still, paid half-a-pound of wax (St. John Baptist), and anyone still persevering in his obnoxious conduct had to do penance by taking or holding the rod tendered him by the alderman. He was also further fined, and if still recalcitrant, ejected from the brotherhood.

If anyone maliciously gave his brother the lie, or was rebellious of his tongue against, or despised the alderman, he too was fined (St. Thomas of Canterbury and Conception). For graver offences the punishment was yet heavier, and anyone striking another at any mornspeche or time of drink, had to pay four pounds of wax (Holy Cross).

The hardest rule to my mind, however, was that which fined a man overcome by the potency of the guild brew* for sleeping in time of drink, or letting the cup stand by him (Conception and St. Edmund).

These regulations were doubtless found necessary by experience, and as there is seldom smoke without fire, we may well imagine these drinking-bouts were not the most orderly affairs, and were not altogether free from jangling, noise, and drunken sleep. No one was to come in a tabard, nor in a cloak, nor barelegged nor barefoot (St. Thomas of Canterbury, Conception, and St. Edmund), nor with his cap or hood on,† nor in any rustic manner (Holy Trinity).

---

* All seem to have drunk ale except the great merchants of Holy Trinity Guild, whose liquor was wine (Richards, 454). The alderman had four gallons, and the dean, clerk and skevyns, two gallons on the first day and half that allowance on subsequent days. From these allowances, no doubt, however, the officials must have had to treat their friends or guests.

† Each brother able to do so was to pay for a livery hood

In the Merchants' Guild there was a janitor, with whom the servants of the brethren had to leave their caps and cloaks while they entered and spoke to their masters. When they had done their business they were to go, but might drink once or twice, standing, before they went.

Having now referred to the feasting customs which formed so important a part of the regulations of the Lynn guilds, we may turn to the religious observances, which are not so prominent a feature here as at Norwich.

The usual ceremony seems to have been to go to church together the Sunday after the feast-day of the guild, and hear a mass; in some cases meeting at a rendezvous 'fairly and honestly arrayed,' and walking thence in procession to the place of worship.

Only one image is specially mentioned in the certificates as being sustained by a Lynn guild, and that is one of St. William, which the Young Scholars kept in a tabernacle, finding six tapers to burn before the same each festival day.

Nearly every guild, however, found six candles or lights; St. Anthony's was a candle of a pound weight burning every festival day in time of service; St. Thomas of Canterbury's, a two-pound candle before its patron saint's image; while a light of five candles, to burn in the church of St. Margaret, was

---

and wear it at every mornspeche and burying (St. George Martyr, and Holy Cross); it was to be kept two years (Shipman).

sustained by the Guild of St. Lawrence ; St. George the Martyr Guild kept five candles burning before the altar of St. George on festival days, and three torches on the principal day at mass, etc., and also found a priest to serve at the altar of St. George.

Provision for the sustenance of indigent members of the guild is made in nearly every case. The members of St. Anthony's Guild relieved their poor brother by each giving him a penny yearly. The Guilds of St. Thomas of Canterbury and St. Leonard provided that if a member came to any misadventure ' by sea, fire, or other manner,' all should meet and help him with a portion of their chattels. The Young Scholars relieved their poor four times a year. Some guilds ordained that each brother and sister should give a penny each mornspeche (St. John Baptist, St. Thomas of Canterbury, and St. Mary). The rule in another society was that each brother and sister should pay the poor man fourpence yearly, till he may help himself. If any brother or sister was in prison, he or she was to be visited and comforted by the brethren (St. Leonard). Should the unlucky man's sufferings terminate in death, he, in common with all other members of the guild, had at least solemn obsequies and decent burial.

Some of the special rules were as follow :

Two torches were kept burning by the body during dirge and mass, until it was buried (St. Katharine). The aldermen were to tell the dean, and the latter to ' hastily bring the wax ' to the dirge, and warn the brothers and sisters to go with the corse to the kirk, and there offer a halfpenny (St. Thomas of Canterbury), If the body were without, or in West Lynn or South Lynn, the brothers and sisters were to be summoned by the bellman.* They were to assemble in their livery hoods.† 'If he die within a mile, and have nought to bring him to the earth,' the alderman and brethren shall go and bring him to the earth at their own costs (St. Leonard). If more than three miles, the alderman should go, or hire a man.‡

In any case the members are to attend the funeral, and a certain number of masses were sung for the dead man's soul; the number varied from twelve to forty, and were to be sung within the third day of the death, under peril of their souls (St. Peter). Anyone not coming, if in health and in town, paid twopence (St. Peter). Their offerings were distributed among the poor in bread.

Of course the guild-feasts at Lynn, though occasionally of great splendour, as we see from the picture of one engraved on the celebrated 'Peacock' brass, still in the church there, could not vie with those of the great St. George's Guild of Norwich. At the table here noblemen and gentles of ancient descent sat down in good fellowship with the merchants and their wives, who were their brother and sister members. Here, no doubt, men of influence in all stations of life met on common ground and discussed measures likely to be of common benefit to the county,

* Shipman.
† Ibid.
‡ Ibid.

and spoke, as their descendants do at this day, in mild and pitying disparagement of those unhappy ones who were born in the 'shires.'

We have plenty of materials with which it would be possible to write the history of the feasts themselves—how the mayor had to give three bucks and a hogshead of wine towards it—how the great pasteboard imitation dragon (afterwards called 'Snap')* came and wallowed before the company for its pastime.

The life of the Norwich citizens, however, was not all feasting, for the unsettled times must have kept them ever alert and suspicious, and, as it were, always in a state of mild siege. The way in which the houses of the better-class citizens were built shows this. A narrow entry, closed by a massive iron-studded door, often with a sliding peep-door, shut in a square yard like the 'quad' of a small college, round which ran a two-storied flint building, which could at a pinch, when well garrisoned, resist any assault to which it was likely to be subjected in a street brawl or town feud.

Specimens of these houses may be seen in King Street and elsewhere in Norwich, but better still at Lynn. For protection against enemies from without, a wall was begun to be put round Norwich in 1294, but it was not finished till 1319. It was not, however, till 1342 that the City was properly fortified, the work being done and the ditches enlarged by one Richard Spynk, a patriotic citizen, who also built the

* Still to be seen frolicking about on Pockthorpe 'Guild-day.'

great round tower at the end of King Street, now known as the 'Snuff Tower.' About the same time the 'Cow Tower,' otherwise the Boom Tower, so called from a boom being stretched from it across the river, to keep out hostile shipping, was erected. It was not till Kett's rebellion, in 1549, that the walls and gates ever came into practical use, and received their first and last baptism of fire, as already mentioned in Chapter IV.

The entries on the Freemen's books of Norwich afford us much curious information as to the number of different trades carried on by the citizens. Over 250 separate trades occur there; an amazing number, and one only to be accounted for by the fact that in olden days, if a country man wanted an out-of-the-way article, he could not get it easily sent him from London, or any other centre, as he can now, so there were probably two or three men in each city who were 'bladesmiths,' 'bridlesmiths,' 'mailmakers,' 'patymakers,' and 'pynners.' The way in which various trades were carried on with others is very curious; *e.g.*, of sixty-nine 'bochers,' thirteen were cooks, and, it is obvious, sold cooked or uncooked food, as their customers wished. Again, of the forty-four bakers, six were brewers and five ostlers. The forty-three smiths were re-divided into locksmiths, bladesmiths, and 'ferrors,' by which I apprehend shoeing-smiths were meant. The 'Brasyers' included pewterers, plomers, and belyaters, or bell-founders; while the scriveners were classed with notaries, text writers, 'lymynors,' and attorneys.

The large number of (barkers) shows how well wooded the country must have been, but the 'raffmen' were not, as Blomefield thought, 'raftmen,' or navigators of floating timber, but a sub-species of grocer — probably tallow-chandlers. The 'freshwater men and fishers' no doubt had plenty of occupation in the old days.

So many of the manufactures of the city were of textile fabrics that the 'merchants' marks,' which were used to stamp the bales of goods, were unusually numerous. They were very usually, also, placed in the spandrils of the doorways of the merchants' houses and on their brasses. Piers Plowman talks of

> 'Wyde wyndowes y-wrought
> Y-wryten ful thikke
> Shynen with shapen sheldes
> So shaven aboute
> *With merkes of merchauntes*
> Y-medeled betwene.'

They served as the coat-of-arms of the merchant, though we sometimes find instances in which a gently-born tradesman—no great rarity then—put his mark on one side and his coat on the other of his doorway or tomb.

As the *nouveaux riches* retired from trade they sank their merchants' marks, and acquired, rightly or wrongly, armorial bearings to which they had hitherto no right. For example, in 1671, it was reported to Clarencieux that 'Both the Mr. Wiggots never knew any coate to belong to them; nor doe not owne any;

but a marke which they wore on a ring.' Six years later we find Alderman Wiggot—no doubt the progenitor of the Lytton-Bulwer-Lyttons—being buried in St. Simon and St. Jude in all the glory of ' Nebulé a chief quartered on the 1st and 4th, two roses on the 2nd, and 3rd a lion passant,' though at Guist we find the same family revelling in another totally different coat.

Several of these marks were really rebuses on their bearers' names; for example, Richard Spynk, the fortifier, had, besides an instrument of war in remembrance of the artillery he mounted on the walls, three birds—of course goldfinches or ' spinks,' or possibly chaffinches, as the writer in N. A., iii., p. 183, thinks. One Caxton bore three cakes over a tun; Richard de Belton, or Bolton, bore three bird-bolts; John Aubry had the letters 'ry' on an alb; and John Curat, a rat over what looks like a tree having a barbed arrow for its root. I think it would be possible, by a careful examination of these marks, to prove that certain combinations of straight lines, which occur in many of them, were meant to show the foreign buyer that the goods which were stamped with them were Norwich goods of a certain class, and that the sub-modifications showed the individual maker.

Besides the merchants and tradesmen, the nobility and gentry, and the more important abbots and priors, had houses or ' inns' in the city. The Berneys had their town-house on the upper side of King Street; so did the Bardolfs, nearly opposite the Gurneys, who were on the other side, and whose gardens no doubt sloped to the river, as did those of the Stapletons and the Boleyns. Bigot's palace was on the corner by the Ethelbert Gate. The Abbot of St. Benet's had his inn in All Saints, and the Abbot of Sibton in Pottergate Street.

The regular public inns were numerous, the two oldest and best known being the Royal, at Norwich, formerly the Angel, and the Maid's Head, once the Molde Fish. The latter change, however, was in very remote times, for it bore its present name in 1472, when Margaret Paston directed that an expected guest should set his horse at the 'Maydes Hedde.' This is, perhaps, from its associations, the most interesting inn at Norwich, being built on the site of the old Bishop's palace, and standing on early Gothic arches. The King's commanders in Kett's rebellion breakfasted here on the morning of the fight in the city. In 1643 it was a royalist resort, Dame Paston's horses being seized here. The first Freemasons' lodge in Norwich was held here in 1724, and I can imagine the horror of the present staunch Conservative occupier when he reads that a Revolutionary dinner was held here in 1791.*

The five most common signs are the Bell, the King's Head, Maid's Head, Half Moon, and White Horse; next to them coming the Jolly Farmers, Plough, Rampant Horse, Feathers, Chequers, Duke's

---

* By the way, was it here that Mrs. Beatson hid herself behind the wainscot of a lodge-room, and heard all about it, as the old Norwichers will tell you? She died 1812.

Head, Horse Shoes, Angel, Dog and Partridge, and all sorts and colours of animals and birds. Of these the Chequers may come from the arms of Warren (Chequey or and az.), and the White Lion, and possibly the Duke's Head, from the Howards, Dukes of Norfolk, whose Norwich house is remembered by the Duke's Palace, which stands on its site.

Some are almost unique, *e.g.*, the Triple Plea at Bedingham, the Hermitage at Acle, and the Cockatrice at Norton Subcourse; while Wheels of Fortune, Black Boys, Woolpacks, Cardinal's Hats, Cherry Trees and Yew Trees are comparatively common. All along the coast we find salt-sounding signs, such as Ship Inns, Jolly Sailors, Fishmonger's Arms, and Mariners, while more rarely Shore-boats and Ferryboats. Wells has its Dogger Inn, and Sherringham its Lobster, being celebrated for that shell-fish, while Lynn once boasted its Dough Fleet—whatever that meant—and still has its Black Joke (*qy*. Black Jack), the Rummer, the Wrestlers, Red Rover, Lattice, Valiant Sailor, Jolly Waterman, Greenland Fishery, Mermaid and Fountain, Hole in the Wall, and Live and let Live, while the Foul Anchor is particularly appropriate to the mariner guest who is overcome by its liquor, and is unable to get away.

Yarmouth has its Barking Smack, Humber Keel, Ballast Keel, Jolly Tar, Three Herrings, Fish Stall House, The Wrestlers, First and Last, Mariner's Compass, and Guardian Angel (!). At Norwich there are, of course, many interesting signs, such as the Bess of Bedlam, Wildman, Norwich a Port, Old

Music House, Castle Steps, Church Style, Lame Dog, Boarded House, Keel and Wherry, Hatchet and Gate, Queen of Hungary, Heart's Ease, Cardinal's Cap, Ribs of Beef, and Buff Coat, many of which relate to bygone bits of local history too long to relate here.

Several well-known inns, such as the Falgate, at Potter Heigham, scorn any sign proper, as does the Woodrow Inn. Of course the best known inn in the county was that at Scole, built by James Peck, a Norwich merchant, in 1655, the sign costing £1,057, and being ornamented with twenty-five strange figures and devices, one of which was a movable one of an astronomer pointing to the quarter whence the rain was expected. There was also an enormous reproduction of the great 'bed of Ware,' which held thirty or forty people. The inn itself is a fine red-brick building with walls twenty-seven inches thick, and with a good oak staircase.

Before leaving the inns we must remember that so many of the Norwich inns were once on the market-place that the street behind the Gentleman's Walk was, and is, called 'The Back of the Inns.' By the way, in Norfolk, in referring to an inn, the natives do not say 'The Angel at North Walsham,' but 'Walsham Angel.' In Dr. Geddes's poem, 'A Norfolk Tale,' 1792, for example, he says:

> 'At *Barford-Cock* I stop to break,
> My fast upon a mutton steak.'

A curious inscription at Wymondham was, I suppose, once outside an inn:

> 'Nec mihi glis servies,
> Nec hospes hirudo,'

which has been translated thus—on the assumption that the last word was a contraction for *hirundo*:

> 'My servant shall not be a dormour [lazy],
> Nor my guest a swallow [go away].

But I think that it should be,

> 'My servant shall not be a dormouse [lazy],
> Nor my host a leech [exorbitant].

Another favourite old parlour inscription was,

> 'All you that stand before the fire,
> To see you sit is my desire;
> That others may, as well as you,
> See the fire and feel it too.'

XI.

THE MONKS AND THE FRIARS.

N the growth of the Norfolk monasteries themselves I have touched slightly in my third chapter, and will now try to show shortly from the carefully kept accounts of their expenditure what the inner life of their occupants must have been.

The materials before me are some detached rolls of the great Abbey of St. Benet's, at Holme, covering a period from about 1359 to 1503; the account-book of the Bursar of Hempton Priory for the year 1500-1; the account of the Keeper of the Cell to Norwich, which was at Yarmouth for 1484-5; and the Cellarer's account of the little Abbey of Creak for 1331-2. Other materials might be obtained, but these form a fairly representative series for nearly 200 years of the busiest time of monasticism.

They do not throw much light on the non-religious duties of the monks. No great copying school is referred to, though there probably was one at St. Benet's. I doubt if the monks or deacons in priest's orders were employed much in actual farm-labour, though the lay brethren may have been. The forge-work, such as shoeing, was no doubt contracted for in most cases, as it was at Creak, where the smith had forty shillings.

The garden—about which some of us would rather hear than of anything else—is provokingly enough hardly touched upon, though no doubt it found employment for some of the brothers. The Yarmouth cell only sold some saffron and saffron roots, but the Deanery at St. Benet's provided wine enough to sell for £5 19s. 2d. in one year; though to one who knows the wind-wasted site now, this seems hardly credible.

No details are given us of the medicines or drugs bought, though we find a trace of the universal rule which sought to mechanically reduce too carnal thoughts and desires by periodical bleedings, in special allowances for the comfort of those who were bled.

Nor is there much about the clothes. There are routine entries as to purchase of liturgical gloves, of altar-cloths and the like; but the only interesting one is where on the Creak roll we find a trace of a large sum paid for 'a cape for rainy weather, with the silk and the making,' which sounds very much like an oiled silk waterproof cape.

The amusements were few and far between.

On Rogation-days the image of a dragon,* to represent the devil or heresy, ran about with a man

---

* Here we have the Norwich 'Snap' again.

inside it, spitting out artificial fire, the terrible effect of which must have been sadly discounted by the fact that a boy ran by its side with a burning candle ready to re-light the fire if it went out.

Every now and again there were feastings of a mild and unexciting character, arising from the spending of the pittances called 'O,' so called from being begun on the 16th December, when the introit 'O Sapientia!' was used; but the real amusement—the glimpse of the busy outer world—was only obtained when a monk was sent out to collect rents, sometimes as far as Leicester and Northampton, or a novice, accompanied by an attendant, was sent to be ordained at Aylsham. The larger monasteries used to send their younger monks to Oxford and Cambridge, and the Benedictines were taxed at one-eightieth of their income to support their 'students' at Oxford. The cook was, of course, often on his journeys after food, sometimes to buy or borrow salt-fish and meat when short at Lent, and sometimes to Lynn or elsewhere to get more succulent food.

The abbot's own life must have been to a very great extent that of a very busy professional man of the present day, having to go hither and thither in search of justice, and even to London 'about the writ called Ad quod damnum,' and having to continually supervise the financial affairs of his monastery. The life of Abbot Sampson of Bury, as chronicled by Jocelin de Brakeland, and re-vivified so startlingly by Carlyle in his 'Past and Present,' is the best known example of the lay life which was mixed up with the religious.

There is, however, one point in the internal economy of monasteries which has frequently escaped attention, but which must have materially lightened an abbot's labours, viz., that of allocating certain properties to support by their rents the expenses of certain branches of the abbey; *e.g.*, one manor would be allotted to the bursar, and another to the sacrist. Of course they accounted for any surplus, and had sometimes to be repaid or allowed for over-payments; but the general idea was a good one, giving the abbot or prior an opportunity of learning the relative administrative ability of his subordinates.

For the accommodation of the prior and the other officials, most of the more important monasteries had 'inns' at Norwich, and sometimes even in London; as, for example, Bromholm, which in 1317 bought a house in All Saints, Norwich, of its neighbour Ralph de Barton, and turned it into an 'inn,' called the 'Holy Cross of Bromholm,' in which its members and others of their order were entertained.

I have just spoken of the journies in search of justice. The rolls prove, if any proof is necessary, how thoroughly bribery had become a part of the judicial system; for there are endless instances of bribes, or 'presents,' sometimes in cash, sometimes in gloves, sometimes in boots. The King's messengers had shilling rings given them, no very great presents, even considering the change in the value of money. Presents to women were generally knives, the superstition against giving any cutting implement apparently not then obtaining.

We hear much of the large amounts given by the monks to the poor, and it is rather startling to find that in 1440 all given by the wealthy mitred abbey of St. Benet's 'in charitable donations at different times' was 2s. 4d., and for 'medicines for the sick' 3s. 4d.! But I think it very probable that the monks had come to the same conclusion about out-of-door relief as modern poor-law guardians have done, and gave much away in kind, either to be consumed on or off the premises.

Themselves they certainly did not stint, especially about 1500. There was goose eaten at Michaelmas (a proof, if one were needed, of the absurdity of the Armada myth), and plum-pudding at Christmas, though 'rese corans' were at the starvation price of $2\frac{1}{2}$d. per lb.

In one case, that of Hempton, we have the bursar's weekly bills. In the first week they had beef, mutton, eggs, sucking-pig, oysters, and fresh fish; and in the third, wild-fowl, veal, beef, mutton, fresh herrings, fresh-fish, salt-fish, oysters, eggs, and a paunch. In other weeks, rabbits, smelts, honey, lamb, 'cockell' (can this be our Norwich 'coquail?'), chicken, and mackerel: so the good canons were certainly not starved. When Lent came round raisins and currants and oil were specially brought forward; and to vary the ordinary salt-fish, shad, salmon, turbot, fresh 'pickerel,' and mussels were provided.

Nor were the condiments forgotten, for we find

purchases of ginger, orris root, cinnamon, saffron, cumin, and on one great occasion even a pound of sugar.

Possibly the best idea one gets of the average contents of the larder of a small monastery is from the 'stock-taking' of the cell at Yarmouth in 1485, which was as follows:

4 coombs 1 bushel of wheat.	11 barrels of beer.
3 good fat wethers.	In beef 8d.
18½ lings.	11½ salt-fish.
2 jars of honey.	½ barrel of vinegar.
½ runlet of malt vinegar.	7 ducks and a drake.
5 hens and a cock.	1 capon.
12 chickens.	150 wood fagots.
450 fir fagots.	3,000 and more turfs.
300 red herrings.	

Of course all through Norfolk the staple fuel was then either large turfs, sedges—*i.e.*, great bundles of sedges, roots and all—or 'flags.'

So much as to the 'cakes and ale,' of which latter, by the way, there would seem to have been a fair if not a liberal supply, if we may judge from the 'O' feasts. Let us hope the want of them did not cause the death of the unhappy monk of St. Alban's, who, according to Matthew Paris, was first beaten and then sent by his abbot to Binham Abbey, which was one of its cells, where he was kept in fetters till he died, and was then buried in them.

Taylor, in his 'Index Monasticus,' says there was a monk's prison, contrived so that the prisoner could see mass, at the end of the south transept of Norwich Cathedral; but I never found anyone who could show it to me.

Nor do I remember anything like either of the curious ground-plans of monks' prisons, which he figures as occurring in any Norfolk monastic ruins. Certainly the rustics will tell you that the 'Cobbler's Hole,' leading out of the north rood-turret of Cromer Church, was where refractory monks were stowed away in a sort of 'little ease;' but as the monks never had an abiding-place there, and the hole is clearly a service or choir book cupboard, this notion need not be seriously combated.

Possibly the grand and well-arched sewers which ran from every monastic establishment, as well as from every castle (see p. 123, Chap. IX.)—and which are so frequently mistaken by rustics, whose ideas on sewage stretch no further than cesspools, for subterranean passages, through which the monks obtained access to the ruins—may also have given some sort of foundation for stories of mysterious prisons.

One thing is certain, that for sanitary arrangements the monks were far ahead of the present generation in giving ample ventilation and plentiful water. The lavatory in the cloisters at Norwich, which ran with clear water, is a curious and easily accessible proof of this; as also is the way in which the 'necessarium' opened boldly on rivers, which then feared no pollution.

When we come to the life of the friars, a very marked difference from that of the monks is discernible. Even allowing for the natural exaggertion and excitement of their early chroniclers, there is no doubt that the early Franciscans were earnest missionaries of the highest type, and came opportunely to fill up the gap caused by the growing sloth and worldliness of the monks, whose predecessors had been probably just as earnest as the friars. In time they too fell, and it should be remembered fell quicker, for much less than three centuries transformed the missionary priest who lived from hand to mouth, the real 'barefooted friar' of the ballads, sometimes into a scheming greedy man of the world—half-politician and half-domestic chaplain—sometimes into a wearisome casuistical philosopher, and too rarely into a Roger Bacon.

There can be little doubt that what first led them away from the paths of poverty was the fatal temptation they had of half-dictating the wills of the poorer and middle classes.

The monks, secure in their endowments and their comfortable homes, do not seem to have much meddled with the deathbed of any but very great lords, while very many of the parish clergy were non-residents or pluralists. When, therefore, the Friars came—who were never afraid of hard work, even when they were falling away—and actually hunted up the poor and the merchants, and forced some better religion on them than the dull routine to which they were accustomed, it is not strange that in the dire hour of death they should have been consulted by the dying man how he should best dispose of his goods for the benefit of his soul, or that, perhaps, an undue share should fall to the lot of he irregulars.

It has been the custom to make out that the parochial clergy and the friars always led a cat-and-dog life, but Mr. Howlett, in his admirable introduction to vol. ii. of the 'Monumenta Franciscana,' has pointed out that frequently this was not so, for in many cases parochial clergymen left legacies to their so-called rivals.

Common alike to the monks and friars was a reverence for the various shrines and holy wells of the county. A list of some of them, compiled by the Rev. R. Hart, in his paper in the 'Transactions of the Norfolk and Norwich Archæological Society' (vol. vi., p. 277), will be useful. The remarks are my own.

1. *The Image of Our Lady of Walsingham.*

This was, of course, the object of by far the greatest number of pilgrimages. Eight crowned heads we know came here specially—Henry VIII. among them, who walked the last two miles barefoot—some few years before the Reformation, when the same image was burnt at Chelsea !—only a few years before he, on his death-bed, in his agony commended his soul to the protection of that same Lady of Walsingham whose image he had destroyed. One king's banner, at least, was hung up before it in gratitude for a victory, and its shrine literally blazed with silver, gold, and jewels, brought as offerings to what was thought the Virgin's favourite English home. There were relics, of course, such as the coagulated blood of the Virgin, and an unnaturally large joint of the Apostle Peter's forefinger, while another attraction was the 'wishing well.' Evidences of miracles were ever at hand, such as a house not built by hands, which was placed by divine power over the wells; and a wicket-gate, less than an ell square, through which a knight on horseback, pursued by his enemies, was safely conveyed by the Virgin Mary, to whom he called in his dire need. Erasmus's account of the whole juggle, the gross ignorance of the monks, and the avarice of the managers of the show, is too well-known to need repetition here. The Milky Way in the heavens is said to have got its name from its showing the way to where the Virgin's blood was exhibited; and the road to the shrine, *viâ* Newmarket, Brandon, and Fakenham, was long known as the 'Walsingham Way,' or the Palmer's Way— as was also that to it from Norwich *viâ* Attlebridge. Taylor thinks that the pilgrims who came to Walsingham from the north of England crossed the Wash near Long Sutton, and came through Lynn; but I fancy it is more probable they took boat across to St. Edmund's Chapel, near Hunstanton, whence there is also a 'Peddar's Road' to Castle Acre Priory. Of course 'peddar's' road here could not mean pedlar's or packman's road, as has been surmised, for the trade between Castle Acre and Hunstanton must ever have been, as it is now, *nil*; but must have meant a road similar to that used by peddars—if, indeed, peddar does not simply mean a person who travels on 'pied,' whether his journey be religious or secular. There were, indeed, many ways to Walsingham, and it would be hard to answer the inquiry in the old (?) ballad,

> 'Gentle herdsman, tell to me
> Of courtesy I thee pray,
> Unto the town of Walsingham
> Which is the right and ready way?'

2. *The Holy Rood of Bromholm.*

When Baldwin, Emperor of Constantinople, was killed by infidels, his chaplain brought over many holy relics to England, and gave to Bromholm, which Matthew Paris says was then 'miserably poor and altogether destitute of buildings,' a great piece of the wood of the true Cross, which very greatly prospered the abbey by the fame of the miracles it wrought. If the rest of the story is no truer than that Bromholm Abbey was then very poor and destitute of buildings in 1206, when Baldwin died, I don't believe much of it; for the abbey was founded in 1113, and the north transept, of work not later than the end of the twelfth century, still stands.

Apropos of the 'Holy Rood of Bromholm,' it is said in E. C. C., p. 225, that a convent of nuns in Yorkshire now have a large piece of the true Cross set in silver in the shape of a Jerusalem cross, which they think came from here, as one of their Superioresses was of the family of Paston, which was intimately connected with the abbey.

3. *St. John the Baptist's Head at Trimmingham.*

I must own to scepticism about this relic. The only time I can find it mentioned is in the will of Alice Cook (died 1478), who directs a pilgrimage to it. This Alice Cook seems to have had a penchant for pilgrimages, for she ordered *nine* to various local shrines, and several of them are known only by their mention in her will. It stands to reason that if the authorities had recognised so magnificent a relic as the Baptist's head, it would have been known and patronized so well that it would not have escaped oblivion merely by an accidental mention in a fifteenth-century will. Possibly there was an *image* of St. John there. Though the head was not there, I can well believe the 'charger' was.

4. *St. Walstan of Bawbergh.*

Hermit and confessor. This saint died in 1016, and at one time six chantry priests and a vicar continually served at his shrine, which was a regularly constituted, respectable, and well-recognised one.

5. *Our Lady at Reepham.*

Of this I can get no particulars, and the same remark will apply to most of the following.

6. *Holy Spirit of Elsing* (St. Spyrite).

7. *St. Parnell of Stratton* (St. Petronilla).

I know of no one of this name in modern history who answers to the description of saint.

8. *St. Leonard without Norwich.*

9. *St. Wandred of Biskele.*

Wandragesilius of Bixley.

10. *St. Margaret of Horstead.*

11. *Our Lady of Pity of Horstead.*

12. *The Holy Rood at Crostwight.*

13. *St. Albert* (Ethelbert) *of Cringleford.*

14. *St. Thomas of Westacre.*

15. *St. Tebbald* (Theobald) *of Hobbies* (Hautbois).

16. *St. Blythe of Martham.*

St. Bleda, mother of St. Walsham, who was buried at Martham.

17. *St. Margaret of Hoveton.*

She was killed in a wood here, called Little Wood, buried at St. Bennet's Abbey, and was said to be a saint.

To these I may add three more.

18. *St. William in the Wood.*

In the Cathedral of Norwich. The shrine of a little boy said to have been murdered by the Jews.

19. *The Scala Cœli.*

In the Church of St. Michael at Conisford, Norwich.

20. *St. Withburga.*

At Dereham, though the Ely monks stole her body away so early that it can hardly be considered a Norfolk shrine in historic times.

As to most of these—in fact all, except the first four and the last three—I think inquiry would show that they were local shrines which had great interest and power to those who lived in the villages in which they were situate, and that when they are mentioned in wills it is by inhabitants of these villages who had moved away, but who had retained their early awe and reverence for the shrine they had known in childhood.

Besides these regular—or irregular—shrines, pilgrimages were made to the graves of worthy but uncanonized bishops, and even to those of their fathers and mothers, and no doubt to many other places where relics were preserved; *e.g.*, part of the shirt of St. Edmund, King and Martyr, in St. Edmund's Church, Norwich; part of St. Andrew's finger, at Westacre; and the Virgin's blood in the chapel of St. Mary of Pity, in Norwich Cathedral.

As well as all these, which one can easily understand could well be venerated by a devout Catholic, there were one or two more which I can hardly believe were ever seriously visited.* I have ever, especially, had my doubts about

The Good Sword of Winfarthing, which is said, I think only by rabid post-reformation writers (*e.g.*, Becon, in his 'Reliques of Rome'), to have had ascribed to it the virtue of shortening a husband's life if a wife, who was weary of her mate, burnt a candle before it every Sunday for a year. Such offerings, in the worst and most corrupt times of the Romish religion, must have been impossible. Nor do I be—lieve that

---

* *E.g.* St. Godric of Walpole, who must have been the champion ascetic, for while hermit he is said to have worn out three suits of iron clothes!

The Smock of St. Audrie, in Thetford, which is another of Becon's stories, was ever really held out as a specific for toothaches and swellings of the throat.

Of the tendency of the people to try to canonize for themselves persons they thought worthy of it there are two curious instances in Norfolk, viz., 'Master John Schorne'* and 'Maid Ridibone.' The former was remarkable as the only layman who put the devil in a boot and kept him there—a feat pictured in several East Anglian rood-screens and windows; and the latter for having been killed by falling through a mill-wheel and yet having no bones broken, and being restored to life by the intervention of St. Alban. There was 'Maid Ridibone's chapel' in Cromer Church.

To all the shrines and places described above, it has been said that 'the stone wayside crosses, once so frequent in the county, served as finger-posts, and that the "Hospitals" were intended as resting-places for pilgrims travelling from one shrine to the other;' but I think the guesses, though plausible enough, are hardly sustained by facts.

Of the Leper Houses, which were once numerous, I do not think any remains now exist. One curious fact about them has, I think, hitherto escaped notice; namely, that those who acted as intermediaries be-

---

* 'John Schorne—gentleman born,
　　Conjured the devil into a boot ;'
so says the old rhyme. Mr. C. Brent of Bromley, has a pilgrim's leaden sign, with the devil's head just showing out of a boot.

tween them and the people were called 'foregoers,' and as such received legacies in Margaret Paston's will, in 1482. By the way, the same will refers to the 'Whole' and 'Half' sisters of Norman's Hospital at Norwich.

XI.

THE PARSONS AND THEIR CHURCHES.

 HAVE spoken before (p. 43) of the difficulty in accounting for the very large number of parishes and churches in Norfolk, and the fact of their being so many must be my excuse for the length of this chapter. Of course the first thing that strikes us is the general poverty of the livings, and the number of cures which many clergy held simultaneously in early days—one may suppose in many cases almost necessarily, for a living could not have been obtained from one. But the scandal which arose from clergy who held benefices in Kent, Surrey, and other counties, so distant that it may be fairly assumed that they never even visited Norfolk, being allowed to hold small livings here must have been very great. One hopes that in many cases they were only presented to prevent the presentation lapsing, and that when indigenous priests could be obtained they were replaced. In many cases the very short interval between the presentation and resignation would seem to show that the stranger

priest simply accepted the presentation because he did not like to refuse anything, journeyed down to see what the place was worth, thought it not good enough, and resigned at once. Take, for example, the case of Aylmerton, to a mediety of which, in less than five months (in 1339), there were *three* presentations, viz., Peter de St. John on 17th July, Walter de Huntingfield on 29th September, and John Keymer on 1st December. In 1396 there were two presentations to the same, and in 1419 three in one year.

With such poor emoluments* and much idle time on their hands, it would be strange if some of the clergy had not got into mischief; but I think few who have not worked at the records themselves have any idea how great was the apparent lawlessness of the clergy in the thirteenth and fourteenth centuries.† Premising that I am not falling into the error of supposing that all those criminals who were found to be 'clericus' and remitted to the Ordinary were ordained priests, I will give a few examples out of many which I have come across.

One Norfolk Crown Plea roll, that for 14 Edward I.,‡

---

* For the poor livings in the gift of the Lord Chancellor, there used to be considerable competition of late years. They used to be called 'run-and-ride livings,' from the haste with which they were sought.

† M. 4, 2, No. 6.

‡ It will be remembered that William of Newbrough, speaking of Henry II., says, 'Finally it was declared in his presence, that during his reign [of which nine years only had then passed], more than a hundred murders had been committed by the clergy in England alone.' 'Roll's Ed.,' i., p. 140.

discloses charges against (1) the Dean of Sparham for accepting a bribe; (2) the sub-Dean of Norwich and his chaplain for illegal rescue; and (3) the chaplain of Hunstanton for murdering another chaplain—of which crime he was found guilty. In another (17 Edward II.), (1) two vicars are charged with murder and robbery; (2) the parson of St. Botulph, Norwich, with illegal rescue of a thief; (3) a vicar with theft; and (4) a parson with theft. In an earlier one (34 Henry III.) the chaplain of Betale is charged with illegal wounding; and in another (52-53 Henry III.) there is a presentment that 'a certain Constance, concubine of John the priest (sacerdos) of Gimmingham, bore a child in the rector's house there,' upon which the bailiff seized her and her bed, and lodged them in the Hall till the priest paid a fine of 40s. to release her. Of course it may be said that concubinage was practically connived at when the early right of the clergy to marry was discountenanced. That this right was an undoubted one at law could, if necessary, be proved up to the hilt; but one instance will suffice, for an official document dated 1237, distinctly refers to Elswyd, a woman having the right to present to the chapel of Panxford, marrying Ralph, the chaplain or curate of Stokesby, and having by him a son named Hermer, who afterwards was presented to the chapel—which, of course, could not have been done had he been then considered illegitimate. Again, we find Richard, son of Bishop William de Beaufoy, ordained and holding high office in Norwich cathedral.

To return to the bad parsons, however, we find in the 5th Edward III. that the chaplain of Guist was no better than a common church-breaker, for he broke into the churches of Dalling, Sall, Weston, Bintre, Norton, and Belaugh and stole chalices, books, vestments, and other valuables, worth £100. He was found guilty, and handed over to the Ordinary, and was no doubt handled by him somewhat rougher than he would have been had he stolen from the laity.

The same roll tells us how Simon atte Wode, parson of Rocklandtoft, broke by force and arms into the house of Oliver, parson of Roudham, and carried away goods to the value of 50s. Later on we read how the parson of Snoring, in 1461, fetched Thomas Denys, the coroner of Norfolk, out of his own house, and he was carried away and murdered. The parson was put into the stocks—a singular punishment for being accessory before the fact to a murder. Again we read in Riley's ' Memorials of London and London Life ' how, in 1416, Wm. Cratfield, late rector of the church of Wrotham, in Norfolk, was presented by a London jury of robbing a Londoner of £12, and was a common and notorious thief, and lurker on the roads, and murderer and slayer. From Fabian's Chronicle we learn that he long haunted Newmarket Heath, but was at last caught and brought with his concubine to Newgate, where he died.

These instances are collected incidentally only, and I have little doubt might be multiplied to an immense extent. Small wonder, therefore, that the parsons generally were held in low esteem, as we learn from Roger Flint, who, when printing a sermon of the Rev. E. Boys, says: 'When a priest and a gentleman meet in one parson, the Church must needs suffer a great loss by his death.'

It is pleasant to see that some of the clergy and officials were well up to their duty, and acted conscientiously; *e.g.*, William Pykenham, in 1479, declining to be a party to Margaret Paston's son being irregularly presented to a family living, returning the mother's presents, and telling her that her desire was 'not goodly neither godly.' So she had to ask a correspondent if he knew 'any young priest in London that setteth bills upon Paul's door,' who would be glad to have it—a curious way of advertising for preferment or employment.

In the time of the Commonwealth many hard things were, of course, said of the parsons, as when the rector of Carlton Rode was accused of being 'an alehouse haunter.' So in 1635 was the rector of Santon, and also of 'swearing, being distempered with liquor, keeping malignant company, and calling the Puritans hypocrites.' Of their rejoicings when the Restoration replaced them in their benefices I have spoken in my sixth chapter. Macaulay's description of the country clergy is not, I think, the caricature which it is often called; and many are the 'good' stories which are told, to the discredit of the parsons of the time of Queen Anne, and of even later date.

The natural depravity of the layman, delighted at catching his spiritual master tripping, has, I fear, caused him to invent many of these. One laughs at the tale how the parson bet out of his pulpit on a dog-fight, which took place in his chancel; how he bribed old women to stay away, so that he need not hold the service; and how he fell drunk into a brook, and protested he would drink that up before he left, without considering the gross improbability of such stories being true. The last tale is now told—a lie of immense circumstance—of a clergyman lately dead, and the beck in Stratton Strawless Wood has been shown me as the scene of the anecdote; but the whole thing will be found in the old Norfolk story-book of the reign of Elizabeth—the 'Anecdotes and Traditions' of the Camden Society.

> 'The good men do lie buried with their bones;
> The evil . . .'

as we have seen, lives after them, and can be recorded; but we can find very little indeed of the histories of the good parsons who wore away peaceful lives in pursuit of duty. They were, no doubt, uneventful.

It has been presumed that they hated the friars, but I think this is only a guess. Certainly all of them did not, for, as mentioned before, we find them leaving occasional legacies to the friars. That they lived very studious lives I doubt, for books were too scarce and too dear for their purses. Of course there were exceptions, and sometimes we find clergymen leaving books by their wills, as when Richard Wygelworth, parson of Waxtonesham, in 1370, left all his library, except 'Sermones parati' and 'Manipulus Curatorum,' to Hickling Priory. Robert Barwell, parson of Thuxton, in 1531, must have had a fair library, for he mentions 'Itercalyn to Jherusalem,' 'The Constitutions Provincial' (two copies), 'Josephus de Antiquitatibus,' 'Postilla super Epistolas et de Evangelia,' 'Gemma Predicantium,' 'The Fall of Princes,' 'Geoffrey de Historia Britanniarum,' and 'The Cronycles of Ynglond,' besides an ordinal, which he left to St. Peter Mancroft, Norwich. Of course many of the city clergy, like the rector of the parish just named, had access to good, and in St. Peter's case to fine, libraries.

I have treated elsewhere* on the library of St. Peter Mancroft, and there is an interesting account of the little rectorial library still preserved in the porch of Shipdham Church, which has many old books, including a Wynken de Worde, but no Caxtons as sometimes stated, to be found in vol. i., p. 184, of the 'East Anglian.'

Still, though their lives must have been humdrum enough in quiet times, when the pinch came, and the cruel test of martyrdom began, several of them did not shrink from it. Indeed, it was a Norfolk man, William Sautre, once priest of St. Margaret's in Lynn, who was actually the first of the noble band of martyrs for the Reformation, suffering at the stake at Smithfield in 1401.

The first who died for his faith in Norfolk was William White, a priest of Ludham, who was burned

* 'Norf. Antiq. Misc.,' vol. ii., p. 359.

in Norwich market-place in 1424. Bilney, too—
'Bilney, little Bilney, that blessed martyr of God,'
as Latimer calls him in his seventh sermon—was
also a Norfolk man, and suffered in the Lollards' Pit,
the other side of Bishop's Bridge.

Bishop Aylmer had, it is said, a narrow escape
from martyrdom, the tale going that in Queen Mary's
time he had to be hidden away in a great wine butt,
which had false partitions, so that while he was inside
his pursuers actually drank wine from the bottom of
it while he sat in the top.

It is some relief, among all the religious murders,
to find a Norfolk man humane at risk to himself
—Sir Anthony Knevet, who was lieutenant of the
Tower, disobeying Bonner, and refusing to rack Ann
Askew. But Bonner himself, on the other hand,
was, to the shame of our county be it said, a Norfolk man, having been rector of Dereham, 1534-1540. Scandal said of him that he was the illegitimate son of one Savage, a priest; but as illegitimacy
was then, as now, a bar to taking orders, this would
seem to have been a piece of spite. Still the story was
told in his lifetime, and there is an entry in Dereham
Register, of no recent date, to the same effect. He
is reported to have been the cause of the deaths by
burning of 200 persons for heresy.

Those interested in the counter-persecution of the
Jesuits will, of course, read Dr. Jessopp's very excellent book, 'One Generation of a Norfolk House,' and
go and see for themselves the 'Priest's hiding-hole,'
in a turret of the east tower of Oxburgh Hall. It is

a little nook 6 × 5 × 7 feet, and entered through a trapdoor formed of a wooden frame enclosing bricks, and fixed on an iron axle.

Of the milder persecutions of the clergy during the Commonwealth I have already spoken, and it was followed by the non-juring agitation on the other side of the question. Both, no doubt, caused much misery and undeserved suffering, as in the case of the Rev. John Gibbs, who was presented to Gissing by Charles II., and ejected as a non-juror in 1690, of whom it is said he was 'an odd but harmless man, both in life and conversation; after his ejection he dwelt in the north porch chamber, and laid on the stairs that led up to the rood loft, between the church and the chancel, having a window at his head, so that he could lie in his narrow couch and see the altar.'

The friction which must have necessarily taken place between the regular clergy and the Puritan and dissenting interest must have always been considerable, and is often amusingly shown by the evidence that has come down to us. The Norwich townsfolk, who affected the Commonwealth side, and especially the apprentices, seem to have set their faces against the cathedral services, and even to have threatened to pull down the organs.

A very amusing and scarce tract in my possession, called 'True Newes from Norwich,' purports to be 'a certain relation how the Cathedral Blades . . . did put themselves into a posture of defence, because that the apprentices of Norwich (as they imagined) would have pulled down their Organs.' It is written in the usual exaggerated and abusive style then so current, and after admitting that there was a rumour that the 'prentices were about to pull down the altar rails and organs, and admitting that the rails were taken down by the Dean and Chapter, asserts that the threat that the 'prentices ' would have a bout with the organs on Shrove Tuesday' was only a joke 'to skare the fooles.' It goes on to say that 500 parsons and priests were ready to resist the attack, and that the gates of the cathedral were shut for two days; and after detailing certain preparations, sets out that, 'In the fourth place there were the musquetiers ready charged with bullets, and one of them had in his musket a bullet split in parts for to shoot the apprentises when they come (say they). Thus they stood all day long shooting and threatening the Rebels that dare come to pull down their organs, when as the apprentises had no intent to come, but were at home about their masters' occasions, and did not intend to foule their fingers about such a company of rake shames: and there they stood like so many Abraham Ninnies, doing nothing but tell how many crows flew over the pinacle.' The writer goes on to accuse some of the defenders of being 'so intoxicated with strong Ale, that was to be sould at the great Cathedrall, that they could not tell what they said or did. Thus, good Reader, thou maist see the folly of these Pipe-mongers,' etc.

Of course, the Puritans did not have all the ridicule on their side; and one can judge how the Cavalier Sir Nicholas L'Estrange, elder brother of the pamphleteer, laughed when he jotted down in his note-book the story about the Puritan chaplain objecting to the running bowl being abjured to go on as told in the last chapter; and when he tells how when a Puritan minister, who had preached a very long sermon, asked a gentleman how he liked it, was told that it was very good, but that it had spoiled a goose worth two of it!

Of the Dissenters it would hardly be within the scope of this little book to treat, but I may point out that they met with as great obstruction from the Protestant Churchmen as the latter had met with from the Catholics. A 'Hell Fire' club was started in Norwich, avowedly with the intention of crushing the Methodists, and, strangely enough, it was held at the Bell, at Orford Hill, now, certainly, frequented by a very different class of customers; a metamorphosis as strange as that which has turned the Maid's Head from a revolutionary house to the steadiest and most respectable High Church and State hostelry possible.

All this, however, is wandering rather widely from my subject, so I will here break off to say something of the *churches* themselves, in which the parsons, as to whom I have spoken in the first part of this chapter, exercised their functions for good or evil.

The first things that strike the stranger-archæologist when he comes into Norfolk are the enormous number of the churches, the fine work that has been put into many of them, and the almost universal use of dressed flint as the material with which they are built. Flint churches and round towers are as common here as they are rare elsewhere; but the reasons for them are not far to seek, for flint is the easiest material to get, and it is easier to build flint into a round tower than into a square one. The great majority of Norfolk churches have (or had before the curse of restoration came on us) a lofty circular tower, often embattled, a long light clerestory, and handsome porches.

Of course we have churches of all sorts and sizes, from the great church at Yarmouth—the largest parish church and the widest ecclesiastical building in England, with its floor area of 23,085 square feet, its length of 230 feet, and breadth of 108 feet—to the little gem of a chapel on the Red Mount at Lynn, which makes up for its small size (floor area less than 180 square feet, being only 15 feet by 11 feet 10 inches) by the most exquisite workmanship.

There are so many magnificent churches in the county, that it is a work of the greatest difficulty to pick out any for special mention without drawing on one the wrath of those who have made particular buildings their special study; but whatever may be the sins of omission in the following list, I am very confident that I have not included in it a single building not very well worthy of careful inspection by any ecclesiologist.

ATTLEBURGH } Fine decorated work.
AYLSHAM

BARTON ST. MARY.—Very singular Norman west doorway.

BEESTON ST. LAWRENCE.—Saxon work.

BURLINGHAM, NORTH.—Early English south porch.

BURLINGHAM, SOUTH.—Considered by Cotman a most interesting church for its stone pulpit with sounding-board, hour-glass and frame, stone reading-desk, and wooden rood-screen, besides a fine Norman doorway. Since Cotman wrote two frescoes have been discovered.

BURNHAM OVERY.—Fine three-light lancet east window.

CASTLE RISING.—Norman west front; Saxon arches to tower; very fine Early English west window.

CLEY.—Fine church, lately well restored; brass of a shrouded figure.

CREAK, NORTH.—Decorated tomb; Perpendicular screen.

CROMER.—Very large Perpendicular church; fine flint and stone panelling and carving on buttresses; galilee.

DUNHAM MAGNA.—Tower; said by Rickman to be Anglo-Saxon.

ELMHAM.—Saxon work.

EMNETH.—Three-light lancet east window.

FAKENHAM.—Very fine church, well restored; lofty tower, with good flint and stone panelling; coats of arms, etc.

GILLINGHAM.—Much Norman work, especially in tower, with fine circular windows. Circular east end.

HADDISCOE.—Circular flint tower, battered considerably; fine Norman south doorway, surmounted by image in niche.

HALES.—Extremely enriched north doorway.

HINGHAM.—Decorated; fine tower; splendid mural monument.

HOWE.—Saxon, as to some parts.

HUNSTANTON.—Early Decorated; Norman font; fine canopied brass, and good monuments.

INGHAM.—Late Decorated; fine monument, dated 1360.

LOPHAM, SOUTH.—Early Norman tower of six storeys, of which the four higher are ornamented with arches.

LYNN.—*St. Margaret.* Transitional Norman; Early English and Decorated tower; the two largest and finest brasses in England.
St. Nicholas. Great west window of eleven lights; very fine and elaborately ornamented entrance to porch.

MARTHAM.—Fine Perpendicular church, with good tower and fine south door.

NEWTON.—Saxon work.

NORWICH.—*St. Julian.* Saxon work.
St. Michael Coslany. Possibly the finest inlaid flint and stone work in England, much recently spoiled by 'restoration.'
St. Peter Mancroft. Very large and beautiful Perpendicular church, with fine and richly ornamented tower.

SALL.—Very large, with aisles and clerestory, transept, chancel, and two porches.

SNETTISHAM.—Beautiful Decorated west window; fine galilee.

SNORING PARVA.—One of the most singular south doors in existence, the head being a round arch, within which is a pointed arch with a bold zigzag.

SWAFFHAM.—Very large (partly Decorated); cruciform; chancel; nave; aisles and transept; and fine tower. For boldness, light, size, and good situation, one of the most striking churches in the county.

TASBURGH.—Thought by some to be Roman, from its resemblance to the church at Brixworth, in Northamptonshire.

TERRINGTON ST. CLEMENT'S.—Cruciform; Perpendicular; very large and handsome; lofty and wide; long clerestory of thirteen windows.

TOFT.—Octagonal tower and lanthorn.

WALPOLE ST. PETER.—One of the finest churches in England; Decorated tower; rest, including magnificent porch, font with cover, and grand chancel, Perpendicular. Rickman says of it, he 'never found a more satisfactory Perpendicular church.'

WALSINGHAM, OLD.—Fine Decorated, geometrical tracery.

WALSOKEN.—Magnificent square tower, greatly enriched; splendid interior of Late Norman work.

WALTON, NORTH.—Early English church, with extremely beautiful details.

WORSTEAD.—North doorway; sound-holes; screen; inscription as to plough light.

Students of special branches of ecclesiology should notice these:

Doorways.—Shingham, Chedgrave, Heckingham, Mintlyn, Mundham, Hales, Wroxham, and Thwayt.

Doors.—Harpley, Cromer.

Porches.—Great Massingham, Worstead, Cromer, and Snettisham.

Easter Sepulchre.—North Wold. This is the largest in England.

Fonts.—Fincham, Belaugh, Kirby Cave, Walsoken, Burnham Deepdale, Shouldham Thorpe, Walsingham, Calthorpe, Hunstanton, Hautbois, and Yaxham. Of these, Yaxham is very unusual, being in 'high florid Gothic,' while Hautbois is Early Norman with interlaced 'Runic' work, and Burnham is Early Norman, if not Saxon. There is a leaden font at Great Plumstead—probably Late Norman—one of the very few in England, and there is a very fine font-cover at Trench.

Roof.—Knapton.

Rood-screens.—Ranworth, Barton Turf, Scarning, Salhouse, Sherringham, Acle, North Burlingham, Cawston, Edingthorpe, North Elmham, Gately, East Harling, Irstead, Lessingham, Happisburgh, Sparham, Stalham, Trunch and Worstead. Of these the two first are magnificent, while of the others Salhouse and Scarning have their saunce bells still *in situ*, and Sherringham its rood-loft and staircase perfect—a feature I have never seen elsewhere.

Mural Paintings.—Unluckily most of these have, when uncovered, faded away so rapidly that, but for sketches taken at once, we should have no memento of them.

At Wyndham was one of fiends; some tantalizing souls in purgatory by offering them cans of water, while others prepared a crop of damned souls by tempting men with purses.

Monuments.—Hingham. A magnificent one to Thomas, Lord Morley, dated 1435, probably the largest and finest mural monument in England, and supposed to be built by the architect of the Erpingham gate; for style it is between Decorated and Perpendicular, and is most richly ornamented. At North Creak there is a very fine Decorated monument, and a very bold and rich founder's tomb at Raveningham. The tomb of Oliver de Ingham, in Ingham, and of Sir Roger L'Estrange, in Hunstanton, are both very fine types. Of late mural tombs, Paston's at North Walsham is a good example.

Brasses.—Of these we probably have the largest and finest show in England. Certainly the two grand brasses in St. Margaret's, Lynn, are untouched for size or beauty of execution—that of the Peacock Feast measuring 8 feet by 5 feet 5 inches. Little less interesting are the brasses of Sir Simon de Felbrigg in Felbrigg Church, of Richard Calthorp and his nineteen children in Antingham Mary, and of Archdeacon Tenison in Bawburgh, Sir Hugh Hastings at Elsing, Sir John Harsick in South Acre, Margaret Castell at Raveningham, Thomas Heveningham in Ketteringham. There is a skeleton brass to John Brigg at Sall, a shrouded brass to John and Roger Yelverton at Rougham, and a very curious one to Thomas Hall at Heigham, representing a coxcomb of 1630 in wrinkled boots and a fashionable wig.

Stalls and Piscinæ.—There is a set of three very fine stalls under a window at Acle, also decorated stalls and piscina at Aylmerton; and other good examples are to be met with at Fakenham, Norton Subcourse, Snoring, Burnham Thorpe, and elsewhere.

Of curious and novel features, I may note that there is a *sexton's wheel* at Long Stratton, and something which I think served the same purpose on the floor of Barningham. The *poor's box* at Cawston is very curious, as is the *acoustic pottery* at St. Peter Mancroft and St. Peter per Mountergate, Norwich, and at East Harling. A very fine *church chest* is at Dersingham, and the *sculpture* over the west door of Rougham—Christ crucified, surrounded by a border of vine-leaves—is very beautiful. The magnificent *bosses* on the roof and in the cloisters of Norwich Cathedral are too well known to need reference. Many of the *gurgoyles* in our Norwich churches, as at Cromer, are very quaint. Several of the churches along the east and north coast seem to have been built with the view of ranging with one another, so that in case of need they could 'pass on a beacon-light' from one tower to another. Certainly, on the north-east of Blakeney and the north-west of Cromer towers, there are platforms or turrets, which are reputed to have served as places on which beacon-fires were lit.

Possibly, however, they served as lighthouses, and it is curious to note that John Puttock, hermit of Lynn in 1349, erected a great cross 110 feet high, which was 'of great service for all shipping coming that way.'

When my reader has seen all or many of the notable churches mentioned in the above list, he may probably have arrived at an opinion of his own about the solution of the difficulty I spoke about when beginning this chapter, viz., the great number of Norfolk churches and parishes. I own to having none, beyond a sort of guess that there was more of emulation than piety in the motive that caused many a squire to build or re-edify his church. Take for example the case of a mother who wrote to a son in 1478, that her cousin Clere had spent £100 on the 'desks' in the choir at Bromholm Abbey, and at Heydon the same; 'and if there should be nothing done for your father [he was buried there] it would be too great a shame for us all, and in chief to see him lie as he does.'

But I doubt if anyone will find a satisfactory reason for the magnificence of the seven marshland churches of Walsoken, West Walton, the two Walpoles, Terrington, Tilney, and Upwell.

None of these places were ever important commercial places, nor can we find out that the builders were men of any vast property or importance in the county; and yet we find glorious churches, many of freestone, of a size and splendour of finish that would make any one of them noticeable in any county. One can understand places like Cley, Blakeney, and Cromer, which, though now insignificant fishing villages, were once important ports; or villages like Worstead and North Walsham, which were once large commercial centres, having large and beautiful churches; but it is hard to say why places which can hardly ever have been more than grazing centres should boast buildings much their superior.

The wonder is, however, that there is anything

The Parsons and their Churches. 199

left of our churches, when one considers the woful ordeal of neglect they went through in the seventeenth and eighteenth centuries, and the more terrible one of restoration under which they are now suffering. The lead was so frequently torn off the roofs to find money to patch up the building, and the fine old bells sold for similar purposes, that the story goes that when, on one occasion, Bishop Wren received an application for a faculty to substitute a lead for a thatch roof, he treated it as a bad and unseemly joke, and threw the paper away, and could hardly afterwards be persuaded that the churchwardens were in earnest.

The worst case was, to my mind—though perhaps I speak under a sense of wrong, as the explosion covered up some of my family burial-places—when the 'Reverend' N. Gill, the lessee of the great tithes of Cromer, was allowed in 1681 to destroy the beautiful chancel of the Church there, on the ground that the nave was large enough, and actually blew it up with gunpowder!

Nowadays, the pendulum of destruction is swinging the other way. Interesting late Perpendicular work, Jacobean pulpits and panelling, and monuments of families who have left the parish, are swept away by the 'restorer,' whose idea usually seems to be to construct a new-looking church (Decorated for choice) with a hammer-beam pine roof, cheap pine open seats, gaudy pattern encaustic tiles, and never a monument on wall or floor. The type is common and most uninteresting. While there is anything left of old work, therefore, it behoves all true ecclesiologists to make as many sketches and church notes as possible—or, better still, to employ the new and easily managed dry-plate process of photography—and all genealogists to copy all the inscriptions. One little crow I may make for myself. I have copied and printed *every inscription* in North Erpingham Hundred (2,509 in number), and have finished and am printing Tunstead and Happing, while a friend has completed and printed Holt. It would be a very little thing for the local clergy, as some slight amends for the ill their restoring zeal has done, to copy the inscriptions and send them up to Norwich to the Secretary of the National Society for the Preservation of Memorials of the Dead, where they could be preserved and indexed.

It will hardly, however, be believed that a member of the committee of the local Archæological Society actually refused permission to the officials of the Memorial Society to copy the monuments in his church!

I cannot, I think, close this chapter better, than by giving a few samples of some of the more interesting Norfolk inscriptions I have come across.

A Norman-French one to a former rector of Thursford, who died 1393, ran thus:

> 'De terre je suis faire et formé,
> Et à la terre je suis retorné,
> Ellertune nome appelé,
> Parsone de Thursford estois,
> Jesus ave de moy pité.'

Of course, everyone is familiar with the modern version of this; but an intermediate one, dated 1607, from Toft Monks, may be new to my readers:

> 'As I was—so be ye,
> As I am—ye shall be ;
> That I gave—that I lost,
> That I spent—that I had ;
> Thus I end all my cost,
> That I left—that I lost.'

One to John Bowf, I forget in what church, runs:

> 'We shall all hence,
> Whither or when
> No man shall know,
> But God above.
> We care for other things,
> Hence we shall fare,
> All cold and bare :
> Thus says John Bowf.'

Laconic, and to the point, is this from Sustead:

> 'Simon Taylor of Metton this stone did make,
> Pray for his soul for Jesus' sake.'

At Colney is a cynical one, dated 1481:

> 'When the bell is solemnly rung,
> And the mass with devotion sung,
> And the meat merrily eat,
> Soon shall Sir Thomas Bettys be forgot,
> On whose soul God have mercy.'

From Beeston I got this—note our dialect in the last word:

> 'Thomas Symson, priest, departed, and lieth under this stone,
> The month of January, alive, and also gone,
> Not for an ornament of the body this stone was laid here,
> But only the soul to be prayed for as charity require.'

An inscription at Foulsham to a lad is curious:

> 'Here I lie John, which livéd but eight years,
> When death me clippéd with his sharp shears;
> Remember me, I pray you, often as ye list,
> And I shall not forget *you* to Master Jesus Christ.'

A very long and elaborate one at Barton is curious for its numerous changes of metre. As in the others, I have modernized the spelling:

> 'Here are buried under this stone, in the clay,
> Thomas Amys and his wife Marger-ay;
> Sometime we were as ye now be,
> And as we be, after this shall ye.
> Of such goods as God had the said Thomas lent,
> [He] did make this Chapel of St. Thomas with good intent;
>   Wherefore they desire of your Charity,
>   To pray for them to the Holy Trinity.
> I beseech all people far and near,
>   To pray for me, Thomas Amys, heartily;
> Who gave a mass-book, and made this chapel here,
>   And a suit of blue damask also gave I,
> Of God the m.ccccxl and v year,
>   I the said Thomas deceased verily,
> And the fourth day of August was buried here,
>   On whose soul God have mercy.'

We get a quasi-comic vein at Wichingham, on Thomas Allyn and his two wives, dated 1650:

> 'Death here advantage hath of life I spy,
> One husband with two wives at once may lie.'

At Edingthorpe, the writer of an inscription to one Oliver Rice, who died 1721, bursts out into politics, anent his relative's Christian name:

> 'Could'st (for thy Land)
> Thou hand to hand
> But Rebel Noll have fought;
> Dear had been then,
> To Englishmen,
> That name now come to nought.'

Of sea-captains' inscriptions this is a favourite type. It comes from Swafield. There are others at Wells and Happisburgh:

> 'Tho' Boreas' blasts and Neptune's waves
> Have tost me to and fro,
> By God's decree you plainly see
> I harbour here below,
> Where I do now at anchor lie,
> With many of our fleet;
> Yet once again I must set sail
> Our Admiral Christ to meet.

From Cromer I got a quaint one, dated 1755:

> 'Farewell, vain world!
> I've seen enough of thee;
> And careless I am what you
> Can say or do to me;
> I fear no threats from
> An Infernal Crew,—
> My day is past, and I bid
> The world adieu.'

For an example of local pronunciation fossilized, this is curious. It comes from Thurgarton; date, 1734:

> 'He was a father to the fatherless,
> He helped the widows in their distress;
> He never was given to worldly pride;
> He lived an honest man, and so he died.
> They were tender parents, our loss was great,
> We hope they both eternal joys will MEET.'

I have often tried to trace the germ of 'afflictions sore,' but this is as far as I have got. It comes from Suffield, and is dated 1758:

> 'Afflictions sore—long time we bore,
> All means did prove in vain;
> Till Death did please—us to release,
> And ease us of our pain.'

I hope no one who goes on collecting Norfolk inscriptions will ever fall into such an amusing blunder as did the author of the 'Norfolk Tour,' who under Neatishead says, 'Here are inscriptions to the memory of Cubet *and Marmore*,' and justifies his statement by an inscription beginning:

'Will'us jacet hic Emmyson, *marmore teste*'!

XII.

THE TOWNS.

PREMISING that the limit of space at my command will only allow me to give some very short notes on some of our chief places, I may as well at once plunge *in medias res*, and begin with our county-town of Norwich. Visitors from London by rail when they near the city, after crossing the river, can see only, on their left, the high ridge of ground on which Ber Street stands, with its old red-brick houses, and it must be owned the entrance is neither imposing nor picturesque.

If I were bringing in a visitor on whom I wanted Norwich to form a favourable first impression, I should arrange that he should come in—as Queen Elizabeth did in her progress—by St. Stephen's Gate, when he would see the old city lying below him, with its grey square castle-keep, and its glorious cathedral spire rising out of the hollow below; but as those for whom this book is written will probably enter by Thorpe Station, I must needs admit at once that they will find this station as dirty, small, and incommodious as any they are likely to find in any other town of the same size.* Nor will they be much better pleased with the first sight of the place. The station-yard is dirty, the 'Foundry Bridge' is narrow and at right angles to exit, and the long 'Prince of Wales Road' which leads from the railway to the old part of the city is, though wide, singularly devoid of architectural beauty, most of the houses in it being of the well-known jerry-builder's type. It is however, like nearly all the city, well paved with wood, Norwich being the first and I fancy the only county-town which has boldly adopted this material, the result being that for driving and walking it is uniquely pleasant. What made the citizens, after enduring for centuries the vilest possible paving—great round ancle-dislocating pebbles —generally without side-walks (my mother, who was brought here for her honeymoon, was laid up for a month from being shown the sights in thin shoes), suddenly rush into the other extreme, I cannot say. There is a mystery about the whole affair, especially in the strange coincidence that the paving stops abruptly when it has reached the doors of influential dignitaries whose houses lie in the suburbs.

However, to return to the road we are on, which, by the way, cuts across the site of the low-lying gardens of the Friars Minor, we may note that by a passage to the right we can work round into the

* Since these lines were written a magnificent new station has been begun.

cathedral precincts. When we get to its end the stranger will wonder at the public spirit that has given the city so magnificent a post-office as that which we see on the left, till he is told that the postmaster has—cuckoo-like—only established himself in the costly premises built for the ill-fated Harvey's Bank.

Stretching in front of us is the wide open slope covered with cattle-pens, known as the Castle Hill; to our left the railway-station-like roof of the new Hall; to our right is the hideous mock-Gothic Shire Hall; and above it, as though frowning down in disgust at the two horrors below, stands the light grey square castle tower. All visitors naturally go up the Castle Mount to spy about the city from its coign of vantage before wandering along the streets; and my reader had better do the same. He will cross a round arch, said to be Saxon, thrown over a dry moat, now used as a garden—and a very pretty garden too, with its wealth of greenery—and walk round the top of the mound.

The whole of the keep has been of late years recased with stone, hardly as white as that which in Norman times is said to have given it the nickname of Blanchflower; but the Norman work—the arcading of stone, the narrow arrow-slits, and such like—has been more or less faithfully reproduced.

Of course only the great square tower—Bigod's tower, as it is called—is old, the one-story abomination to the right being modern. There is little to see inside, so it is hardly worth while to take the trouble to get a magistrate's order to view the hollow shell, and the very few articles of interest, which are chiefly a few wall inscriptions cut by prisoners, something like those in the Tower of London, though much older. One poor Bartholomew describes how he is confined 'saunz resun,' and I dare say he was neither the first nor the last who could have said so. It is curious that, in the reign of Elizabeth, kinsmen and namesakes of such men as Cecil and Throgmorton should have been in duress here. It is a prison still, but clean and orderly; not as it was in 1629, when thirty-two prisoners were packed together so closely that they had no room to lie down together for six weeks. However, the inside is soon seen, and the visitor should, when he gets out, walk round the top of the mound till he passes the hideous roofs of the Sessions House which lies below, and looks down on the tops of the houses in the Prince of Wales Road. To the left, the foreground being hidden by the trees planted on the side of the mound, which rise up level with one's eyes, is the great grey cathedral, with its beautiful spire shooting up, even from its low marshy site, far higher than where we are standing. Behind it, and now, luckily, ever to be its unbuilt-on background, are the green and brown patches of Mousehold Heath, where the rebels camped in Kett's time. Right and left, as far as eye can see, are the red-tiled houses, contrasting picturesquely with the green tree-tops, which occur so frequently between them, and even now give some reason for Norwich's old name—the 'City of Orchards.' You can hardly count the flint and stone square-towered churches, for they are almost as numerous as the hideous red-brick chimney shafts.

Still walking on to the left, we notice how the houses below follow the shape of the mound we are on, and are really built on the bank of one of its outer ditches, for you can see the deep drop of the earth, now mostly bricked in, and used as gigantic areas. Still farther, and we look up to the fine tower of St. Giles's Church, built on the highest ground in the city; and, if we wait long enough, we shall see the new cathedral of the old faith gradually rising hard by it on the finest site in this city, and, perhaps, in any other. If I were the Duke of Norfolk—duke, by the way, of a county in which I don't think he has a house to live in, though he is building this worshipful one—I think I should set up a *replica* of the old cathedral, as it was first built in the damp meadow of Cowholm. No modern architect is likely to improve on it.

Farther along still, we look down 'Castle Steps' on to the Market Place, and catch a glimpse of St. Peter's grandly ornamented tower through the trees, which just about here are poor and thin and lanky, and would be all the better if they were topped, for we should then have a fine view *of* the city, while those below *in* the city would be able to see the castle.

At last we work round to nearly the place we began, and get a view of the upper part of the Cattle Market, backed by the dingy old houses of Ber

Street, and recrossing the castle ditch re-enter the plain. Some of these days, when the new buildings which disfigure the castle are removed, this castle ditch will make one of the finest possible recreation grounds for the citizens. Fancy what an arena for athletic sports it would be, if the broad path at its base were black-ashed, and bicyclists allowed to ride, and athletes allowed to train on it at stated times!

If the visitor is lucky enough to come to Norwich on 'Tombland Fair Day,' he will see a collection of live-stock which will make him open his eyes, and, indeed, he will see a fine show nearly every Saturday. He will note with pleasure how very clean and comfortable the cattle-stalls are, but with other feelings the way in which the bullocks are unnecessarily knocked about. It seems to be articles of faith with the drover, first, that all the drove should be compelled to arrange themselves in a circle, with their noses all touching, and their tails radiating outwards with mathematical accuracy; and, secondly, that if a bullock stands perfectly quiet, he has some deep and vicious design in doing so, and must be promptly thrashed for it.

If we turn to the left, at the base of the Castle Mound, by Castle Meadow, we shall get a better view of the remains of the outer ditch which we noticed from the top, and see how strangely it has been adapted to modern use. In one place a charming little bit of greenery—a hanging garden—has been made on its side; and just past this we see the back of the Royal Hotel, with its long narrow yard.

We may now turn down the narrow way known as the 'Back of the Inns,' which runs parallel with the 'Gentleman's Walk' of the Market Place, and, turning up Hog Hill, reach the end of Ber Street. This is the oldest, and widest, and dirtiest street in the city, and stands high over the river on a very commanding site; but it will, I fear, never be very attractive to visitors, as the inhabitants of its courts are the roughest lot in the place, and their language is more remarkable for its easy colloquial power than for its elegance. Nor are there any very interesting houses in it, for the very old houses are gone, and for three centuries or so it has not been a favourite place for the rich merchants or the county gentry.

On its left is St. Michael at Thorn, still with a thorn-tree in its churchyard, as becomes it; while at its very end, raking it like a fortress of the church, stands St. John at Sepulchre.

If we went straight on we should go through the gap in the old wall, where Ber Street gates once stood, on to Carrow Abbey, which once stood just outside the city, in a pleasant place above the winding river. There are a few crumbling foundations just laid open, and the parlour of the last abbess, but they are hardly worth the trouble of seeing.

If we turn to the left, just past the wall, we can keep along its side down to the river, and note how the 'Snuff Tower,' one of the old flint bastions of the city wall, would have commanded the approach before gunpowder was invented.

To our right is the great manufactory of mustard

(and votes), known as the Carrow Works,* which is very well worth seeing indeed to those interested in machinery; but such of my readers as are fonder of old work should follow me to the left down King Street—once called Conisford Street. It runs on a lower ridge of the river-bank than Ber Street, and is much more interesting. On its left are several churches, the first being St. Peter's, Southgate, which is in a shameful state, going wholly to ruins, and its tower falling fast; a strange contrast to St. Ethelred, which we come to next, and which has been recently well and tenderly restored. The good east flamboyant window and the traces of Norman work here should be noticed; but the next church is the real treat for the antiquary, for St. Julian's is the oldest in the city, its tower being thought to be Saxon.

Farther down on the left there is a curious early inn 'sign,' a long, highly ornamented carved label over the doorway, with the inscription 'Princes In' on it. Opposite is the 'Music Hall,' built on the site of Moyses the Jew, who lived in the reign of Rufus, from whose grandson Isaac it took its old name of Isaac's Hall. I think it clear he was the victim who lost his head to King John, and in any case he lost this house to him. Few houses in the city have had a more memorable history than this. It was once the Yelvertons' town house, then the Pastons', and lastly the home of Chief Justice Coke. Its two

---

* The owner is a very worthy man, and most liberal and fair to his army of workmen. I have never heard a man so well spoken of by his *employés*.

fine windows and its staircase should be specially noticed. There are many other interesting houses in this street, and you will catch many a picturesque glimpse of the river under you, through the courtways and open doors; but time presses, and I can only specially draw attention to the archway of the 'old Barge' with its great door well calculated to resist the attack of any street rufflers.

Crossing the foot of Castle Meadow again, we will now wend our way to the cathedral. It lies in the poorest situation that could have been chosen, in a flat plain almost enclosed by a horse-shoe bend of the river, but for many reasons is one of the most interesting cathedrals in England. The open space in front is Tombland, and that gateway is the Ethelbert Gate, so called from standing near the site of a church dedicated to St. Ethelbert, which was burnt in the great riot between the monks and the citizens in 1272. The inlaid flint and stone panelling over the arch is very fine, but not all old. Farther down is the beautiful Erpingham Gate; through it we see the west and worst front of the cathedral.

I am not here going to try to describe the building, but the visitor must wander through it carefully, and not miss the grand cloisters, the finest in England, nor the lavatories in the south-west corner, the fine massive Norman pillars and arches, the Norman transept, the misereres in the choir, the sealed altarslab in the Jesus chapel, and the elaborate bosses on the roof, both of the cathedral and the cloisters. If the visitor cares to climb the 313 feet of the spire,

he will get such a view over the level country round—
with, if it is a fine day, the glint of the sun on the
sea at Yarmouth, twenty miles away—as will well
repay him.

Leaving the cathedral one can either pass down
through the Lower Close, and cross the river by
Sandthorp or Pull's Ferry, where there is an interesting water-gate, or come out again by the Erpingham Gate and re-enter Tombland.

The tumble-down old-curiosity-shop at the corner
of the church alley opposite will no doubt tempt a
Londoner to take home some remembrance of the
old city; and he might do worse, for prices range
cheaper here as yet than in London, and there are
no Wardour Street goods made up. He must not
forget to peer in at the open gateway of the big
cheese-factor's a little lower down, and peer at
the two great wooden images which are said to
have come from Sir Thomas Erpingham's house
hard by. The turn to the right at the end of
Tombland—where carriers' carts, a strangely per-
isstent remnant of bygone days here, have their
regular rendezvous—would take us by the gateway of
the Bishop's Palace (well worth looking at) and St.
Martin-at-Palace, to the old stone bridge at Bishop's
Gate; but if we are to continue our walk round the
city we will keep straight on.

Here the road narrows, and by a natural sequence
the drivers of all vehicles (and I may say Norwich
drivers are exceptionally reckless) become more reckless than ever, and urge their horses on with a

peculiar local cry, which I can only formulate as 'Eh! eh!! hip ar!' which sends them along at a speedy hand-canter, puzzling indeed to the walking Londoner accustomed to proprietary rights in the roadway. To the right is the 'Maid's Head,' the best and one of the oldest inns in the place, which is built on arches, on which once stood the old Bishop's Palace, and which has a very fine original Jacobean carved oak bar.

Passing over the river and turning to the left we get into Colegate Street, noticeable for several fine old houses. That on the right once belonging to Mayor Bacon—flint and stone—is the very one which had the ragged staff stuck up on its gates after Kett's rebellion was put down, and so gave such great offence to the common people smarting under memories of Warwick. On the same side of the way is St. Michael's of Corslany—noticeable anywhere for its inlaid flint work—the finest work of its sort in England, but which was sadly mauled by the hand of the 'restorer' last year. From here one may work round by St. Miles's old Bridge, which is said to have had a dragon's mouth as a keystone to its arch, and an inscription,

'When dragon drinks
Heigham sinks,'

meaning that when the floods pent up by the so-called 'New' Mills—juveniles of some four or five centuries—reached the top of this bridge the inhabitants of the low-lying suburb of Heigham, hard by, might look out for themselves.

Turning from the river up Fisher's Lane we get on to the high ground again at the top of St. Giles, which is to a great extent honeycombed under the houses and roads by tunnels probably worked ages and ages ago by the masons of the castle and the cathedral for the sake of the chalk. One stretched, and perhaps still stretches, right up from Paragon Hill to St. Giles's Church; and it would be just as well for those who will soon be building the new Catholic Cathedral to find out by experimental shafts that their site is not undermined by some of these hollow ways. If we turn to the left by the old gaol, now so soon to be replaced by the new cathedral, and keep on, we come to Chapel Field, once noted for the 'Chapel in the Field,' and now for its being the Norwich public recreation-ground, and a very cockneyfied and badly laid-out one it is, too. Fragments of the old city wall may be seen by its side, but of no particular interest; and St. Stephen's Gates, to which we come next, have now no gates at all. As I have said before, this is the best entrance into the city, and the street which leads us down to it has one or two objects of interest, especially the old thatched inn, the Boar's Head, on the right, and a very finely ornamented plaster ceiling, in Messrs. Barwell's counting house on the left. A short twist to the left along Rampant Horse Street, at the corner of which is the large church of St. Stephen's, and again to the right, brings us into the Market Place, one of the largest in England. The recently restored church of St. Peter Mancroft, with its grandly ornamented tower, will be an object of as great interest to the spectator as the funny pepper-pot-looking cupolas (?) with which the restorer has thought fit to surmount it will be of disgust. Over the way the Guild Hall, with its armorial carving and alternate flint and stone work, with some relics of Nelson, is worth attention, and the Fish-market, with its dirt and stinks, a careful avoidance.

Want of space prevents me saying much more of Norwich. If a visitor would see it aright he should come in about midday on a summer Saturday, stroll round the Castle Hill and see the Norfolk beasts, and wander up London Street, and along the 'Gentleman's Walk,' and see the Norwich beauties—squires' wives, parsons' daughters, and all. If he goes away and says he has seen better cattle or fairer women elsewhere—well, don't believe him.

There are plenty of pleasant excursions out of Norwich. The visitor may stroll down past Charing Cross, and keeping on along the lower road, pass the quaint well fountain known as St. Lawrence's Well, the inscription on which tells us,

> 'This water here caught
> In sorte as yowe (*) se,
> From a spring is brought
> Threeskore foot and thre,'

—and so on. Unluckily the Elizabethan-carved front is all that is left, for the deeper new wells of Bullard's brewery have drained the spring, and the brewer—

(*) Good Norfolk.

good Conservative though he is—has not yet been gracious enough to connect the pipe with his new water. Keeping on, the stroller will presently come to the Dolphin at Heigham, now an inn, but once the residence of the royalist, Bishop Hall, who retreated here when the Puritans ousted him from his palace. The outside has a date and a good shield of arms, and the inside rooms are very quaint, with capital oak panelling, plaster ceiling, and fine doors, while behind are the remains of what must have been a pleasant garden, sloping down to a river still clear and pretty, and now a public bathing-place. I remember noting down on one chill October day the pencil remark of a local wit on the side of the dressing-place: '11 October. The water is damp and unpleasant this morning.—E. G.'

Straight on one may wander on to Cossey, with its park, where the Jerninghams have been seated since the reign of Elizabeth, and have staunchly carried on their old religion. Great patrons to art, and literature too, they have been; and Norfolk antiquaries must ever be grateful to them for the friendly help found in their hall and library by 'F. C. H.,' Dr. Husenbeth, a writer of more than local reputation.

Another way out of the city is up Magdalen Street, noticing the Blind Hospital on the left, past the 'Greenhills,' with the fine grove of roadside trees, patriotically bought for the city by a gentleman whose name I ought not to have forgotten; and straight on by St. Faith's—where there are remnants of Horsham Priory—to the lovely woods of Stratton Strawless. If any tree-planter gets weary and faint of heart at the poor progress his young trees make, he should come to Stratton for fresh courage. The land hereabouts was barren and poor and flat a century or so ago, when the Marshams began to plant here, and the Petres at West Wick, a few miles away to the east, but now the two bits of scenery that strangers notice and admire most in Norfolk are Stratton Strawless Woods and West Wick Pond. What Sandringham will look like in about a hundred years' time, when the Prince's planting has matured, I should very much like to, but doubt if I shall, see.

Another excursion the visitor must not miss is that due south to Caister, which is the largest Roman camp in England, the walls enclosing thirty-five acres. Real existing walls too, obvious to the merest layman, and not to be taken on faith from a guide-book. Those who know the castle at Burgh by Yarmouth, will form some idea of the size of Caister if I tell them that that fine castle is only *one-seventh* the size of Caister. Yet another stroll out of the city is that of King Street, over Trowse Bridge by the cattle lairs, turning in by a nice old flint house with red-brick windows, and a date '1604.' This takes you along the river, by the ruins of the old Bishop's country house and some very pretty scenery, to the ruined church of Whitlingham, the tower of which stands high and conspicuous on a knoll above the river.

Of course, in this rough sketch of what may be

seen in and near Norwich, I have missed dozens of objects of interest. The churches of St. Stephen, St. Andrew, and St. Giles, each fine enough to make special sights of in any other town, the splendid flint-work of the Old Bridewell, the Old Man's Hospital in Bishopgate Street, the Bishop's Bridge, ' Kett's Castle '—St. Andrew's Hall—the charming corner by the Briton's Arms at Elm Hill, the brasses at St. John Maddermarket, and the beautiful 'Stranger's Hall' hard by, all deserve special visits if time can be spared, while on no account must the Norwich visitor pass the very interesting, if very miscellaneous, collections preserved in the Museum. It is a modern building as far as the exterior is concerned, and though some people say that the 'Chapel Room' was once part of the old Duke of Norfolk's Palace, which stood either on or very near this site, I do not think there is anything to support the conjecture, for the ornamented ceiling is of much later date. Things are rather mixed, but the collection of birds, and notably of the *Raptores*, hawks and such like, would shame the British Museum collection, and a wonderful collection of *Fungi*, set up and coloured by Mr. T. J. Munns in a most life-like way, would attract attention anywhere. The antiquities proper are mostly in the gallery of the Chapel Room; amongst the most curious are some 'Anglo-Saxon' funeral urns, and some pilgrims' bottles and greybeards. Those interested in bibulous history should see the fine specimens of black-jacks, and the whiteware jugs or bottles, with blue inscriptions: 'Whit(e),

1648;' 'Claret, 1648.' A stone instrument like a small quern, found in Wayford Wood, Stalham, and a mould for casting pilgrims' signs from Walsingham, should not be passed over. Of Kett's rebellion there are two reminiscences—bits of sheet-lead rolled up, found in 'Kett's Castle,' and probably intended to be used as shot, and a dagger, found in Dussin's Dale, at Sprowston, now corruptly called Ossian's Dale. Among miscellaneous articles are a pair of embroidered gloves from Paston Hall; a long rusty and very early sword found in the river by Thorpe; some Exchequer tallies; a fine ornamented spearhead from Plumstead Parva; and a servant's badge, with the Walpole crest. A splendid copy of the printed Sarum Missal, by Jehan de Pres, and a good MS. copy of Wickcliffe's Bible, will interest bibliographers.

To geologists the magnificent collection of objects from the 'Forest Bed' of Cromer will be of the deepest interest, for nowhere else can be seen anything like it. There he will see the stool of a fossil tree; great teeth, jawbones, and shoulder-blades of elephants, mastodons, and mammoths. One tusk is ten feet long, and two feet eight inches round, and the animal must have stood about seventeen feet high.

So much for Norwich. There are seven other centres round which one may conveniently gossip, leaving Yarmouth for my next chapter on the 'Broads' (XIV.), and arranging that a visitor who follows the sequence of my 'mardle,' as an East

Anglian would call it, will see nearly all that is most noticeable in the county.

Starting from the Foundry Bridge Station the rail takes one along the river by the pretty village of Thorpe, and soon after turns up north through varied scenery to Salthouse, which is the first station on the line, and so on to Wroxham, where it crosses the river, and a first glimpse can be got from the carriage of a Norfolk pool with its water-lilies and reeds. Beyond the bridge, if it is summer, one will see the masts and sails of dozens of pleasure-yachts and wherries moored along the banks on either side, for this is the station most convenient to Norwich men from which to begin their sailing up the Broads. Farther down the line we see Sloley on our left, and pass Worstead Church, which is noticeable for four hideous modern tulip-like pinnacles which deface its tower.

Here we should call a halt to see the interior of the church, which is a magnificent one, raised by the liberality of the merchants who founded here the 'worsted' trade. The tower arch screen with its quaint inscription, the bosses in the aisle roof, the splendid south porch and the fine tracery of the 'sound-holes,' all render this church particularly interesting to the architect; while to the student of history the smallness and poorness of the present village, which we know from the records must once have been an important place, will be noteworthy. There is an old dated sampler by ' Rebekah Dawber, 1726,' hanging up in the Ship, near the church.

Continuing our journey we pass the beautiful woods of West Wick, with the 'gazebo' peeping through them on our left, and soon run into North Walsham, a quaint little red-brick town nestling in a hollow, with its great broken church tower showing conspicuously from the rail. If the excursionist is a walker he should by all means come on to 'Walsham,' as the natives call it (calmly ignoring the fact of there being another place of the same name not far off), by road and not by rail.

The road by Sprowston and Crostwick is rather interesting, with its bits of English scenery; an open common close eaten down by geese, a bridge over a brook, and a wooded hill, bringing us to the placid little river Bure, at Coltishall Bridge. Coltishall has an antiquarian notoriety about it from Henry III. having declared its inhabitants free from villeinage of blood or body, and its bridge is one of many which the ghost of Sir Thomas Boleyn has to cross in its headless penitence for his share in his daughter's death. Farther down the road we pass to the right of Scottow, and keeping along some well-wooded country, and under a natural roadside avenue, reach the hideous arch crossing the road at West Wick. Just by its side to the right is the way to the church, well worthy a visit for its interesting interior and the monuments to the Berneys and Petres. The present Petres, by the way, are so only *ex parte maternâ*, for their real name is Varlo. As mentioned before, the Petre of his day was a great tree-planter, and probably no better effect has ever been produced than by his skilled landscape gardening here. Where the road dips through the park two ponds have been skilfully cut, one higher than and draining into the other, and their banks planted so naturally and well that no stranger would imagine that the charming spot was wholly designed by man, but that it was the remnant of some primæval wood. Farther on we pass through pleasant pine-plantings till we see in the crook of a side-way on our right the tall single-shafted cross which marks the slaughter of Litester's men by Bishop Spencer in 1381, and soon after spy the two railway stations at 'Walsham,' lying under us on the same side of the way.

North Walsham, considering it was almost wholly burnt down at various times, is a picturesque and interesting place, with its market 'cross,' its old-fashioned butchers' shops, and its little out-of-the-way alleys and streets. The Angel is a comfortable and roomy inn near the church, and the Scarborough House, the only private house of note, though new-fronted, still contains some fine oak-work inside, and carved arms outside. Unluckily the church has suffered much, partly from restoration and partly from want of it; but its great length (159 feet) and fine proportions make it very interesting. Within are a few brasses, and a gorgeously grand mural monument to Sir William Paston, the judge who died in 1608, but who is more worthily kept in remembrance by his foundation of the Paston Grammar School here. The south porch should be specially noted, having much very elaborately carved stone-work about it.

Resuming our railway ride, we pass the two churches of Antingham on our left, and on our right the well-known Antingham Ponds, dear to pike-fishers, whose 'Jordan' they often are, and which form the head of the river Ant. Of course the old story of the two churches in one churchyard having been built by two sisters who quarrelled, and determined each to have a church of her own, is told here as elsewhere. In the parish of Thorpe Market is the next station, Gunton, and it is singular, by the way, that not one of the stations on the line to Cromer is really built in the parish whose name it bears. Gunton Park is celebrated for its head of game and its fine gardens. Pheasants tamer than most barn-door fowls are uninteresting birds, but the greenhouses and orchard-houses, though nothing in themselves, are known all over England for the flowers and fruit got out of them by the ability of Mr. Allan, who has in him no trace of the reticence and incivility of most Scotch gardeners. The hall was burnt out not long ago, and is not yet rebuilt, and very picturesque it looks with its great gaunt shell pierced by rows of empty windows. It would make a capital ruin, and might just as well be left as it is, and a smaller house, more suitable to the fortunes of the Harbords, be built elsewhere in the park.

While at North Walsham, and before proceeding to Cromer, for which see the next chapter, the visitor will be well rewarded for his pains in walking or driving to Aylsham, by having some lunch at the Black Boys, one of the old coaching-houses, going to see the church, said to have been built by John of Gaunt, and noticing its large size, its good lych-gate, and the fine tracery of its aisle windows. One excursion hence can be made to cover two interesting seats, namely Wolterton—which, however, is interesting more for its associations than for its beauty, it having been built by *the* Sir Robert Walpole, with what is usually thought peculated public money—and Blickling. The latter has a rare history of its own, having been at different times owned by Harold, by the Bishops of Norwich, and by Sir Thomas Boleyn, father of the ill-fated Anne.

A sheet of water about a mile long in the middle of a beautiful and well-wooded park, is a fitting adjunct to the noble red house, built in the reign of James I., with its fine ceiled galleries and carvings, and its grand staircase. In the church there are plenty of interesting monuments, and especially one to the Cleres, with a lot of fudged heraldry, which passed muster for nearly 300 years before I took the liberty of analyzing and exposing the Clere pedigree and quarterings alike. By the way, another 'splendid impostor' in the way of coats of arms is to be seen, not far off, at Barningham Northwood, where the Palgraves forged their blazonings even more impudently than these Cleres did. Aylsham should not be finally left without a visit being paid to the very curious church of Burgh, with its many peculiar features, and its fine lancet windows—so uncommon in Norfolk.

Returning to the East Norfolk Railway, the next station past Gunton will be Cromer, and a very pretty one it is—perhaps commanding the finest view of any station in England, the rails leaving off at the very edge of a high hill overlooking the town and the sea and the lighthouse. Cromer I shall describe in my next chapter. From Cromer a pleasant ramble westward along the cliffs brings us through Runton round the Beacon Hill to Beeston Abbey, or what few ruins are left of it. All along here is said to be a favourite haunt of the ghost dog 'Shuck,' who, inconsistently enough, is at once headless and saucer-eyed. The neighbourhood is full of superstitions and stories. There is a ghostly light* seen at intervals to cross a field near Runton Mill and bury itself in a copse where once human bones were found; while the Aylmerton Pits, round which a ghostly woman is seen 'weeping and wringing her hands,' are not far off. Sherringham, with its lovely woods and most interesting church—which has, I think, the only instance in England of a perfect 'practicable' rood-loft and gallery *in situ*—must not be missed. Farther on is Weybourne, still the best anchorage on the coast, deep water running right up to the shore—which gave rise to the old rhyme, already referred to, as to the advisability of would-be invaders of England landing here.

* I went specially to see it last year, but could not.

Perhaps no village has more traces of its early inhabitants than Weybourne. There are British hut-dwellings, a Roman kiln, and some Saxon work in the church.

Near here, too, is Muckleburgh Hill, one of the many 'burgh' hills along the coast, for we have passed Incleborough, and are coming to Warborough by Salthouse, and to Garborough and another Warborough by Stiffkey. The sea here begins to recede from the road—salt marshes from one to two miles across intervening—and the scenery generally loses the up and down aspect which makes the pedestrian once and for all heartily abjure the popular idea that Norfolk is a flat country all over. Cley, which stands on the mouth of the little river Glaven, is now a dead-alive sort of place, like some of the old towns on the south coast, the silting up of the harbour having ruined a port which once promised to be of as great importance as Yarmouth. The church is a very fine one, with some good brasses, and a fine font sculptured with the seven sacraments. In the churchyard rests Captain Grieve, who helped Cloudesley Shovel to burn out the Barbary Rovers in Tripoli. Fair accommodation to the wayfarer and winter wild-duck shooter can be had at the Fishmongers' Arms, a roomy, old-fashioned house.

Blakeney, a little farther on, is just such another place as Cley; but the church is better placed, and has several points of interest, specially the turret outside the tower—which, like that at Cromer, is said to have been used as a lighthouse—and a chamber over the chancel, which is the only one I have ever seen. There is nothing left of the Carmelite Friary, in which flourished John de Baconsthorpe, the 'Resolute Doctor,' whereof it was said that his height was only that of his penknife and his pen and his inkhorn and his sheet of paper and his book:

'Scalpellum, calami, atramentum, charta, libellus.'

Morston, whose inhabitants are so proverbially slow that they are known as 'Morston dodmen,' or snails, need not detain us; but Stiffkey, with its 'tumulus' and the ruins of the hall begun to be built by Sir Nicholas Bacon, is worth waiting at before we tramp on to Wells-by-the-Sea. The 'Stewkey' people are not so slow nowadays as their Morston neighbours, for 'Wood of Stiffkey' is just now our fastest English amateur run but anything up to a quarter of a mile. A sleepy es w town is Wells, but having been selected for a railway station because its harbour is not quite choked up yet, there is more going on than at Cley or Blakeney. The church is, or was, a notably fine one, and the oak carving on the vestry door is very noticeable. Unluckily it was burned down a few years ago, having been struck by lightning, and is now but the shell of its former self, though remarkably well restored by Mr. Herbert Green of Norwich. All the monuments were destroyed; but luckily I had copied and printed them a few years before the fire, so they are not lost to posterity.

Returning to Wells, after this egotistical digression,

I would advise a visitor to put up at the Railway Arms (the Globe is dearer and no better than it used to be), and after looking at the ample quay, peering about in search of the water, which may be seen at high tide, and trying some of the celebrated Burnham oysters, which now run Whitstables hard in price, let him pause in his coast-line journey, and take the train south. A twenty-mile journey will enable him to see, perhaps, as many objects of antiquarian interest as he could find in any equally long jaunt in England. First he comes to the Danish camp at Warham, and then to the great Benedictine Abbey of Binham, which was founded before 1093. There is a great deal still left of it, especially the Norman nave and the Early English west front, which is very fine, and the general effect from a little distance is striking.

Walsingham, with its priory, which was founded about the same time as Binham, was known all over the Christian world for the wonders said to have been done by its image of 'Our Lady of Walsingham,' to which so many pilgrimages were made, that not only the earthly way to it was known as the 'Walsingham Way,' but the 'Milky Way' in the heavens was supposed to point it out to travellers. To the impositions scathingly satirized by Erasmus, to the 'wishing wells' said to have sprung up by the Virgin's command, to the little hatch through which a knight and his charger were miraculously passed through by the Virgin in dire need, one need do no more than refer. Excepting those of the Refectory, the ruins are insignificant and disappointing, and being in the Lee-Warners' park, are not always accessible to visitors, though they may be peeped at through the railings.

A couple of miles off we come to the historic manor-house of East Barsham, once the seat of the Calthorpes, an old Norfolk family, but now a farm-house. It is one of the finest existing specimens of the domestic architecture of the Tudors, the moulded brickwork of the fabric and the beautifully ornamented chimney-stacks being especially noticeable. Why it has not been thoroughly restored and used as the 'Hall' again, it is hard to say. It was built by Sir William Fermor, who, if I remember rightly, was one of the commissioners for plundering church goods in the reign of Edward VI., and whose family died out in a way which would have delighted Spelman.

Farther down south we reach Fakenham, a particularly clean and pleasant market-town, with several good old-fashioned inns, especially the Crown.

Of course the church is the only public building of any note, and it is a very interesting one, with a battlemented flint and stone tower, a fine west window, a beautiful Perpendicular font, and Transitional piscina and sedilia. It is one of the few churches that has not been spoiled by injudicious restoration, for what the rector has done, chiefly at his own expense, has been well done, but not so well done as to obliterate the old work. All over the church may be seen the crowned 'L,' showing how the town was once the head town of the Duchy of Lancaster in this country.

Yet another short stage by the rail brings us to North Elmham, one of the oldest towns, if not the oldest, in the county. It was a cathedral town in 673; and Roman remains having been found here, it was, no doubt, a place of importance from the earliest times. The see was, however, early removed to Thetford, and thence to Norwich; but the Bishop long retained a palace here, of which recent excavations show considerable traces. The 'warlike' Bishop Spencer had license to embattle it 500 years ago, and the moat may still be traced. Bishop Herbert de Lozinga, 'the church builder,' founded the church in the reign of the Conqueror; but, excepting in the chancel, there is no Norman work left. There is, however, something of nearly every other style, and the church is a fine, light, and lofty one.

Another short bit of railway travelling, and we reach East Dereham, the only town of any extent or importance in Mid-Norfolk. Two very different personages lived here at different times — Bishop Bonner and Cowper. The former was vicar here, but whether a 'native' or not I cannot say, for there has been much that is apocryphal written about his parentage, the validity of his consecration being denied on the ground that he was illegitimate.

Like Beccles and other East Anglian churches, there is a 'clocker' or 'clocher,' a square, massive bell tower, in the churchyard, standing away from the church. ' St. Withberga's Well,' once a miracle-working spring, is also in the churchyard. She was what Bonner was said to be, a love-child, but became Prioress here in the latter half of the seventh century; and dying in the odour of sanctity, her body became a powerful agency for miracles, so much so that the monks of Ely came over in 974 and stole the body for the use of their cathedral (pious fraud *they* called it), but the miracle-license was transferred to the well by the real owners.

Here is a very pretty view from the churchyard for the lovers of the picturesque, and two good inns for the refreshment of the worldly-minded, while the sentimental may visit with advantage the tomb of the melancholy Cowper in the church. His madness is satisfactorily accounted for by the fact that he once paid a prolonged visit to Happisburgh. From Dereham it is a pretty drive through Scarning (where the visitor will see a fine rood-screen, with a saunce bell or 'ting-tang' *in situ*, and a curious vestry, and may hear the best preacher in the county if it is Sunday) to Castle Acre, one of the most interesting places in the county. Here are the ruins of a most magnificent Norman priory, and the earthworks of a very fine Norman castle. The priory ruins are most extensive, and some of the additions are very fine, noticeably the grand Perpendicular west window; but there is little left of the castle, though its earthworks are immense, and may have been British. It is hardly likely that such a position would have been overlooked by the Romans; indeed, we find their traces here, and the so-called 'Peddars' Way' was straight from Castle Acre to the sea.

Pentney Priory and Blackburgh Priory both lie between us and Lynn; but there is little left of their ruins. The latter is in the parish of Middleton, where there is an interesting tower, now habitable, called Middleton Tower, which is all that is left of Lord Scale's castle. Three or four miles on, along a very excellent road, is Lynn, formerly Lynn Episcopi, but now Lynn Regis.

Lynn is usually guessed at to mean 'Lyn,' a lake; but though I used to agree with this derivation because of a lake-like appearance of the wide rivermouth, I have come round to think that it must have been a transplanted name; for in all old documents it is spelt Len, and we find places of that name in Denmark. As a specimen of an old-world town which has very little outgrown its old boundaries, and which has but few suburbs, Lynn is very interesting. It has several shows for the antiquary—from the great chapel of St. Nicholas, which is 200 feet long, and has an eleven-light west window, to the small chapel on the Red Mount, which is only 17 feet by 14 feet. The big chapel was nominally a chapel of ease to the mother church of St. Margaret, and was built in 1160, but practically rebuilt about 1419. Its curiously decorated south porch is one of the finest in England; while the sedilia, the nave roof, and the 'St. Peter's Door' should all be carefully studied. In any other town this fine building would obtain a deservedly special attention; but it is comparatively dwarfed by its mother church St. Margaret, which is a cruciform building 240 feet by 132 feet, founded by Herbert de Lozinga, the well-known Norman church-building bishop. It is said to have had its foundation on wool-packs; but I fancy this only came from some donation of wool, or of a wool-subsidy in aid of a partial rebuilding. Whatever it was built on, its foundations certainly settled very much directly, for the tower leans over in such a Pisa-like way that it makes a nervous spectator quite uncomfortable to go inside it, and look up, though the protecting piers have been there in their present position a trifle over 700 years or so. Within the church are a very fine decorated screen, a fine Elizabethan pulpit, and the two largest and most interesting brasses in England, both dating in the fourteenth century—one to Adam de Walsokne, which shows a vintage going on; and the other to Robert Braunche and his two wives, which displays a 'Peacock Feast.' There were originally two more—one to Walter Coney and another to Robert Attelath—which were equally fine, but which are now gone. The tremendously long clerestory should be specially noticed, and the clumsy modern building which obscures the view of the church from the High Street, especially anathematized by all good antiquarians.

Opposite is the Guild Hall with its elaborately checkered flint and panelled front, reminding us of the similar building at Norwich. It is much cut about and divided; but the Stone Hall, with a large-light Perpendicular window, is worthy of attention. Within are a lot of curiosities, such as the 'Red Book,'—said to be the oldest paper book in England, and certainly a very old one. 'King John's' cup and sword are usually shown as having been given to the town by Cœur de Lion's brother, whose Wash experience gave a colour to the vulgar tradition; but though no antiquary who saw the articles believed the story for a moment, no one proposed a plausible reason for the articles being called 'King John's' till Mr. S. A. Gurney, a local antiquary, very plausibly suggested that they were so-called from King John *of France*, not of England, who, while a prisoner, often accompanied Edward III. and Philippa on their royal progress; and as we know Edward III. visited Lynn, the suggestion seems a sound one, the more especially as the cup and sword are of this date. The 'Chapel on the Red Mount'—no doubt on the *Rood* Mount, was built just about 400 years ago; and is, perhaps, the most beautiful and most elaborate specimen of the architecture of the latter part of the fifteenth century that can be found anywhere. The outside is nothing —a poor casket for so fine a gem; but the details of the tiny inside are very lovely, especially the fan-tracery, which resembles, but is superior to, that of King's College Chapel, Cambridge. The Grey Friars Tower not far from us is all that is left of this priory here; but is still perfect, and is a very light and beautiful brick-building with stone facings. The great squat strong stone south gate is very interesting, and it is seldom that so fine a city gate can now be seen. Of old houses with quaint courtyards, of 'Queen Anne' houses of grand size and design, and of deserted staithes and curious corners, the visitor will find plenty. He should specially notice the Dutch-looking Custom House on the quay, which is thought a good deal of by architects interested in the work of this period. The Globe in the Tuesday Market Place is a capital and comfortable inn—perhaps the best I have ever stayed at.

Lynn must not be finally left without a visit to what was the Wash and the 'Seven Towns of Marshland,' as Clenchwarton, Tilney, Terrington, Walpole, West Walton, Walsoken, and Emneth were called in the reign of Elizabeth. The Wash is practically non-existent; for where King John's treasure was lost is now reclaimed and fertile land, and no one need now hang about the Cross Keys waiting for the low tide and a mounted guide to show him the shortest and safest way across the sands to Lincolnshire. The attraction of this district is not in the scenery, which is flat and level as the sea itself, but in its magnificent churches. Nowhere else in England can be found in so small a district five such churches as Walsoken, Wiggenhall, Walpole St. Peter, West Walton, and Terrington St. Clement's. It is difficult to give even a guess how a purely agricultural district like this should have been able to find the funds to erect such churches, or to sustain them when erected· Any one of these five would be the pride and glory of many a county town, and it is hard to say which of the five is the finest. Perhaps Walsoken should be named first for its great size, its very fine Norman work—especially in its chancel arch—and its quaint staged tower, Early English below and Decorated above; but Walpole St. Peter is equally celebrated for its beautiful Perpendicular architecture, its strange passage under the altar and corresponding high altar platform, its range of twenty stalls, and its 'Think and Thank' legend round the base of the font. West Walton, with its beautiful detached Early English tower, 60 feet or 70 feet away from the church, and its extremely beautiful nave and wonderful carvings; and Terrington Clement's, with its cruciform church and staged tower and fine late font-cover, are equally notable, the latter especially for its great slightly detached tower, and its long range of thirteen clerestory windows. Still some will prefer Wiggenhall Magdalen, partly Decorated and partly Perpendicular, its old glass, its rood-screen, and other points of interest. It was in the adjoining parish of Wiggenhall St. Germans that the great sluice burst in 1862, and let the flood in over an immense tract of this country, which is so low-lying that the chancel floor is said to be 8 feet under high-water-mark!

When one leaves the marshland country on the south-east journey back to Norwich, nothing much must be expected, either in the way of scenery or fine buildings. Swaffham, of course, must be seen, for it is a clean little market-town, with wide and pleasant streets. Its great cruciform church, long and light, with fine tower and clerestory, is indeed worth going miles to see; while the 'Black Book of Swaffham' is almost as early a paper volume as the 'Red Book' of Lynn, referred to before. The visitor well read in pedlar-myths will probably disbelieve the story of John Chapman, the local pedlar, who was told in a dream to go to London Bridge, and when he got there was sent home to dig up a crock of gold in his own back garden, at Swaffham. Something of the same sort, it will be remembered, was told of Beggar Smith, whose glass effigy has just triumphed over that of a vestry clerk at Lambeth.

A pilgrimage down south over the bleak sandy downs—the 'rabbit and rye' country, as it used to be called—should be made to see the 'Grimes Graves,' near Brandon—earthworks spreading over more than twenty acres, about which so much has been written; but Brandon itself, which is half in Norfolk and half in Suffolk, is not a very interesting place, its old industry, that of making gun-flints, having naturally enough died out of late years.

Farther down the river is Thetford, also planted on both sides of the river, but a vastly more important place than Brandon, for it was once the capital and cathedral town of East Anglia. It has been guessed to be *Sitomagus*, and certainly many traces of Roman occupation have been found here. But the great 'Castle Mound,' steep and high, with its grass-grown sides, so difficult even in times of peace to climb up, is the chief object of interest in the town. There are no traces of buildings on it, and the platform at the top is so small that the generally received theory that it was thrown up as a refuge against the Danes is obviously untenable. The labour and energy necessary to create such a mound must have been enormous, and surely would have been expended in comparatively recent times, such as those in which the Pirate-Danes harried our country, to more practical use. That the mound is mainly artificial I have little doubt; but whether it was a burial mound or not cannot be now discovered without deeper excavations than are likely to be allowed. The ruin one sees from the railway station is a comparatively recent gateway leading to the ruins of Bigod's Cluniac monastery, which are still very well worth inspecting. St. Mary's Church, said to have once been used as the cathedral of the diocese, is now wholly gone. There are other places between this and Norwich which a visitor with plenty of time on his hands might dawdle over, such as Rushford, with its most interesting 'College,' well restored; and Shadwell Court, which should be looked at more in pity than in anger, as the worst specimen of the mock-Gothic manor-house ever built. Merton Hall, by Watton, is a charming Elizabethan house, preserved with great taste, and environed by the most lovely 'wild' garden; but it is right out of the way of anyone wending back to Norwich or Yarmouth, as we are supposed to be. Diss is a clean little town, with the very unusual feature of having a fine lake, 'Diss Mere,' of five acres or so in its middle, which makes it a very picturesque place for this part of the world. Harleston and Loddon are much about the same sort of places as Diss, without its mere. The church at Loddon is a fine one, with an enormously long clerestory.

XIII.

THE WATERING PLACES AND COAST LINE.

SUPPOSE one has to consider Yarmouth a Norfolk watering-place, though in my individual capacity I resolutely decline to do so; and for that reason propose, as I shall have to describe it in my next chapter, to omit it in our journey along the coast-line, in search of real watering-places.

If there is anything more unpleasant to me than Yarmouth, it is the first three miles of road out of it, which runs as straight as a die alongside, but out of sight of the sea; for a more dusty and uninteresting walk I defy anybody to find in the county.

Eventually we get to Caister, noted for its lifeboat station, which shares with the Yarmouth beach boats the honour of rescuing, or trying to rescue, the hundreds of sailors who are yearly wrecked on the roads. Caister Castle, the red-bricked tower which lies away to the left, was built by Sir John

Fastolf about 1440, and has had a stirring, if short, history of its own. Rumour goes that it is a facsimile of the Duc d'Alençon's castle, in France, and was built with his ransom when Sir John took him prisoner. Here long lived William of Worcester, the first of our antiquaries who 'took notes,' and who was physician to the old knight. How the Pastons acquired the castle, and how they were besieged there in a quiet and business-like way by their enemies, till the castle was taken from them with some loss of life, but without any officious unneighbourly intervention of the Sheriff and the Posse Comitatus, is it not all written in the 'Paston Letters'?

A coast-path, sometimes path and sometimes road, takes us along to the low Marrum Hills—covered with the blue-green grass which, the natives will tell you, it is death by Act of Parliament to destroy—past Winterton and Somerton, till we get to Horsey Gap.

Both here and at Winterton the bank against the sea is of so slight a character, and the inland marsh country has sunk so much through the drying up of the bogs and the peat, that some extensive works seem absolutely necessary to prevent a recurrence of the former sea-floods which have been so disastrous in this district. There is not enough left of Hickling Priory to make it worth one's while to cut inland and see the ruins. But Ingham, with its beautiful late decorated church, its founder's monument with helmet *in situ*, and the ruins of the priory for 'the order of the Holy Trinity and St. Victor for the redemption of captives,' is well worth a visit.

Keeping along the coast we see below us, on the sands, the ruined tower of Eccles standing up from the beach like a solitary tooth. It was abandoned nearly three hundred years ago, for the parish was practically gone—through the irruptions of the sea—two thousand acres having been known to be lost. Singularly enough the stout, honest work of the old church builders, with their dressed flints and iron-like mortar, seems to have acted as a breakwater; and by banking up the sand has saved what little there is left of the village. If the tide is down, the walk to Happisburgh (Hasboro) along the sands is a very pretty one; if it is not, the visitor had better make a wide sweep and get on to the hard road, as the walk along the Marrum Hills is a tedious and unpleasant one.

On this road, perhaps, better than anywhere else on the coast, can be noticed the effects of the heavy east winds, which always seem to be blowing on to the land—the hedgerow trees being bent inward and twisted into fantastic shapes, as though frozen while being blown almost to the ground by a heavy gale. Nothing but maple and ash seems to recover itself, and grow straight again. We soon get a glimpse of Happisburgh Church tower standing high on a hill, while to its right are the two 'Happisburgh Lights.' Happisburgh is the first place which we come to along the coast, that may be considered as a nascent watering-place. The view from the cliffs is a fine one, and the sands are very firm and good for bathing, though there is, or was, only one machine. Some few houses let lodgings, and good accommodation can usually be had at the 'Hill House,' which is a roomy and well-conducted inn, with a pretty bowling-green.

There are, however, certain objections to the place, which should be stated by an honest chronicler. There is only one little general shop; no meat is to be bought except at arbitrary and erratic intervals; the seven miles that divide the place from North Walsham, where are the nearest railway station and doctor, are over the vilest roads that I have ever had the hap to come across, chiefly consisting of sea-beach; no newspaper or book has ever been seen in the village; everyone is expected to be in bed at nine; and dulness reigns supreme over the district. Cowper used to come here, and Cowper afterwards went mad, and I don't at all wonder at it. As a substitute for Spain or Chili, I may conscientiously recommend the place to absconding city accountants, for no one would ever dream of looking here for anybody. One should not, however, leave it without having a careful survey of the church, which is still a very fine one, though it was most shamefully 'restored' in 1863, every monument but one in the church (it is said there were hundreds of them) having been covered up by the new tiling—an act of vandalism which I venture to think is unparalleled in the whole county, and one which would not be ventured upon by the most impudent parson of the present generation. The tower has luckily escaped the attentions of the architect and his employer; indeed, it would have been hard for them to have found an excuse to lay hands on so perfect and handsome an erection. It is 107 feet high, square embattled, and of flint, with tracery still in the windows and sound-holes. The two courses of base ornament should especially be noticed, the first being trefoiled stone arches filled in with square flints, while the second is a range of particularly handsome flowing ornament.

Keeping along the coast from Happisburgh north, the first object of interest is, of course, the ruins of Bromholm Abbey, which is only about three miles as the crow flies, but vastly more 'as the road go.' The road 'go,' in fact, very strangely along this coast, for there is no roadway running parallel with the sea, as is the case nearly always on other coasts. There are plenty of roads like those running from Ruston through Walcot, and from Witton to Bacton to the sea, which we must suppose originally joined in with some seaside road. But here there can be very little doubt that the seaside road they once joined has itself been swept away by the inroads of the ocean. The ruins of the great abbey of Bacton, otherwise Bromholm, founded early in the twelfth century by William de Glanville, are very well worthy of special notice, and the best account of them will be found in Harrod's 'Castles and Convents of Norfolk.' Antiquarians will remember that this was the abbey that owned the great piece of the true cross which was embedded in the 'Holy Rood of Bromholm.' There is a beach and bathing-place at Bacton, and two or three people who are fonder than I of extreme and remote seclusion have built them houses on the edge of the cliff, and, I have no doubt, enjoy themselves in their own peculiar fashion.

The walk from Bacton to Paston by the road is a very pretty one, and though the hall of the Pastons, so well known in history, is now gone, the church which bears their name is a very picturesque one, with its square low tower and thatched nave, barely peeping above the trees which closely embower it. It is a large building of rough flint with decorated windows and a new lych-gate, but it is chiefly noticeable for its churchyard, which is one of the prettiest I have ever seen, and is a model for the adoption of country parsons, with its magnificent growth of Gloire de Dijon roses and Virginian creepers. Though the hall is gone, the hall-barn is not, and a grand barn it is, built 303 years ago of dressed flint, with an elaborate timber roof that would shame many a West-country and Midland church. While so near Knapton, it would be a great pity not to strike a little inland to see its beautiful church roof, noted all over England for the boldness and elaborateness of its design. A stupid local tradition makes out that the roof was found in the wreck of a Spanish ship which came to grief on the coast hard by; but the startling coincidence of the dimensions of the roof with those of the older edifice on which it was providentially placed, makes the story rather hard to believe.

Mundesley is the first of our few Norfolk watering-places which is worthy of its name; in fact, a good many people would cavil at its being called a watering-place at all, for I don't think there is any bathing accommodation beyond the bare sands and the hotels, and lodgings are not very grand. The Ship is a clean and respectable inn close to the sea, but there is more accommodation in the Royal, which is clean and comfortable, most of it being let off as lodgings. The sands are firm and good, though the sea is making terrible inroads all along the coast. The old village is prettily situate, huddled round the banks of an impetuous little river, which is distinctly visible to the naked eye after heavy rain, but which in bygone days must have had much more water in it, for it has cut a deep and sharp channel down to the sea. From Mundesley the cliff heightens fast, and beautiful views of the sea can be obtained from the rises of the road, and especially at Beacon Hill, a rugged furze-grown and wind-blown spot, which is said to be the highest land in Norfolk. A couple of miles inland, and below us, is Gimmingham, the head of John of Gaunt's possessions in Norfolk, where he had a park and a palace, now unhappily untraceable.

Continuing along the coast, through a deep-cut lane which does duty for a road, and which is literally embowered with vegetation, we come to

Trimmingham, a pretty village with a grey old church which has suffered severely from the ruthless hands of 'Restorers.' Once it is said to have held the head of St. John the Baptist, and pilgrimages used to be made to the relic. From the absence of any mention of so celebrated a relic in any but local wills, I expect, as I have already said, that 'head' meant an artificial image or representation only.

The walk along the coast is through deep-cut lanes, winding strangely along to Sidestrand. The old church stood on the edge of the cliff, but has lately been dismantled and rebuilt farther inland, with what I must consider very questionable taste. Half the money that the new church has cost would, if it had been spent judiciously in groins and piles on the beach below the old building, not only have saved it, but have checked the inroads of the sea along this coast. This, however, would not have gratified the instincts of the meddlers and muddlers. The same unhappy taste to disturb existing buildings is shown in the next village of Overstrand, where the old church has been left to ruin so as to form an excuse for the erection of a new church in the same churchyard, which jars the eye sadly.

If we strike the cliff path by Kirby Hill, we shall soon, after climbing over some breezy downs, covered with short, close turf, see Cromer lying beneath us as in a cup, with its great grey church standing out masterfully over the red-tiled roofs of the old town. If one stops and sits on the cliff opposite the 'new' lighthouse tower and looks down, one will see evidence everywhere of how the sea has been coming in and wasting the land. Some works have at last been started to stay it, and none too soon, for the cliff here falls away landwards almost as abruptly as it does towards the sea ; and if this narrow hog-backed slip of land ever goes, it won't be very long before the sea will run right up to the picturesque railway station that stands on the knoll to our left. The visitor need not be a conjuror to guess that the grand church, which was 180 feet long, with a tower 160 feet high, and which for delicacy of ornamentation has no equal in the county, was never built for the accommodation of the few fishermen who formed the inhabitants of the village before it became known as a watering-place. The houses of those who built it lie out to sea, covered with seaweed, and visible only at very low tides, when the streets can clearly be traced.

Still farther out to sea are the remains of a yet older village, called Shipden, once a port of importance along this coast, but which, with its church, succumbed to the waves 500 years ago. A piece of the flint tower of the church is occasionally visible at low tides about 400 yards out to sea, and is now called 'the Church Rock.'

Cromer itself, though perhaps not so important a port as its predecessor, Shipden, must have been a thriving and busy place, for I find letters addressed from the Privy Council to its Mayor, and there was an Admiralty Court held here for a long time. As late as 1528 it sent out thirty ships, trading

The Watering-Places and Coast-Line. 251

chiefly to Iceland and Norway, and carried on a great North Sea fishing trade also. But 'the rages and surges of the sea' proved too much for the engineers of the period, and the pier, which was partly used for a jetty and partly as a protection against the water, gradually fell into bad repair, and, being washed away, left the place at the mercy of the waves. The few fishermen who were left could not afford to keep so enormous a church in repair, and the lessee of the great tithes, himself a clergyman, actually obtained leave from the Bishop of Ely to destroy the chancel, which he accomplished by blowing it up by gunpowder, as the honest work of the old masons was too strong for his villainous hands. A scheme has now been made for re-erecting the chancel and strengthening the tower, and, if this is done, the view from the tower end through the chancel arch will be grand indeed.

As a watering-place, Cromer is chiefly noticeable for the firmness and extent of its sands, which afford unlimited bathing accommodation, the great beauty and variety of the neighbouring scenery, and its old-fashioned air of comfort. Lodgings and everything else are outrageously dear in the season; and long may they remain so, keeping out of the place the cockney hailing from London and elsewhere! There are no amusements except those provided by Nature. The best inns are Tucker's, the Hôtel de Paris, and Chapman's. Under the first-named are some old vaults, but the town having suffered so severely from fire and water, there are no old houses of any interest. The history of the growth of Cromer as a watering-place would be an interesting one, if it ever could be written. A valuable contribution to it would be a delightful little book of some fifty-seven pages, published in 1806, by an anonymous writer, and entitled 'Cromer: a Descriptive Poem,' and consisting of some 700 lines of the blankest verse I have ever had the luck to come across. Its dedication to Mrs. Wyndham, of Cromer Hall, is, however, neat: 'Of Cromer it has often been doubted whether the spectator derives a greater pleasure from the sublimity of its sea views or the beauty of its landscapes; and of you, madam, it is difficult to determine whether you are more to be admired for the dazzling attractions of your person or esteemed for the amiable qualities of your heart.' After this one mechanically turns to the list of subscriptions to see how many copies taken by the dedicatee rewarded the dedicator, but unluckily there is no subscription list in my copy. Of its originality, two specimens will suffice:

> 'No foot is heard upon the jetty's base;
> I am alone, and leaning o'er its side
> I gaze in silence, thinking on the deep,
> Its dangers and its wonders and its paths,
> Dark, trackless, and unsearchable by all
> Save by His eye Who,' etc., etc.

But this is good:

> 'Quiet the steady *Sociable* proceeds,
> No danger in its course, and in the rear
> The humbler vehicle, that bears displayed,
> In letters legible to every eye,
> The Stamp of fiscal avarice.'

He means a taxed cart.

Later on the place became a sort of rendezvous for a clan formed by the allied Quaker families of Buxton, Gurney, Hoare, and the rest of them, who must be credited with great taste in discovering the beauties of the place, but whose invasion of it by no means tended to the general comfort of other visitors. However, now that the rail is open to Norwich, one need no longer be refused the right to purchase articles of food in *market overt* on the ground that Mr. X., Y. or Z. *might* want them!

Beyond Cromer to the west there are lodgings to be had at Runton, which will spring up into a watering-place directly the new coast-line rail is opened; as will, no doubt, Sherringham and Weybourne, two charmingly pretty places on the seashore, described in my last chapter. Holkham, near Wells, has a good inn, the Victoria Inn, at the very gates of Lord Leicester's Park, and visitors might do worse than stay here and spend a few days exploring the results of the woodcraft of 'Coke of Norfolk,' who, by his planting, turned a barren waste into one of the finest demesnes in England. There are no cliffs here, the coast-line being sandy 'meals' swarming with rabbits.

Fourteen miles or so on by the pretty coast road, or an hour by rail, brings us through Burnham Thorpe, the birthplace of Nelson, and the Roman station of Brancaster to our last watering-place—Hunstanton. We come first by the road to the old town where is the hall once inhabited by 'Strange Lying Roger,' as

Sir Roger L'Estrange's name was once anagrammed, the Cavalier pamphleteer and plotter. The beautiful Decorated church, which has been admirably restored and looked after by the owners of the advowsons, descendants in the female line from the L'Estranges, whose monuments are so interesting. The nave roof and the Norman font should be especially noticed. A mile or so on we come to the new town, which was to have been called 'St. Edmunds,' but which has firmly declined to be so labelled. It is a very ordinary waterside place, with lodging-houses, piers, terraces, and so on; and is much frequented by excursionists from the Midlands. The Golden Lion used to be the best house, but is eclipsed by the 'Sandringham'—a pretentious but fairly comfortable London-terminus-looking hotel. The view westwards across the sea is a fine one, and 'Boston Stump' on the Lincolnshire coast is clearly visible on a fine day.

There is no good bathing along the coast, but the road to Lynn (already described) is a very pretty one indeed; and if the visitor has a good horse, a bicycle, or a tricycle, he is strongly recommended to use it instead of the railway, which is as slow and inconvenient as any in England. Heacham and Snettisham churches and Ingoldisthorpe Hall are all very worthy of careful examination. Between Dersingham and Sandringham the county is open, and is being well planted by the Prince of Wales, who I hope may live long to see the delightful results of his hobby. Sandringham itself is nothing to see.

It was bought vastly dear, and has had a tremendous lot of money spent on it, and is still a very poor place for the heir-apparent. Gunton or Blickling would have been much more suited for him, and with the same money spent on them would by this time have been little palaces.

Castle Rising is the last place of interest we pass through before we reach Lynn. Its church is, perhaps the finest and most compact instance of Norman work I know, with its magnificent west front, which has been so often engraved. The castle with its Norman keep almost perfect, and its earthworks which Harrod thought Roman, but which may have been still earlier, are worthy of very special study. The she-wolf—Queen Isabella—was long kept here by her son, but not in the strict custody that has been said; and I need hardly say that the story of the subterranean passage between the keep and the Red Mount at Lynn, through which the King is said to have secretly visited his mother, has not the faintest foundation on fact.

XIV.

THE BROADS AND MARSHES.

T is painful for one who has known and loved the Broads as long as I have, in common honesty, to say that their charms have been grossly exaggerated of late. To read some of the word-painting about them you would think that you had only to leave Yarmouth and sail up the North River to get at once into a paradise of ferns, flowers, and fish, where you could not fail to fill your basket or bag; or to see, at all events, myriads of wild birds of the rarest sorts in the air, shoals of fishes in the water, and any quantity of rare water-plants on the bank. The first few miles will effectually disillusionize any stranger who has been taking in the 'Swiss-Family-Robinson' sort of rubbish referred to above, for he will be disgusted with the very muddy flint walls of a tediously winding river dragging itself along through a flat uninteresting marshy country, varied only by drainage-mills in various stages of dilapidation, and by telegraph-poles. Even when at last Yarmouth

Church finally disappears, after having come into view about a dozen times through the windings, and the river wall with its rats and dirt changes into the regular river scenery, he will see nothing particularly pretty. On either side of the river there is a long strip of marshy land locally called the ' Rond,' covered with coarse poor wet grass and fringed with the blue flowers of the wild Michaelmas daisy. Then comes a new-looking grass bank and great stretches of marsh or water-meadow with hundreds and hundreds of cattle fattening on it. Nor is the Yare much more interesting; for, except that behind the water-meadows rise fairly high hills mostly wood-covered, and obviously once the banks of the old estuary, the view from the water differs little from that just described. The first thing to catch the eye of the stranger is always the local barge, here known as a wherry.

The wherries are long low boats, built on lines much resembling those of the Viking's Ship found in 1880 at Sandefjord. They carry one enormous brown sail only, draw very little water, and sail nearer the wind than any yacht; while for speed they can go as fast as anything. It is, indeed, a sight to see a 'light' (*i.e.*, unloaded) big wherry 'roaring' down over Breydon with a wind, and one that would not be forgotten easily by the owner of many a crack South-country yacht that tried to keep with her. Many are large boats; the *Wanderer*, for example, being eighty tons. The wherrymen who work them load and carry the cargo, and get 8d. out of every shilling of freightage; the other groat going to the owner who finds and repairs the wherry. Sometimes a man will make £1 a voyage between Yarmouth and Norwich, and the quasi-partnership between the men and the masters is based on a very sound principle; for it is obviously to the former's interest to make as many voyages and earn as much money as possible, the result being that the men are most skilled watermen, and very sober and industrious. Unlike London barges and canal boats, the snug little cabin for the man and his wife is in the stern—a much more comfortable arrangement, for all the draft wind is avoided. During the last few years it has become the fashion for private parties to hire one of these wherries instead of a yacht, and as they can go where few yachts can, and as their accommodation is roomy in the extreme, with headway all about, the fashion will no doubt spread. They can be hired ready fitted out for private parties at about £7 10s. a week from Cubitt and Walker, of North Walsham, or from Mr. H. George, the hon. secretary of the local yacht club at Surbiton Lodge, Gorleston, who is also agent for several yacht-owners. Yachts of all sorts can be hired at Hart's, Thorpe by Norwich, or Tungate at Icehouse Lane, Bracondale, and Loyne's patent boats with oilskin covers for sleeping under (capital things in the real summer-time) of the patentee at Elm Hill, Norwich. They are, however, veritable rheumatism-traps in the late autumn and winter, and are always open to the objection that if rain comes on suddenly the boat and its contents get drenched before there is time to get the coverings up, and that they are no protection in a 'smurry' day. Besides, it is all very well, but sailcloth and oilskin do not keep out the cold like good thick planking. The last winter I slept out in my own boat—a round-topped old 14-tonner—and was as snug and as warm as could be; while the water we had washed up crockery in after supper froze $\frac{3}{4}$ inch thick just outside the cabin door. A pleasure-wherry is undoubtedly the most comfortable boat on which to see the Broads, the six-feet headway being delightful. The wherries have quite superseded the 'keels' which used to be the only boats sailing on these waters, and which carried a great square sail on a mast stepped nearly amid-ships; whereas the wherries have theirs right into the bow. Whether the keels were identical with the Newcastle keels I don't know; but they were quite distinct from the wherries, as is evidenced by the Norwich public-house sign of the 'Keel *and* Wherry.'

Anyone wanting a short run up the Broad district from Yarmouth can always get a lift in one of these wherries if he walks down to the limekilns, past the bowling-green, and makes terms with a wherryman who is just through the bridge and about getting his mast up again; and he is sure to have a pleasant day's outing at a very moderate price, and hear some good stories if he can persuade the man to talk, which, by the way, everyone cannot. The wherrymen are great at old jokes and tales, and have certain standing formulæ of greeting on meeting another coming up or down; *e.g.*: 'There you go!' which should apparently be answered, 'There you blow!'

They tell tales, too, of various simple members of their fraternity; such as how when one man dropped a kettle overboard while sailing, he ran to the side of the boat and cut a 'snotch' with his knife to mark the spot and so be able to find it again; and how another, when complaining that his berth was higher at his heels than his head, accepted the tendered advice to turn the head of his wherry round, without, however, finding much relief thereby. Sometimes one sees a big lumbering, flat-bottomed, round-nosed barge from London, Rochester, or Harwich coming along which has been chartered right through, but which can only go with a fair wind, as she is not handy enough to tack on these waters.

The pleasantest way to see the Broads, and so avoid the unfavourable impression which a start from Yarmouth gives you, is to take the rail to Wroxham Station, and start down the river from the staith hard by. It is hardly worth while to go up the river, for it rapidly narrows and shallows, and though pretty, is scarcely navigable, still small yachts can get up to Coltishall, and row-boats and canoes even farther. From the station at Wroxham you can see the river-banks dotted in the summertime with yachts and pleasure-wherries as close as they can be moored, there not unusually being fifty at the same time placed, bow to stern as close as possible, on both sides of the river. Wroxham is, in fact, *the* headquarters of Norfolk yachting, from the convenience of the rail landing one at once into the prettiest part of the scenery. But it is very badly supplied with shops and other victualling accommodation, so food for the voyage had better be provided from Norwich (Snelling's in Rampant Horse Street, or the various chief hotels, make up hampers of all sorts of provisions; and Grimmer, in St. John's, supplies very reliable potables), or from North Walsham, which is the nearest station, and where the hostess of the Angel will victual any-one very well, and reasonably. It may sound as though I am unduly impressing on the intending cruiser the necessity of getting his food and drink on board before starting; but except by accident, when one *may* get fowls and eggs, there is no place between Wroxham and Yarmouth where eatable food or drinkable drink can certainly be obtained. Good water, too, is very scarce, and I am beginning to doubt whether the wherrymen's simple expedient of taking it out of the river is not better than drawing it from doubtful wells. There are several waterside inns at Wroxham, the best being the King's Head (Jimpson's), which has improved of late years.

Starting down river, we soon come to some closely-wooded country, the bushes and trees of which run down to the water's edge, and are a great nuisance to those who delight in sailing only, but are very pleasant to those who love nature and would rather dawdle along and notice everything, than rip along with one's deck at an angle of 45° to the horizon. In the recesses of the little pulk-holes are great clumps of the Osmunda regalis, the great king fern, seven and eight feet high, but luckily extremely inaccessible, and therefore not likely to be soon stolen away. To the right are the entrances, or 'gatways,' to Wroxham Broad, a fine sheet of water, more open than most of the Norfolk Broads, and with fewer inlets and creeks. 'Wroxham Water Frolic' used to be a great institution, and the regatta which followed it is still a successful one. The Broad is a great place for fishing in summer, and skating in winter.

All along the marshy banks of the river are innumerable little pools, or 'pulks,' interspersed with marshy islands, the haunt of pheasants in the summer and autumn, and of coot in the winter. On very many of these are wild black-currant bushes, growing and fruiting well—a fact which proves the soundness of the horticultural dictum that the black-currant grows best in a damp, shady place. The natives tell you that the seeds are brought by birds; but as in some spots near here, such as 'Black Currant Carr,' the bushes are very plentiful, it may indeed be doubted whether the plants are not indigenous.

Twisting and turning, the river goes on till we catch a glimpse of the large trading village of Horning—or rather Horning 'Street'—on the left bank. There is some sleepy business done here with malt, and there is a decent river-side publichouse at which it is sometimes possible to obtain food of some sort or another. Whether the fact of half the population being employed or interested in the malthouses renders their children rabid anti-teetotalers,

I don't know; but it is undoubtedly the fact that never a yacht or a pleasure-boat goes by Horning Street without being favoured from the bank, by boys and girls alike, with a somewhat garbled and inconsequential version of 'Hey, John Barleycorn,' sung prettily enough to a running accompaniment for coppers. A few thousand years hence, when the river has silted up, and its bed is dry, future generations of antiquarians will wonder extremely at the enormous quantity of copper coins of the reign of Victoria I. which will be found there.

Whilst on the subject of malt, by the way, I would recommend those strangers who sail on these waters to let their watermen have a liberal allowance of the local public-house ale *per diem*, rather than try to supply their wants with a better article obtained from Norwich or Yarmouth, and which would be quite wasted on them. Over the bibulous propensities of the watermen one would fain draw a veil; but the usual unpleasant results of drink are generally absent, for they are apparently able to drink not only any 'given,' but any 'taken,' quantity with impunity. My readers may think me joking, but I can assure them that I know of a well-authenticated case of a Yarmouth waterside loafer, who was allowed to help himself, taking down a soda-water tumbler of neat brandy in two appreciative gasps, and walking away quite untouched.

These Yarmouth loafers—Yarmouth pirates as they are termed, half in joke—who press their services on every boat going up the North River, are a tremendous nuisance. To hear them talk, Scylla and Charybdis were child's-play to the unassisted novice who tries to get, unaided, through the suspension-bridge; and woe be to the yachtsman who leaves his victuals and drink near the lime-kiln for half an hour unguarded, or guarded only by a friendly waterman! I had two bottles of whisky and a bottle of wine consumed by friends of my man* one night while I was away, and the only satisfaction I had was being able, the next morning, to sternly refuse his urgent entreaties for soda-water to cure what was obviously an uncommonly bad headache.

This, however, is all wandering sadly from Horning Street, so we will go on once more down the river. The gap to our right is the entrance to Ranworth Broad, one of the prettiest of the Broads, being better backed up by woody slopes than most of them are.

It is, however, its church and its contents that make Ranworth so well known, for 'Ranworth rood-screen,' with its magnificent panel paintings of twelve saints, and its fine parcloses, is perhaps the best in England. A little farther down, and to our left, is the little river Ant; and up this we must diverge for a while, if we want to see the fine Broad at Barton—the chief home of the water-lilies, and one of the few remaining habitats of the swallow-tail butterfly. Every boat, however, cannot squeeze

* I need not say that was before I was lucky enough to come across the veteran Tungate.

under Ludham bridge, which is a standing disgrace to the road authorities, for when there is much water out it simply stops the passage of any large wherry. Last year I heard how a pleasure-wherry just scraped through, when down came a lot of rain, and she could not get back again; and the unlucky hirer had to pay £7 or £8 a week, and feed his men, for the privilege of staying above. Irstead Church should be visited for its font, and Barton Turf for its rood-screen, second only to Ranworth; and in a light-draughted boat, a trip up past Wayford Bridge (on the knoll above which is a Roman camp, the 'Devil's Ditch'), and on nearly to North Walsham, is a pleasant and very quiet one. All up this river Ant the fishing is very good indeed, lots of perch and rudd being catchable—*crede experto*—by the veriest novice elsewhere accustomed to failure.

For some time before we re-enter the North river, we see the great ruined gate-tower of St. Benet's Abbey, standing out among the level marshes dotted all over with innumerable fattening cattle, and passing by it, moor off the fragments of a massive flint wall, no doubt the remains of the monks' *necessarium*, which makes a most convenient landing-place just before we reach a low little old building, now unluckily divided into two cottages, once undoubtedly the porter's lodge, or water-gate. Within it are some old arches, but the visitor should evade paying a fee for being shown 'the brass of the last abbot,' which is kept in one cottage, but which is really a layman's inscription-brass only—of, I think, the sixteenth century—of the usual type. Second only in date to Thetford of our Norfolk monasteries, St. Benet's at Hulme is said to have been founded by the Saxons about A.D. 800, and to have been refounded by Canute in 1020. Standing in what is still a most lonely and inaccessible part of the marshes, it must have then been the very place for real retirement from the cares and troubles of the world; but as it was far from human help, its occupants no doubt thought it necessary to fortify themselves against the attacks of marauders, and built themselves a strong place of refuge, which, it is said, had to stand a siege by the Conqueror.

Except the old tower, which long served as a water drainage-mill, and which has some good work still left in it, and the massive foundation of the abbey church, there is little left of what was once the home of the mitred Abbot of St. Benet's, who was one of the most powerful persons in England in his day. The size of the precincts can be seen from the top of the tower, the circle of trees showing it well. It encloses an old orchard, and has two or three oblong stews, or fish-ponds, now grown up with weeds.

A mile or two past the abbey, and we come to another river, the Thurne or Hundred Stream, which joins us also on our left. To be more correct, one should say we join the Hundred Stream, which is perfectly straight with the latter part of the Bure, and which I cannot help thinking was once *the* river of the district, but which has probably been affected by some of the numerous subsidences of the peaty bog.

It is well worth our while turning up the Hundred Stream, leaving the pretty little village of Thurne on our right, and Womack Broad—nearly grown up—and the Grange, or Bishop's Farm, at Ludham, on our left. The house was burnt down in 1611, and with it, unluckily, certain records relating to presentations and institutions, and 'all the auditt rolls and divers evidences of the Bishoprick.' It must have been a rather extensive building, with a steward's chamber, pantry, buttery, great hall, tailor's chamber, woman's chamber, dining-parlour, gallery, and a great number of bedrooms, and a dove-house and 'ferret-house' outside.

Farther up we come to Heigham Bridge—an old stone building—leading up to Potter Heigham, supposed to be so called from some Roman pottery having been here. But it used to be called Potteres Heigham, and may have been only so called from a former owner's name in contradistinction from Heigham by Norwich. It is curious that there is a Potter Hanworth in Lincoln also in the thick of a Danish settlement. Why the local proverb should run: 'Blessed are they who live near Potter Heigham, and doubly blessed those who live in it,' I can't say. The biggest hawthorn-hedge I ever saw is up the road, nearly opposite the Falgate Inn, so called from a representation of a gate hanging over the road—a fal-gate meaning, according to some, a fald or fold gate; to others, a 'falling gate,' *i.e.*, a hanging gate to a common, which, being hung over, shuts to with a bang by its own weight when you have passed through it, so that no animals can wander off the common. Just above the old stone bridge is the new railway bridge, carrying the light line from Yarmouth to North Walsham; and the double obstacle will, I fear, deter many from sailing up to Hickling Broad, the largest if the shallowest of any of our lakes. There is very little left of Hickling Priory—founded exactly 700 years ago—but what little remains is curious.

Farther on still one may get up, in a row-boat—or a small sailing-boat, if well handled—to Horsey Mere, with its 'Horsey Pike—none like,' the last and most lonely of the Broads, and separated only from the sea by a mile and a half of sand-bank. The sea came in here once, and I hope it never may again; but as the 'fresh-water-land' keeps on subsiding, the bank will be more liable to go.

When we rejoin the main river, we have on our left the two Flegg hundreds, of which nearly every village bears an obviously Danish name. Winterton and Somerton seem exceptions, but it is curious to notice that there are places of the same names in the north of Lincolnshire, among an equally dense Danish settlement.

Acle Bridge, which is the next old bridge we come to, is a mile or so from Acle Town, the way to which is along a desperately straight and uninteresting marsh road. The church is a fine one, and the churchyard, with its lime avenues, pretty; but the town is best known from its celebrated priory, founded by Roger Bigod. Some broken ground nearly opposite the church is all there is to show of the priory. Possibly the cut from the river, ending at the 'Hermitage Staith,' shows the locality of some retreat of which we have now no record.

Below Acle the characteristics of the 'Broad' scenery gradually vanish. One no longer sees the broad green leaves of the water-lilies flapping up from the water as the wind catches them, looking for all the world like a duck getting up. The bog-beans float more rarely on the top of the water, and even the tall, red-brown 'reeds,' and the lighter-coloured 'chate,' or flowering grass, begin to disappear. The villages are quaint, clustering close to the water's edge; but the scenery gets barer and barer, and we soon become disagreeably aware of mud-banks, of unsightly flint walls, and dilapidated drainage-mills, till at last we see Yarmouth steeple in the distance. We shall see it appear and disappear plenty of times, for the river winds in and out like an eel for the last few miles, till we risk the terrible perils of the suspension bridge, and moor against the staith of the Bowling Green, just opposite the mouth of Breydon Water. For some time past, of course, we have been in salt water, and any night one may see the phosphorescence which some say comes from the animalculæ, but which, ever after I passed one awful night here, moored by mistake between the outfall of a sewer and a cargo-load of putrid herring-guts on the other, I believe arises from other causes.

Without any exception, Yarmouth is the beastliest hole any boating-man can have to stay at. The Bowling Green is the best mooring-place, but bad is the best, and if by luck one can, in coming from the Norwich river to the North river, or *vice versâ*, catch the tide across Breydon, one should certainly do so, and not wait a night here. If this cannot be done, it will be as well to make a virtue of necessity and stroll over the town, and revictual, if one wants to do so, in the splendid market—one of the best in England. In this case, the first thing to do, whether one lands by the limekilns or at the Bowling Green, is to keep along the side of the river— noticing the old tower hard by the water-side, which ended the city wall—till one reaches the wide open space fronting the swing bridge. This is generally called the Hall Quay from the town-hall, which stands facing us at its end. The present town-hall is a fine big place, and stands on the site of an older one, built in 1715, which had a curious portico, supported by Tuscan pillars.

The celebrated Yarmouth Hutch—which contained the equally well-known Hutch map, showing the country as it was before the river contracted—is a fine specimen of old work, with massive locks and bars. Before we come to it, however, we should look at the interior of the Star Inn, a fine Elizabethan building, with flint panelling outside and oak within, some of the carvings in the first-floor rooms being very good. Gurney's Bank, near this, was once occupied by Mr. Dawson Turner, who is well-known for his large, if not very valuable, collections to illustrate our county history. His illustrated copy is now in the British Museum, but is not much consulted, for the original sketches are poor and usually inaccurate.

If we turn to the right, we follow the river along the South Quay—a wide and pretty walk, nearly a mile long, shaded with lime-trees, and thronged with busy workers. It is a free quay, and from its banks the great herring-boats, with their massive timbers, can be seen to advantage.

To our left is a particularly fine Elizabethan house, formerly belonging to C. J. Palmer, a wealthy and able local antiquary, who, besides other good work, published a very elaborate set of working-drawings of the beautiful ceilings, panelling, and other details of his house. The story that the execution of Charles I. was determined at a secret meeting of the Roundhead leaders in this house is unsupported by any evidence whatever, and the probabilities are greatly against the story. The story most likely arose from the fact that the house once belonged to a son-in-law of Ireton's.

If we keep on along the quay, we shall notice many fine old houses, once the habitations of great merchants who were not ashamed of living over their counting-houses, and who by so doing were able to afford to put up buildings which shame our degenerate villas. Most of them, however, are in a sad state of decay, and the walk is rather a dreary one till we get into the opener country past the barrack and the South Star battery to Nelson's monument, which stands near the racecourse. It was built in 1817, and is a finer column than most monumental columns are, and carries a figure of Britannia looking out proudly over the seas our local hero guarded so well. Nelson landed here after two of his more important victories, hence the choice of this spot.

Walking round the racecourse, which in due season provides the usual excitement for fools who incorrectly fancy they 'know something,' and the usual emolument for betting-men and others who have a sounder and better-grounded knowledge of the value of such information, we come to the end of the long spit of land on which Yarmouth stands. Opposite us is Gorleston pier, and a fine sight it is on a windy day to see the various fishing and trading craft trying to round its stubborn-looking head, and escape from the roaring water of the 'Road' outside.

When we have repassed the racecourse on its other side, and walked past the barracks, we reach the modern quay, the sea-front of Yarmouth, a very fine and wide promenade indeed, with grand sands, and many excellent houses facing them. To see it aright, one should do so about 4.30 a.m. on a fine summer morning. Later than this the throngs of cockneys will begin to emerge from the numerous small lodging-houses, and render the place unsavoury.

Yarmouth is nothing more or less than a big Margate, and is rapidly becoming the Londoner's paradise. Here he will find everything his soul loveth. Shrimps and public-houses everywhere, comic songs and horse-play all day long, and in the season a beach simply packed with a noisy crowd—good-humoured enough, I will admit, but having remarkably little appreciation of the sea or scenery. The steamers from London bring down shoals of them, on whom the voyage, if rough, operates like the physic which used to begin a prize-fighter's training, and leaves them fresh to begin their week's pleasure with clear consciences and empty stomachs.

Once at Yarmouth they stop there, as close to the beach as they can; and I don't think I have seen half-a-dozen excursionists exploring the country more inland than half-a-dozen miles.

To the passing visitors like ourselves there are several objects of interest which must not be missed, and especially the great church and the toll-house. The latter will be the best to see first, as we shall find it at the end of Row No. 108.

It is a most interesting thirteenth-century building, partly used for municipal purposes and partly as a prison. The outside door is very curious, and so is the outside staircase leading to a sort of open balcony, lit by a two-light Early English window. Within, the rooms are quaint in the extreme, but the cells and stone-yard, which until quite recently were used not only for criminals but for prisoners for debt, are some of the vilest holes in which human beings were ever left to rot.

Passing through the market-place, which is one of

the finest in England, and is always (and especially on market-days—Wednesday and Saturday) very well stocked with flesh and fruit, fish and flowers, we see the largest parish church in England in front of us, standing up over a pretty lime avenue. Indeed, Yarmouth church is larger in area than many of our English cathedrals, as may be guessed from its length being 230 feet, its nave alone being 80 feet. It was built by Herbert de Lozinga, Bishop of Norwich, just after he had founded his cathedral. Unluckily but little of the Norman work is left, for the church was practically re-built and re-consecrated in 1286. It had no less than nineteen chapels, and it was proposed before 1348 to increase its already enormous proportions by adding a 'Bachelor's Aisle,' which was to have been 107 feet by 47, and a doorway 40 feet wide! Owing to a pestilence, however, this building got little farther than its foundation, and was abandoned. Within the church the great organ—with its 49 stops, 7 couplers and 3,188 sounding pipes—the Crowmer and Fastolf monuments, and the old library, all attract and deserve attention.

Leaving Yarmouth, after getting a last glimpse of the flint front of the Star, and of the local walking-stick-carrying policemen (a species as curious as their grey-trousered *confrères* at Brighton), we will cast off from the Bowling Green, and not forgetting a big jar of pure water from its hospitable pump, and some fresh food and vegetables from the market-place, sail, if the tide serves, over Breydon Water, a wide, muddy, salt-water lake, formed by the junction of the mouths of the Yare, which runs down from Norwich, and the Waveney, which comes from Thetford, Bungay, and Beccles. The channel is marked out by white posts, and must be very carefully kept, for though in years gone by a boat could be sailed on its north side almost as far as where we see the train puffing leisurely along its embankment, woe is now to the yacht or wherry that goes much outside the posts at low water, for on to the 'putty' she will go gently but firmly, and there stay till the next tide floats her, or the local pirates have got her off *nolens volens* the owner, and extracted what they can from him.

Breydon, for those who care for a real bit of sailing, and don't mind a breeze and some choppy water at times, is a real paradise; and, let favourable circumstances arise, it is pretty to see boats of all sorts coming out from the town 'by one, by two, by three,' of all sorts and rigs, and availing themselves of the chance. Given a hard winter, again, and Breydon becomes the happy hunting-ground of all the gun-owners of the district, for, from its position and the feeding-ground its long mud-banks afford, it is as good a non-preserved place for fowl as can be found. It is also a special locality for those who take a pleasure in exterminating the rarer sorts of water-birds. Luckily, however, the professional shooters, whom you will see stealing along in their slate-coloured punts, look with no great favour on amateur gunners; and I have known them shoot off their big guns at nothing in particular, just to alarm the ducks rather than let the visitors have a chance.

To the left, just as we get out of Breydon we see the grey walls of Burgh Castle, which, though not in our county, must not be passed by. It was built A.D. 46, no doubt to command one mouth of Breydon (which must then have been much longer and wider), while Caister by Yarmouth dominated the other. Which of the two was 'Garianonum,' let Spelman and Camden fight about : enough for us that the Roman station is perhaps as perfect in parts as any other in England ; and though it will not compare for size with Caister by Norwich, its walls are fourteen feet high and nine feet thick, and enclose five acres of ground. The view from it is strange and lonely as one looks down over the wide stretch of water and low-lying land, with the sluggish river winding below. Keeping up the Waveney, or more technically the ' Beccles River,' we pass by St. Olave's, and under its bridge, and are reminded of the tale of the Danish saint, Olaf. Inland to our east, and in Suffolk, is the celebrated Fritton Decoy, so noted for its wild-duck and its fish.

Of the parson here it is said that being a Norfolk man, and moved here, he replied to the bishop when asked how he was, that he was as well as a Norfolk man 'suffocated'[*] could be. He too it was who, when a too-long-staying visitor unwarily commented at dinner on the great convenience of the adjoining railway stations to people who wanted to come to Fritton, replied sententiously, ' Ah, and it's perfectly marvellous how useful they are to go away by !'

[*] ' Suffolk-bated ' (please laugh).

Another railway bridge is at Somerleyton, an estate bought by Peto, the contractor—(the ' Bardolph and Peto' of his neighbour Borrow's biting joke) of 'S.G.O.'—and then just before we get to Oulton we can turn up to the left and get on to the only Suffolk ' Broad '—Oulton, otherwise Mutford, and otherwise more euphoniously 'Lake Lothing,' a great rendezvous for yachts, for it is only two miles or so from Lowestoft, a nice place for those who like it, and anyhow a convenient marketing-place. The 'Broad' itself is always picturesque with the white sails of yachts, and on its north bank is the house where George Borrow wrote most of his books. It is a pretty place, backed up with a pine plantation, and his readers will well remember his masterly bit of wordpainting about it, and his old mother, and his good horse.

At the 'Lady of the Lake' (Kemps), a comfortable little inn, is a vine planted outside the house and brought in through the wall into the kitchen, the windows of which it covers, as it used to cover the ceiling—a veritable horticultural curiosity. Turning back into the Waveney and going up-stream, if the sluggish flow is worth such a name, we see on the Norfolk side the very strangely shaped four-storied tower of Wheatacre Burgh, or Burgh St. Peter, which serves as a landmark for miles. The church is well worth a visit, for not only does one get a fine view all over the marshes—which, strangely enough, seem lower inland than near the river, as though the river was flowing between artificially raised banks—but the interior of the building deserves inspection. The font is a very handsome octagonal one with a shafted base; the roof is luckily untouched, and so is the rood-staircase, and a very fine piscina, and equally good sedilia. It is, however, the tower which is the peculiar feature of the church, for it batters *four* times, the lowest course being partly flint and stone panelling in lozenge-shaped panels, the next two modern brick, and the fourth partly old stone. Roman remains have been found here, and it has been conjectured that the 'Burgh' points to a Roman station. In the low-lying ground behind—about four miles off—are what ruins are left of Aldeby Priory, but it is not worth while going either to see them, or the birth-place of Tawell, the Quaker murderer, and the first victim of the electric telegraph.

A few miles on and we reach Beccles, a very pretty and quaint Suffolk town, huddled up on a high bank above the river. Here we may well turn back, for the sailing above is not so good, but not before admiring the fine detached clocher of Beccles church, which I take to have been built by the same architect as that of Cromer and Happisburgh churches, for the very unusual flowing ornament on the second base course running round the tower is identical with that at Happisburgh, and the still more unusual hollow canopy-work in the buttresses I have seen nowhere else than at Cromer. The visitor should also try to see the inside of Ros(e) Hall, a beautifully oak-panelled Elizabethan house, occupied by Mr. Robinson, the well-known athlete and ex-champion pole-jumper, which is past the Fauconberge Grammar School. In the street that runs parallel to the river there are some charming and well-preserved 'Queen Anne' houses, and, indeed, I do not know a more sleepy, middle-aged, pleasant town in which to waste a summer's day than Beccles.

Turning down stream again, we sail back to St. Olave's, and turn up the 'New Cut,' which joins the Waveney and the Bure, and substitutes a two or three mile straight canal for a thirteen mile *détour* round by Burgh Castle. Very nice sailing this cut is *if* the wind suits you, and very nice healthy exercise by the way of towing it gives you if it doesn't. It comes out at Reedham, a little village on a bank, with a great history; for it was here that Lodbrok, the Dane, is said to have been inhospitably treated when he was blown across from Denmark in an open boat, with hawk and hound, and was murdered by a huntsman of King Edmund. His sons, Hingar and Hubba, are said to have come over to avenge him, and to have in return converted King Edmund into a martyr, the story whereof is to be seen on so many East Anglian rood-screens, and therefore must be true. The church lies high above the river and is full of interest, so one must go to it.

From the little hill or big mound on which it stands we get a wonderful view over the marshes, where the long straight cut and the winding river contrast strangely. Under us, if tradition is truth, is a subterranean passage leading to the hall, which may be the remains of some Roman work, for Roman coins have been found here, and there is some Roman brick built into the chancel. The churchyard is very picturesque, being well sheltered on one side by a close growth of trees which show out very markedly in so treeless a country. It is indeed a little oasis in the wilderness, for the parson is clearly a man of taste as well as a good gardener, having succeeded in getting great tea-roses—Maréchal Niel, Gloires, and others—to grow against his church, in spite of the bleak open situation. On the other hand, an ordinary necessarium has been erected against the church—an instance of profanation it would be difficult to match. Though the nave is only thatched the tower is a very fine one, and as perfect as the day it was put up. It is early Perpendicular, with flint and stone work best of the way up, and has a fine exterior stair-turret. The Berney chapel is very interesting, especially for a fine Elizabethan monument to Henry Berney, Esq., who died 1584, of the usual type, husband and boys kneeling on one side, and wife and girls on the other. It is of the Berney family (who were afterwards baronets) that the rustics used to say that they had to bear the bloody hand on their arms because one of them 'whipped a boy to dead.' There is also a nice brass of a lady with a butterfly headdress. The whole church has been carefully and conscientiously 'restored,' and not 'destroyed,' and is left open at all times. It is pleasant to note this, and to be able to record the results of the cultivated taste of a stranger, for I do not even know the rector's name.

The Broads and Marshes.

Coming down again into the quaint little village, we see that it is built on two or three terraces or ridges of the detached hill by the river, a hill low in itself, but very noticeable among the marshes. It is inhabited mostly by shipwrights and fishermen, who live alongside the low staith, which is hardly raised above the river. There are a few small shops, and occasionally butcher's meat may be bought; but, as in most other remote parts of Norfolk, butcher's meat forms but a very small portion of the dietary of the lower classes.

It was while loafing about at Reedham that I noted down from the mouth of a friendly wherryman the following absolutely unique and hitherto entirely unpublished list of the forty-eight reaches ('raches' he called them) between Breydon and Norwich, which I subjoin for the benefit of posterity:

1. Borrow [Burgh] Flats.
2. Barney Arms.
3. Fi' Mil' House.
4. Tilekil' Rache.
5. Six Mil' Rond.
6. Six Mil' House.
7. Seven Mil' House.
8. Bowlin' Alley.
9. Eyht Mil' Trees.
10. Reedham Town.
11. Taylor's Rache.
12. Reedham Ferry Rache.
13. Hardley Cross.
14. Cross Rache.
15. Little Head.
16. Darty Hole Rache.
17. Devil's House Rache.
18. Limpenhoe Rache.
19. Cantley Red House.
20. Cantley Rache.
21. Under Langley.
22. Langley Uppershot Rache.
23. Langley Lowershot Rache.
24. Hassingham Deke.
25. Buckenham Rache.
26. Buckenham Ferry.
27. Buckenham Horseshoes.
28. Ashentree Rache.
29. Rockland Rache.

30. Rockland Dig [Dyke?].
31. Trane.
32. Coldham Hall.
33. Brundall Short Rache.
34. Brundall Long Rache.
35. Ditches Deke.
36. Grace House [*i.e.* Cart-grease Manufactory].
37. Surlingham Ferry.
38. Horse Shoe Rache.
39. Six Mil' Staith Rache.
40. Underhills, or Jimmy Norton's Rache.
41. Bramerton's Woods End.
42. Posick [Poswick] Rache.
43. Posick Grove.
44. Thorpe Short Rache.
45. Whittingham Rache.
46. Cave Rache.
47. Thorpe.
48. Cut.

I don't suppose my particular wherryman's memory was faultless, so submit this list as a draft to be corrected. Wonderfully nice fellows many of these wherrymen are, and I hope their business will never be superseded by steam, for the big brown or black sails leaning stately and steadily over up and down the river are strangely picturesque.

Steam on these placid waters seems sadly out of place; most of the steam launches are noisy puffing abominations, and of the two pleasure-steamers, though one, the *Jenny Lind*, is respectably quiet, the *Jumbo* has made its bad name known to everyone who knows the Yare. A great big brutal paddleboat, which keeps on a steady Juggernaut-like progress, wholly regardless of sailing-boats or fishing-punts, swamping the first and spoiling the sport of the occupiers of the second, while its wash tears away great pieces of the 'rond,' is a public nuisance, and ought to have been indicted as such long ago. A duck-gun full of grey peas let go at the steersman at a safe distance would have done much good; but we have a little chance of peace and rest now, for she has recently swamped an influential solicitor and his family. Boats which ply to a cathedral city should avoid swamping solicitors who live in its close, and I shall be very much surprised and disappointed if the ugly nuisance is allowed up the Yare next year.

These, however, are very wide digressions, and we will go on up the river. The little river—brook, we should call it elsewhere—is the Chet (pronounced soft), which is sometimes navigable up to Loddon, but you must have a fair wind to get up it, for it is little better than a dyke—and, after all, I never knew of anyone who ever wanted to go to Loddon, so it does not matter.

The single-shafted stone cross on our left is Hardley Cross, the boundary of the jurisdiction of the city of Norwich. Here, yearly, the officials of the corporation make their solemn proclamation: 'If there be any manner of person who will absume, purfy, implead, or present any action,' etc. They do not know (nor do I) what 'absume' and 'purfy' mean, but that is immaterial. Once the town clerk was asked what he would do if anyone came forward and said he wanted to absume and purfy. 'Tell him to go and do it at once,' was the official's safe reply.

Buckenham Ferry is simply a riverside public-house, and when we get by it we come to the openings of two little broads—Rockland on the left and Strumpshaw on the right. The latter is nearly grown over, and it is hard to shove one's way in the 'jolly' up the very narrow reed-overhung channel still left. After a mile or two's hard work, however, you break into an acre or so of, perhaps, as secluded and lonely water as there is still left in England, and lovely in an inverse proportion to its size.

Still farther down the river is Coldham Hall—the riparian population living in two or three cottages, and a small, red-brick public-house, famous for Norwich bean-feasts and fishing competitions. There are plenty of fish here for those who know how to catch them. Last time we put up here there were two men pulling them out at about six a minute (they caught one hundred and twenty!), and my wife and the skipper meanly went and moored alongside them, hoping to share their luck, and were rewarded, for three hours' labour, with *three!* Of course the successful fishers had baited heavily. There is a good boat-builder's yard here, and if the sailor has come to grief, or wants to build or convert a boat, he might do worse than give Gibbs a turn.

A little farther down to the left is the entrance to Surlingham Broad, the nearest broad to Norwich. It is not a large one, but it is very pretty, and has plenty of watery lanes and avenues, bowered over with reeds and flowers of all sorts, and, except when there is a bean-feast on, is as quiet and pleasant as any of the more secluded broads.

Straight in front of us, as we go on farther still, we see Brundall Hall—a fine, big white house, looking out of a grove of trees right down the river towards

Yarmouth, and on about as fine a site for a house as any in the country. Brundall itself is a little place on a green hill, sloping down to the river, with the railway running at its foot.

Bramerton Wood End is the white, farmhouse-like building on the left, with a high bank behind it; while on the opposite side, to the right, is Postwick Grove, a pretty wooded hill with some old trees. The ruined church on the top of the hill to the left is Whitlingham, and very picturesquely it stands.

Soon after the banks lower, and by Crown Point it is low and marshy—a strange site for the Bishop's country house, the ruins of which peep through the trees. The village to the right is Thorpe—the Richmond of Norwich—which is extremely well situate on the water's edge. Up on high, on the hill behind, is a big tower, with a wart-like little turret growing out of it. This, down south, we should call 'Taylor's Folly,' but for all that it commands the best view in Norwich—bar that from the cathedral. We do not, however, wind round by it, for the railway cut keeps straight to the left, and soon lands us first to the railway, and then to Carrow Bridge. No traces of the once famous Abbey of Carrow are visible from the river, though there are some still existent on the high ground. The round flint tower up the hill to the left is the 'Snuff Tower,' while that on the bank to our right is the 'Boom Tower,' and both no doubt form part of the patriotic work undertaken for his city by that good burgess, Richard Spynk, in 1342. Colman's mustard-works occupy hundreds of yards of the bank before we get to Carrow Bridge, and form a small town by themselves; but the other waterside manufactories are, with one exception, of no importance, and nothing need be noticed but the picturesque backs of the old buildings in King's Street, till we get in sight of the new 'Foundry Bridge,' and end our water-trip literally at the gates of the Thorpe station of the G. E. R.

XV.

THE SUPERSTITIONS, FOLK-LORE AND DIALECT.

HE earlier traditions and semi-political prophecies, treated at length in vol. i., pp. 209 *et seq.*, of the 'N. and N. A. S. Trans.,' and by myself at pp. 18, 19 of my 'Tourist's Guide' to the county, are now almost wholly lost and forgotten. People still mysteriously hint, as I have already said, that

> 'He who would Old England win,
> Must at Weybourne Hoop begin;'

but all the old tales, how a traitorous mayor shall let a French king in there; how the Danish duke with sixteen great lords shall land at 'Weybourne Stone,' and fight a disastrous battle there, and how the miller with three thumbs shall hold three kings' horses on the Rackheath Road, during the progress of a terrible fight, which shall kill off nearly every man in the county—are now clean forgotten. Most of our prophesying is done out of penny almanacs, and our best-known local herbalist and simple-culler (that I should live to write it!) gets his stock-in-trade from Covent Garden by rail! We have 'cunning men' still, but they are not powers in the land like 'Allen the Prophesyer' was in 1551, of whom Underhill, in his 'Autobiography,'* says that 'this Alen was called the God of Northfolke before they received the light of the Gospel.' The present cunning man is literally what his name implies—a man more able and cunning than his neighbours, and who adds to his income by imposing on them. He should be careful, however, if he wants to sustain his reputation, to have 'no visible means of subsistence,' or his character will suffer. Not long ago a small farmer near Dereham, being perturbed in his mind about a bad arm and some pigs, both of which he considered 'overlooked,' had himself driven over to the house of the cunning man whom he wished to consult. On asking for the wizard, the latter's wife replied that he was 'troshing' (threshing) in the barn, upon which the client promptly told his driver to turn the mare's head round, for he could be no cunning man if he did hard work.

Of 'carriage-and-four ghosts' we have specimens at Caistor, Pulham Market, Great Melton, and Blickling. The latter is the best story, for there are duplicate carriages, in one of which Anne Boleyn is driven, headless, down the avenue; while in the other her father, Sir Thomas, has to cross forty county bridges, pursued by all the fiends of hell for his share in his daughter's death. The ghastly story of the

* Cam. Soc., p. 330.

self-moving coffins is about Blickling, too; while not far off Lady Dorothy Walpole, the 'Grey Lady,' walks systematically at Rainham. She is described as a young and interesting woman who was forced, against her will, to marry Lord Townsend, in 1713, and I was told by a kinsman of hers how he saw the apparition. The 'lie with circumstance' was related, one windy and wet night, at the now closed 'Chequers,' at Brandon, with such detail and so many solemn asseverations, that I hardly dared sneak off to bed. Subsequent researches, which convinced me that so far from the lady dying of a broken heart, she lived long and ended a very prosaic life very quietly, have led me to disbelieve the whole story. Indeed, if we believe her other kinsman the gossip and the 'Wentworth Papers,' she was very little, if at all, better than she ought to have been. Of course, the recent appearance of a tall, priest-like figure to a well-known antiquary, while dozing over his books at Mannington Hall, is well known to Norfolk men.

How an escaped female lunatic, in white, ran barefooted and silent, but for her shrieks, alongside the gig of a hard-headed auctioneer, and temporarily converted him to a full belief in the uncanny world, is a well-known North-Norfolk joke, as also is the trick played with a black ram and a chain, which was turned out to meet some farmers, so as to represent the 'Shuck Dog,' the great, black, fiendish animal that patrols the northern coasts nightly, and which brings death within the year to anyone who meets it.

The fishermen, particularly, are very superstitious, and don't care to be out of doors after dark, on the land. Their prayer is curious*:

> 'Pray God lead us,
> Pray God speed us,
> From all evil defend us,
> Fish for our pains God send us;
> Well to fish and well to haul,
> And what He pleases to pay us all.
>   A fine night to land our nets,
>   And safe in with the land—
>   Pray God, hear my prayer.'

The only appearance, if it can be called so, which puzzles me, is a 'light' which has been showing lately at Runton, near Cromer. It is said to issue from a hedgerow, cross a field, and disappear in a fir-spinney. Many credible people have seen it, and a superstitious glamour is cast over the matter by a statement that it goes into the ground just where some human bones were once found. I believe myself that it may be the reflection of Cromer revolving light, cast on a bank of fog or vapour, which may appear under certain atmospheric conditions. But this theory, and that of " Will-o'-the-wisps," is scouted, because the ground is high and dry, and well drained.

Another inexplicable story is that told both of Rainthorpe and Ashwellthorpe Halls—how a stranger came into the hall in bygone times and planted an acorn, which grew into an oak of large size then and there, and

* E.C.C., p. 274.

> ‘Tew gostlings, young and green,
> Then there came " whewting " in,’

and carried away the oak out of the hall.

Of ‘Men of Gotham’ stories, I think the most amusing is that about the ‘Holt knowing ones,’ who being annoyed by the hooting of an owl, caught it and put it up a waterspout in the church tower, in the full assurance that it would be drowned the next rainfall, and who were extremely disappointed to see it emerge at the other end and fly away.

I have collected from all sources open to me the following epitome of the FOLK-LORE of Norfolk, which may be divided as follows:

DEATH, AND OMENS OF DEATH.

1. The limp corpse foretells, or is a warning of, another death.—*Vide* Henry Daveney in *Notes and Queries*, 1st Ser., vol. x., p. 156; and Rev. A. Sutton, Rector of West Tofts, *ibid.*, p. 88. Compare Grose's 'Superstition,' p. 48. This seems common in Durham and elsewhere in England.—*Notes and Queries*, 1st Ser., vol. x., p. 253.

2. If you bring yew into the house at Christmas amongst the other evergreens, you will have a death in the family before the end of the year. —Forby, p. 413.

3. If a branch of may, or whitethorn, is brought into the house, it brings with it misfortune and death.—*Notes and Queries*, 4th Ser., vol. i., p. 550.

4. If you overturn a loaf of bread in the oven you will have a death in the house.—Forby, p. 414.

5. A failure of ash-keys portends a death in the royal family.—Forby, p. 406.

6. If you watch in the church porch on St. Mark's night (25th April) you will see the apparitions of those who will die or have any dangerous illness during the following year.—Forby, p. 407; and *vide* 'Norf. Arch. Original Papers,' vol. ii., p. 295.

7. To hear the cuckoo's first note when in bed, betokens illness or death to the hearer or one of his family. If a cuckoo light on touchwood or on a rotten bough and cuckoos, betokens death. —'Norf. Arch. Orig. Pap.,' vol. ii., p. 301.

To Courtship and Marriage, etc.

1. A clover of two if you put in your shoe,
The next man you meet in field or lane
Will be your husband or one of the name.
G. A. Carthew, in *Notes and Queries*,
1st Ser., vol. vi., p. 601.

2. Bishop, bishop, Barnabee,*
Tell me when my wedding be!
If it be to-morrow day,
Take your wings and fly away.

---

* Otherwise 'Bishee, bishee, Barnabee,' etc. (F. C. Husenbeth in same vol. of *Notes and Queries*, p. 286), and 'Buskye, buskye, Byrnie Bee,' etc. (E. S. Taylor, E. A., p. 301).

> Fly to the East, fly to the West,
> And fly to him that I love best.
> > *Notes and Queries.*, 2nd Ser., vol. vii., p. 198.

3. A humble bee flying in at the window betokens a stranger coming. If it has a red tail, a man ; if a white, a woman.—*Notes and Queries*, 4th Ser., vol. ii., p. 221.

4. A long stalk in the tea-cup betokens a tall, a short one a little, stranger.—*Ibid.*

5. If one blows at the tuft on a seeding dandelion, you can tell how many years it will be before you are married by the number of puffs you take to blow all the seeds away.—Forby, p. 424.

6. If you take a leaf of the yarrow plant and tickle the inside of your nose, saying—

> Yarroway, yarroway, bear a white blow,
> If my love loves me my nose will bleed now.

And if your nose does bleed, your lover does love you.—*Ibid.*

7. If a young woman on St. Mark's Eve goes out alone into the garden at midnight and sows some hempseed, saying at the same time—

> Hemp-seed I sow—hemp-seed grow,
> He that is my true love
> Come after me and mow—

the figure of the future husband will appear with a scythe and in the act of mowing.—Forby, p. 408.

8. If a young woman on St. Mark's Eve, while quite alone, bakes the 'dumb cake,' made of an eggful each of salt, wheat-meal, and barley-meal, before the fire, a little before midnight, and fasts and holds her tongue during the operation, the sweetheart will come in exactly at midnight and turn the cake. The door must be left open.—Forby, p. 408.

9. When an old maid dies the steeple nods.—*Notes and Queries*, 2nd Ser., vol. iii., p. 199.

The spire of Great Yarmouth is said to have got crooked through a virgin having once been married in the church.

10. They that wive
     Between sickle and scythe
     Shall never thrive.
            'Norf. Arch. Trans.,' vol. ii., p. 203.

This probably relates to its being unlucky to waste any time during the harvest.

To Certain Days in the Year.

1. Candlemas Day:
   (*a*) On Candlemas Day, if the sun shines clear,
   The shepherd had rather see his wife on her bier.
            E. S. Taylor, in *Notes and Queries*, 1st Ser., vol. xi., p. 239. Also see 'Norf. Arch. Trans.,' vol. ii., p. 294.

This is an allusion to the mortality among the

ewes and lambs during the consequent bad weather. It seems a modern version of the old Latin proverb:

'Si sol splendescat, maria purificante
Major erit glacies post quam fuit ante.'

See also F. C. Husenbeth in *Notes and Queries*, 1st Ser., vol. xi., page 335, and distich in the 'Norwich Domesday' on St. Swithin's Day, quoted in *Notes and Queries*, 2nd Ser., vol. vii., p. 450.

(b) As far as the sun shines in on Candlemas Day,
So far will the snow blow in before old May.
Ibid., also 'Norf. Arch. Trans.,' vol. ii., p. 294.

(c) The farmer should have on Candlemas Day
Half his stover [turnips—new version] and half his hay.—*Ibid.*

(d) At Candlemas cold come to us.—*Ibid.*

(e) Candlemas Day the good huswife's geese lay,
Valentine's Day yours and mine may.—*Ibid.*

(f) You should on Candlemas Day
Throw candle and candlestick away.
Ibid., also see 'Norf. Arch. Trans.,' vol. ii., p. 294.

(g) When Candlemas Day is come and gone,
The snow won't lie on a hot stone.—*Ibid.**

(h) All the Christmas evergreens must be re-

---

* The sun by Candlemas Day has so much power that the snow won't stop long unthawed.

moved on Candlemas Eve, or some misfortune will happen.—Forby, p. 415.

2. St. Valentine's Day:
 (a) For an account of St. Valentine's Eve at Norwich, see *Notes and Queries*, 1st Ser., vol. x., p. 5. For old custom of 'catching valentines,' see Forby, p. 423.

 (b) At Ryburgh, on St. Valentine's Day, the children go round the village for contributions, singing—

> God bless the baker!
> If you will be the giver
> I will be the taker.
> *Notes and Queries*, 4th Ser., vol. v., p. 595.

 (c) On St. Valentine
All the birds in the air in couples do join [jine].
—Forby, p. 418.

3 St. Mathias's Day (24th Feb.).
 (a) This is the farmer's day.—'Norf. Arch. Trans.,' vol. ii., p. 295.

 (b) If the bushes hang of a drop before sunrise, it will be a dropping season; if the bushes be dry, we may look for a dry summer.—*Ibid.*

 (c) St. Matthew get candlesticks new
St. Matthi lay candles by.—Forby, p. 418.

4. St. Mark's Eve:
 (a) The brakes drop their seed at midnight. The top rolls up quite close and the seed falls.—*Ibid.*

(b) The appearances of all who are to die or be married can be seen at midnight in the church porch.—*Ibid.*

5. Ash Wednesday:

    Wherever the wind lies on Ash Wednesday it continues during the whole of Lent.—Forby, p. 414.

6. Good Friday:

    (a) If work be done on Good Friday, it will be so unlucky that it will have to be done over again.—'Norf. Arch. Trans.,' vol. ii., p. 296.

    (b) One must not wash on Good Friday. This is in the Bible. Christ once went on Good Friday for a walk, and asked a woman for a draught of water, and she gave him water with soapsuds in it. Therefore, etc.—[Told me on Good Friday, 1874, by my servant, Susan Abbs, from Runton.]

    (c) Cake baked on Good Friday never gets mouldy. It is good for diarrhœa. The same is said of Good Friday bread.—Forby, p. 402.

7. Easter:

    Baked custards should be eaten at Easter and cheesecakes at Whitsuntide.—*Notes and Queries*, 3rd Ser., vol. i., p. 248. A tansey pudding on Easter Sunday.—Forby, p. 422.

8. Midsummer Day:

> Cut your thistles before St. John,
> You will have two instead of one.
>
> Forby, p. 418.

9. Holyrood Day:

> On Holyrood Day the Devil goes a-nutting.— Forby, p. 418.

10. Michaelmas Day:

> If you do not baste the goose on Michaelmas Day, you will want money all the year.— Forby, p. 414.

11. St. Andrew's Day:

> St. Andrew the king
> Three days and three weeks before Christmas comes in.
>
> Forby, p. 418.

12. Christmas :*

> (a) At Christmas Eve, at midnight, animals rise and turn to the east. The horse will stay some time on his knees, and move his head about and blow over the manger.—' Norf. Arch. Trans.,' vol. ii., p. 296.
>
> (b) The rosemary blooms on Old Christmas Day.—*Ibid.*
>
> (c) If you bring yew into the house at Christmas with the other evergreens, there will be a death in the family before the end of the year.—Forby, p. 413.

* For Christmas carols see *Notes and Queries*, 4th series, iii., p. 90 : 'Oh ! here's to the one ho !'

(d) At old Christmas the days are longer by a cock-crow.—Forby, p. 418.

13. Childermas Day:

On whatever day of the week the 28th of December falls, that day is an unlucky day for the ensuing year.—Forby, p. 405.

To the Weather, etc.

1. First comes David and then comes Chad,
And then comes Winneral [St. Winnold] as though he was mad;
White or black or old house-thack [thatch].
Notes and Queries, 1st Ser., vol. i., p. 349.

2. If the ash is out before the oak it foretells rain.—*Notes and Queries*, 2nd Ser., vol. x., p. 256.

3. The grass that grows in Janiveer
Grows no more all the year.
Forby, p. 418.

4. Night rains make drowned fens.—*Notes and Queries*, 1st Ser., vol. vi., p. 601.

5. Ne'er cast a clout till May be out.—*Notes and Queries*, 1st Ser., vol. vi., p. 601.

6. A wet Sunday a wet week.—Forby, p. 416.

7. Saturday's change and Sunday's full
Never brought good and never wull.
F. C. Husenbeth, in *Notes and Queries*, 2nd Ser., vol. ii., p. 316; and 'Norf. Arch. Trans.,' vol. ii., p. 297.

Another version is in Forby, p. 417:

> 'On Saturday new or Sunday full
> Was never good and never wull.'

8. A Saturday's moon
   If it comes once in seven years comes too soon.
   Forby, p. 416.

9. Another version is:

   > On Saturday new and Sunday full
   > Never brought good and never wull.
   Forby, p. 417.

10. When the weirling shrieks at night,
    Sow the seed with the morning light,
    But when the cuckoo swells its throat
    Harvest flies from the mooncall's throat.

This is in *Notes and Queries*, 1st Ser., p. 614, called the 'Wilby Warning,' but from its phraseology I should say it was decidedly modern.

11. When a sun dog (two black spots) comes on the south side of the sun there will be fine weather, when on the north side there will be foul. The sun then fares to be right muddled and crammed down by the dog.—'Norf. Arch. Trans.,' vol. ii., p. 297.

12. If you see the old moon with the new there will be stormy weather.—*Ibid.* (*Vide* Ballad of Sir Patrick Spens.)

13. If it rains on a Sunday before the church doors are open, it will rain all the week more or less,

or else we shall have three rainy Sundays.—*Ibid.*

The old version used to be :

> If it rains on Sunday before mass,
> It rains all the week more or less.

14. If it rains the first Thursday after the moon comes in, it will rain more or less all the while the moon lasts, especially on Thursdays.—*Ibid.*

15. If there be bad weather, and the sun does not shine all the week, it is sure to show forth some time on the Saturday.—*Ibid.*

16. If Noah's Ark show many days together there will be foul weather [I do not understand this].—*Ibid.*

17. On three nights in the year it never lightens (clears up) anywhere, and if a man knows these nights he would not turn a dog out.—*Ibid.*

18. If the hen moult before the cock, we get a winter as hard as a rock ;
    If the cock moult before the hen, we get a winter like a spring.—*Ibid.*

19. If the evening star rides low in the summer (*i.e.* with the leading star of the bear's tail above it) there will be a bad crop.—*Ibid.*

20. If the cuckoo on the last week he goes keeps on the top branches of the oaks and makes a noise, it is a sign of a good harvest, etc.; but if he keeps on the lower branches it is a bad sign.—*Ibid.*, p. 301.

To Various Subjects.

1. Them that ever mind the world to win,
Must have a black cat, a howling dog, and a crowing hen.—*Ibid.*, p. 302.

2. Cutting your nails on Monday means health; Tuesday, wealth; Wednesday, news; Thursday, new shoes; Friday, sorrow; Saturday, seeing your sweetheart the next day; Sunday, the devil.—Forby, p. 411.

3. White spots on the nails are lucky.

4. It is dangerous to let blood in the dog-days.—*Ibid.*, p. 413.

5. It is very unlucky to burn green elder.—*Ibid.*, p. 414.

6. It is unlucky not to wear at least some new article of dress on Easter Sunday.—*Ibid.*

7. It is unlucky to burn the withes or bands of faggots.—*Ibid.*, p. 415.

8. Dogs howling is a sign of ill-luck.

9. It is unlucky to buy bees; they should be obtained by barter.—*Ibid.*

10. It is unlucky to turn a loaf over in the oven.—*Ibid.*

11. It is unlucky to leave a candle to burn in the room by itself.—*Notes and Queries*, 1st Ser., vol. xii., p. 488.

12. It is unlucky to have rooks build near your house.—Forby, p. 414.

13. It is lucky to see the moon over the left shoulder. —*Ibid.*, p. 415.

14. If you bring a few flowers into a house at a time there will be but few chickens there.—*Notes and Queries*, 4th Ser., vol. i., p. 550.
15. Down corn, down horn.—W.R., 1866.
16. If you swear, you will catch no fish.—Forby, p. 414.
17. Fish are plentiful when fleas are plentiful.—*Notes and Queries*, 3rd Ser., vol. viii., p. 288.
18. If snakes could hear and slows could see,
    Nor man nor beast would ever be free.
    Ibid., 4th Ser., vol. vii., p. 547.
19. To cure hooping-cough, catch a house spider and tie it up in muslin and pin it over the mantelpiece, and when it dies the cough goes away.—*Ibid.*, 2nd Ser., vol. i., p. 386.

QUAINT SAYINGS.

The late Rev. E. Gillett, of Runcham (E.G.R.), had a most amusing collection of these, which he told me he intended publishing under the title of 'A Latch of Links;' but his untimely death prevented this, and I do not know where his MS. is.

A long collection of East Anglian proverbs, etc., will be found at pp. 427-435 of Forby.

Those in the text marked 'W.R.' are, I think, new, and are from my personal observation.

1. He has no more sense than a May gosling.—W.R.
2. On and on like a pig in a harvest-field.—W.R.
3. The kettle call the pot black-face.—W.R.
4. At fifty years of age a man is either a fule or a doctor.—W.R.

5. The last of eleven stone of hemp.—W.R.
6. He lies like a tooth-drawer.—W.R.
7. Sunday saint and week-day devil.—W.R.
8. As wooden as a pump.—W.R.
9. As lame as a tree.—W.R.
10. As old as Carlton Common.—W.R.
11. As deep as Chelsea (Reach).—*Notes and Queries*, 2nd Ser., vol. iii., p. 258.
12. Tew eager, like Farmer Cubitt's calf as drotted tree moyles to suck a bull.—W.R.
13. No more ear for music than Farmer Ball's bull, as dossed the fiddler over the bridge.—W.R.
14. A man who has had four wives is said to have shod the horse all round.—*Notes and Queries*, 4th Ser., vol. iv., p. 300.

The Local Rhymes

I have been able to collect, are neither numerous nor particularly amusing, viz.:

1. Halvergate hares, Reedham rats,
    Southwood swine, and Cantley cats,
    Acle asses, Moulton mules;
    Beighton bears, and Freethorpe fools.
     Notes and Queries, 1st Ser., vol. ii., p. 150.

2. Blickling flats, Aylsham fliers,
    Marsham peewits, and Hevingham liars.
     E. S. Taylor, in *Notes and Queries*,
     1st Ser., vol. ii., p. 150.

Superstitions, Folk-Lore, and Dialect. 305

3. Gimmingham, Trimmingham, Knapton and Trunch,
    Northrepps and Southrepps, all in a bunch.
    Ibid.

4.   Cromer crabs,
    Runton dabs;
    Beeston babies,
    Sherringham ladies;
    Weybourne [Cley] witches [bitches]
    Salthouse ditches;
    Langham fairmaids,
    Blakeney bulldogs, [*var.* bowheads];
    Morsta dodmen,*
    Binham bulls,
    Stiffkey trolls [*var.* blues]; †
    Wells bitefingers, ‡
    And the Blakeney people
    Stand on the steeple,
    And crack hazel-nuts
    With a five-farthing beetle.
    C. W. Barkeley, in *Notes and Queries*, 4th Ser., vol. iv., p. 331; as added to from my own collection.

5. Rising was, Lynn is, and Downham shall be,
    The greatest seaport of the three.
        J. N. Chadwick, in *Notes and Queries*,
          1st Ser., vol. iii., p. 206.

° Dodmen—snails.
† Blues—mussels.
‡ A Wells sailor is said to have bitten off a drowned man's finger to get his ring.

6. Rising was a seaport town,
　　And Lynn it was a waste;
　　But Lynn it is a seaport town,
　　And Rising fares the worst.
Ibid.

7. That nasty, stinking sink-hole of sin,
　　Which the map of the county denominates Lynn.
Ibid.

8. Caistor was a city ere (when?) Norwich was none,
　　And Norwich was built of Caistor stone.
Ibid.

9. 　　Denton in the Dale
　　And Arborough in the Dirt,
　　And if you go to Homersfield
　　Your purse will get the squirt.
Fuller.

10. 'Twixt Lopham Ford and Shimpling thorn
　　England shall be won and lorn.
　　Old Court-Book of Shimpling Manor.

The Dialect[*]

Of Norfolk has been exhaustively treated upon—per-

---

[*] A long list of all authors on this dialect will be found in the Appendix to the 'Prompt. Parvulor.,' p. lxxxii. The more important works on the subject are Forby's 'Vocabulary' (2 vols., 1830), with Supplementary Volume by the Rev. W. T. Spurdens (1858); 'Promptorium Parvulorum' (ed. by A. Way for the Camden Soc.), and Gnatt's 'Etymological and Comparative Glossary' (compressed in his 'Guide to Yarmouth and Lowestoft,' 1866); 'Sea Words and Phrases along the Suffolk Coast,' *East Anglian*, iii., p. 347, and iv., p. 109; 'A Capful of Sea Slang,' *East Anglian*, iv., p. 261 (these two articles were by the late Edward Fitzgerald; 'Additions to Forby,' by the Rev. F. Gillett, iv., pp. 128, 156; and 'Norfolk Words not in Forby,' by the Rev. G. J. Chester, 'Nor. Arch.,' v., p. 188.

haps too much so—by many writers, who have included in their vocabularies many words which are common to the whole of England. What will strike the stranger's ear as being most unusual in the fields will be 'deke, holl,' or 'hull' (*e.g.*, 'he hulled it into the holl;' *i.e.*, threw it into the ditch), 'pulk, dolestone,' 'par-yard,' 'largess,' 'ligger,' 'pightel,' 'levenses and fourses,' 'driftway,' and the right of 'shackage.' Up the rivers and broads, as he is 'quonted' along in a wherry, he will notice a man on the 'rond' 'dydling.' In the evening he will probably see either the 'roke' or an 'eynd' rise, and may hap to sail under a 'perry wind,' or be upset by a 'Roger's blast.'

Indoors he may be sent to bed in either the 'parlour-chamber' or the 'kitchen-chamber,' the floor of which will be wiped up by a 'dwile.' The goodwife may be 'haffling and jaffling' with a neighbour, and come in and tell you she thinks her very 'dis-improved,' as she is not 'jannock' now, and is tolerably sure to give her children either 'coshies' or 'loggetts' to quiet them if they make too much 'dullor,' while she pours you out a glass of ale from a 'gotch' into a 'beaker,' and she 'froizes' you a pancake. A Norfolk man will say to you, 'Come to *mine*,' or tell you he had been to '*his*'—house being understood in each case. He will talk of a 'mawther' who may or may not be his 'dafter,' and if he is speaking to two or three will call you 'together.' He cannot pronounce 'h' when it comes after 't,' so is compelled to say 'tew' and 'tree' for two and three, and 'trew' for through; while his vocative appellation for a man is 'bor,' and for a woman 'mor.' Lastly, I regret to say he always, and in the most unblushing way, says 'wulgar' for vulgar.

'That gate *hang* high;' 'but *hinder* none.' Inscription at Kimberly to Jno. Jenkyns, Mus. Doc.: 'Under this stone rare Jenkyns *lie*.'

The following specimen of dialogue was given me the other day as being taken down from the mouth of an East Norfolk gardener. Emphasized as italicized.

'As I was *jump*ing t' holl from *Farm*er *Thirk*ettle's little *pigh*tle inteu t' rhoed, she come up teu me and say :

'"Can I get trew *here* ?"

'"Iss," said I ; "but it is no *mat*ter of a rhoed."

'"Whawt?" said she.

'"It's only a *drift*way like," sed I.

'"Eh ?" sed she.

'"Nobbut a *pack*way," sed I.

'"Oh," said she ; "and which way deu I go?"

'"Yew go as the *rhoed* go, for tew or tree hundred *yard* till you come teu a *par*yard," sed I.

'"Teu whawt ?" sed she,' etc., etc.

Of dialect ballads we have few. There is an amusing one, telling how Giles Jolterhead, a joskin raw, took his 'darter Dinah' to the Norwich Festival, printed in 'E. A.,' ii., p. 67 ; and the Rev. E. Gillett translated the 'Song of Solomon' into Norfolk, for Prince Bonaparte, in his polyglot version of that poem. The most readable of all the dialect stories of the present day are 'Giles's Trip to London,' and the rest of the series ; these are very clever and deservedly popular, and have run to a great number of editions. The difficulty in getting the country people to let you take notes of their local words, or, indeed, to use them in your presence at all, is very great. There are, indeed, some more sensible than others, and among them is my old skipper, Tungate, who sails my old boat, called the *Lotus*. Here are some notes I have taken down from his mouth, and as he is about seventy-seven, and is pure-bred Norfolk, they may be depended on. Sickles, in Norfolk and Suffolk, used to be slightly toothed or ragged-edged—a sharpened sickle ought to be called a 'rape (reap) hook.' A 'flagg' is the top spit of a marshy meadow; a 'turf' is cut *down* after the 'flagg' is skinned off. It is always 4 inches by 4 inches by 3 feet long. Six score go to the hundred. 'My father used to cut 'em and lay 'em one hundred and twenty in thirteen minutes, but I got to do 'em in eleven minutes and a half.'

'Hay (have) you got the guy rope?'
'Undernain' = Underneath.
Dingling about = Hanging or swinging about.
'Then in her byes' = Then in her best.
'I will stick-lick him' = I will beat him with a stick.
'He *driv* home' = He drove home.
Hakes = Hooks.
Poyles = Piles.
Moyles = Miles.
Roding line = Roeing line.
The gun was 'loaden.'
Wretts = Warts.
To lig = To lie (hence *ligger*).
Musharoom = Mushroom.

'I cast him such a dab,' 'I punched him good tidily.'
'I rew him' = I rowed him.
Ganging = Going.
'We are not so *pent* for half-an-hour' = Pressed.
'We har tew hev' = We ought to have.
Jiffling = Fidgety.

INDEX.

ABORIGINES, the, 1
'Absume and purfy,' 283
Acle, 268
Acoustic pottery, 197
Advertising for clerical preferment by 'setting bills upon Paul's door,' 184
Ale drinkings, 151
Alen, 'the god of Northfolke,' 288
Antingham, two churches and ponds, 225
Armada, preparations in Norfolk for resisting, 79
Ascetic, the Champion, 177 n.
Ash-Wednesday, folk-lore as to, 297
Aulepimen, 107
Aylmer, Bishop, escapes martyrdom by hiding in a wine-butt, 187
Aylmerton, shrieking-pits, 1, 227
Aylsham, 226

Bachelors, the comely, of Norwich, 71
Bacton, otherwise Bromholm Abbey, 246
Barn, the great, at Paston, 247
Barningham, 226
Barsham, East, manor-house, 231
Barton Broad, 265
Bawbergh, St. Walstan of, 175
Beacon towers, churches used as, 197
Beccles River, 276
Beccles, 278
Beer, 263
'Bees,' American: query derived from our Norfolk beeves, 111
Bill of fare, monastic, 168

Bilney, the martyr, 187
Binham Abbey, 230
Biskele, St. Wandred of, 175
'Black currant car,' 262
Blakeney, 228
'Blanchflower,' a nickname of Norwich castle, 34
Blankest verse on record, the, 252
Blickling, 226
Bondsmen in blood, 106
Bonner, Bishop, was rector of East Dereham, 187
Books, 130
'Borough Hills,' 16
Boom tower, the, 285
Bosses on the roof of Norwich Cathedral, 197
Bowls, saying of a Puritan chaplain as to, 134
Bramerton Woods End, 285
Brandon, 239
Brasses, noticeable, 196
Breydon Water, 274
'Broads and Marshes,' the, 256
Bromholm, the Holy Rood of, 174
Bromholm, otherwise Bacton, Abbey, 246
Brundall Hall, 284
Buckenham Ferry, 283
Burgh Castle, 276
Burgh St. Peters, 277
'Burgh' and 'Borough' Hills along coast, 228
Burghers, fortified houses, 156
Burnham and its oysters, 230
Butcher's meat, a man who had never tasted, 109

Caister Castle, a Roman work, 219
Caister Castle, by Yarmouth, 242-3
Calthorp, how Sir Philip, gave a shoemaker a lesson in fashion, 144
Candlemas-day, folk-lore as to, 294
'Carriage-and-four Ghosts,' 288
Carrow Bridge, Abbey, and Works, 285.
Castle Acre, 233
Castle Rising, 255
Castles and Castle building, 33
Cenimagni, 2
Chantries, growth of, superseded foundation of monasteries (?), 42
Chest, fine church, at Dersingham, 197
Chet, the, 283
Chevage, 107
Chivalry (?), 128
Christmas, folk-lore as to, 298
Church-breaking by a chaplain, 183
'Church Rock,' the, at Cromer, 250
Churches, the overstock of, 43
Churches, nearly all of flint, 191
'City of Orchards,' the, 208
Civil War, 85
Clere pedigree, early part of, fabricated, 31, 226
Clergy, lawlessness of the early, 181
Clergy, their early right to marry, 182
Cley, 228
'Clocher,' the, at East Dereham, 232
Coast roads, lost (?), 246
Cockell=coquaille (?), 168
'Cocking,' 133
'Coke of Norfolk,' 253
Coldham Hall, 284
Coltishall, 223
Cossey Park, 218
Courtship and marriage, folk-lore as to, 292
Cricket, 135
Cringleford, St. Albert of, 176
Cromer, 249
Cromwell, his Norfolk descent on his mother's side, 91
Crostwight, the Holy Rood of, 176
Crown Point, 285
'Cunning man,' the, 288

Danes, conjectured pre-Roman settlement of, 3
Danes, the subsequent or Pirate, 19
Danish surnames still in Norfolk, 20, elsewhere in England, 21 *n*.
Death and omens, folk-lore as to, 291
Decoys, 131
Denmark, coincidences of place-names in, with place-names in Norfolk, 4
Dereham, East, 232
Devil, the, conjured into a boot, 178
'Devil's ditch,' at Smallburgh, 16
Dialect, the, 306
'Dick Merryfellow,' his political squibs, etc., 104
Dietary, 126-7
Diss, 240; Mere at, 241
Dissenters, 190
Doors, noticeable, 195
Doorways, noticeable, 194
Druids, 2
Drury, Captain, the 'only general' on the king's side in Kett's rebellion, 64, 65, 66, 68
Duels, 139
'Duke's Palace,' 73
Dunmow Flitch, first won by a Norfolk couple, 110
Dussin's Dale, 58, 66
Dutch and Walloon strangers settled in Norwich, 1565-75, their surnames now traceable, 78

Easter, folk-lore as to, 297
Easter Sepulchre at North Wold, 195
'Eastern Association,' Norfolk's part in, 85
Eccles, 244
Elections, 95-105
Elizabeth, Queen, her progress through Norwich, 70
Elmham, North, 232
Elsing, Holy Spirit of, 175

Fakenham, 231
Fisherman's prayer, the, 290
Flegg Hundreds, Danish (?) place-names in, 9
Flegg Hundreds, 268
Flint churches and round towers, 191
Folk-lore, 291
Fonts, noticeable, 195
Forest-bed, the, 221
Freeholders, great number of small, 23
'Freemen,' great number of, in Norfolk and Suffolk, 21
Friars, the life of, 170
Fritton decoy, 276
Funeral etiquette, 143

Garianonum, 276
Gentlemen to be reduced in number to the number of white bulls, in Norfolk, 57
Gentler life, the, 122

Index. 313

Gentry, guilty of murders, 136
Ghostly light at Runton, 227
Gimmingham, 248
'Gladman's insurrection,' 56
Good Friday, folk-lore as to, 297
'Good Sword of Winfarthing,' the, 177
'Grey Lady of Rainham,' 289
'Grimes Graves,' 1, 239
Guilds, increased as foundation of monasteries ceased, 42
Guilds, 146; good customers to the church, *ib*.; rules of, 147
Gunpowder used to blow up a church, 199
Gunton Park, 225; Hall burnt, 225
Gurgoyles, 197

Happisburgh, 244-5
Hardley Cross, 283
Hare pedigree, early part of, fabricated, 31
Harleston, rising of, 1570, 69
Harvest-homes, 117; songs, 118
Hautbois, St. Tebbald of, 176
Hedge, large hawthorn, 267
'Hell Fire Club' at Norwich, 190
Hickling Broad, 268
Hickling Priory, 243, 268
Holkham, 253
'Holy Rood of Bromholm,' 174
Holy Spirit of Elsing, 175
Horning, 262
Horsey Mere, pike, 268
Horstead, St. Margaret of, 176; our Lady of Pity of, 176
Hospitality, 127
Hospitals, 178
Hoveton, St. Margaret of, 176
Howard pedigree, early part of, fabricated, 29
Hundred Stream, the, 266
Hunstanton, 253

Iceni, 2
'Ingham' and 'Ington' terminations, who brought in the, 11
Ingham, 243
'Inns,' private, 125
Inns and inn signs, 160-1
Inscriptions copied, 200; specimens of Norfolk, 200-4
Irstead, 265

James I., his hunting, etc., at Thetford, 94
Jesuits, 187

Jews, persecutions of, 46; as to St. William of Norwich, 46; at Lynn, 47; at Norwich (Jurnepin), 48; caricature of, 51-2
'Jews' Ways,' by Burnham and Burgh Castle, 16
'John Amend-all,' 56
'Johnny Raw,' in 1381, 52
Jordan Fantosme's Chronicle quoted, 123
Justice, sale of, 167

Keels,' 259
Kett's rebellion, 58-68; causes of, misconceived, 1596, 58
Kett family, 60 *n*.
'King John [of France]'s sword,' 236
Knapton Church roof, 247
Knevet, Sir Anthony, refuses to rack Ann Askew, 187
Knights, cheaply made by James I., 141
Knights Hospitallers at Carbrooke, 43
Knights Templars at Haddiscoe. 43
'Knight's fee,' estimate of 800 acres approximately correct, 23

Lake-dwellings at Wretham Mere, 1
'Leeches,' want of skill of the old, 142
Leper-houses, 178
Libraries of the early clergy, 186
Litester's rebellion, 52
Litigation, love of, 113
Local rhymes, 304
Loddon, 241
Ludham bridge, 265; Grange, 267
Luxury shown by furniture, etc., 124
Lynn, guilds, rules, etc., of, 147, *et seq.*
Lynn, 234; brasses, 235; King John's sword, 236
Lynn, siege of, in 1643, 88

Macaulay's description of the country parson vindicated, 184
'Maid Ridibone,' 178
'Maid's Head' at Norwich, 160, 190
Mannington Hall ghost story, 289
Manor Rolls, curious entries in, 113-15
Marriage-making, prosaic, 129
'Marrum Hills,' the, 243
Martham, St. Blythe of, 176
Martyrs, William Sautre of Lynn, the earliest English, 186
'Master John Schorne,' 178

Mercenaries, Italian, employed to suppress Kett's rebellion, 63; one hung, 63
Merchant's marks, 158
Merton Hall, 240
Michaelmas goose long before the Armada, 168
Middleton Tower, 234
Monasteries, the growth of the, 37; built in groups by families (?), 39; relative number of different orders, 41
Monastic account rolls, 164-5
Monks and citizens, riot of, 1272, 52
'Monks and the Friars,' 164
Monuments, noticeable, 196
Monuments of North Erpingham, Tunstead, Happing, and Holt Hundreds copied, 200
'Mount Surrey,' 73.
Mundesley, 248
Mural paintings, noticeable, 195

Nelson's birthplace, 253
'New Cut,' the, 279
Non-jurors, persecutions of, 188
'Norfolk Miscellany,' or 'Robin's Panegyrick,' 101
Norman Conquest, the, 23
Norman landowners, analysis of the chief holdings by, 24
Norman surnames still in Norfolk, 27
Norman pedigrees, examples of fictitious, 28
North Walsham, 224
Norwich, description of, 205-18; castle, 207; cathedral, 213; museum, 220
Nursing, paupers nursed at expense of parish, 117

'O,' pittances called, 166
Organs at Norwich Cathedral threatened to be pulled down by the 'Prentices, 189
Otters, once plentiful, 131
Oulton Broad, 277
Our Lady at Reepham, 175
Our Lady of Walsingham, 172; image and relics, 172-3
Overstrand, 249
Oysters, Burnham, 230

Palgrave quarterings fudged, 226
'Palmer's Way,' 173
Parish Church, Yarmouth, the largest in England, 191
Parsons and their churches, the, 180

Paston, 247
Paston Letters, 243
Pastons, often besieged in their houses, 138; possibly deserved it, 139
Peasant life, the old, 106
'Peddar's Road,' 173
'Peddar's Way,' 17
Pedigrees, examples of forged, 29
Persecutions and risings, 46
Pilgrimages, the chief, 177
'Pilgrimage of Grace,' followed by small local rising here in 1537, 57
Pirates along Norfolk coasts, 84
Pirates, the Yarmouth, 263
Plantations, 219
Poaching, early, 115
Poor's box at Cawston, 197
Porches, noticeable, 195
Potter Heigham, 267; Falgate, 267
Prayer, the fisherman's, 290
Priest's hiding-hole, 187
Printing, early, at Norwich, 77
Prophecies, old, 287
Proverbs, local, 303
Punt-shooting, 275
Puritans, 190

'Rabbit and rye country,' the, 239
Race meetings, 132-3
Rainham ghost story, 289
Ranworth Broad, 264; rood screen, ib.
Reaches on the Norwich River, list of, 281
Rebuses, 159
Rector, highwayman, a, 183
Red Mount Chapel at Lynn, 191
Redman's conspiracy, 69
Reedham, 279
Reepham, our Lady at, 175
Restoration, so called, of churches, 199
'Robin's Panegyrick,' 101
Roman settlements, 14; coins, 16; surnames (?), 18
'Rond,' the, 257
Rood-screens, noticeable, 195
Roof, noticeable, 195
Rotten borough of Castle Rising, 102
'Rough' element in early homes, 135
'Run and ride' livings, 181 n.
Runton, 253
Rushford College, 240

St. Bennet's Abbey, 265; scheme for seizing, 55
St. Faith's fair, scheme for rising at, 55

Index. 315

St. George's guild at Norwich, 155
St. John the Baptist's head at Trimmingham, 175
St. Leonard without Norwich, 175
St. Mark's eve, folk-lore as to, 296
St. Mathias's day, folk-lore as to, 296
St. Olave's, 276
St. Parnell of Stratton, 175
St. Valentine's day, folk-lore as to, 296
St. Walstan of Bawbergh, 175
St. Wandred of Biskele, 175
St. William in the Wood, 176
St. Withberga's Well at East Dereham, 233
St. Withburga, 176
Sandringham, 254
Sautre, William, of Lynn, the earliest English martyr, 187
Saxon settlement, 18
Sayings, quaint, 303
Scala Cœli in St. Michael at Conisford, 176
Scanring, 233
Scole inn, 162
Scottow, 223
Sculpture, 197
Sermon, how a, spoiled a goose worth two of it, 190
'Servi,' few in Norfolk, 21
'Seven marshland churches,' the, 198-237
Sewers often mistaken for subterranean passages, 123
Sexton's wheel at Long Stratton, 197; and at Barningham (?), 197
Shadwell Court (hideous), 240
Sheffield, Lord, slain in Kett's rebellion, 63
Shepherds, a dinner to thirty master, 131
Sherringham, 227
Ship-money, 85
Shipden, 250
Shrieking-pits, 1
Shrines and Holy Wells, 172
'Shuck Dog,' 227, 289
Sidestrand, 249
Sitomagus, 239
'Smock of St. Audrie,' the, 178
Snuff tower, the, 285
Spencer, Bishop, 'the warlike,' 55
Sporting anecdotes, 133-4
'Squire Papers,' 87
Stalls and piscinæ, noticeable, 196
Stratton, St. Parnell of, 175

'Subterranean passages,' usually sewers, 123, 170
Suffolk, countess of, curious escapade of, in 1442, 56
Sun-dogs, 300
'Superstitions, folk-lore, and dialect, 287
Surlingham Broad, 284
Swaffham, 238; the pedlar and the crock of gold, 239
Swedish or Norwegian settlements (?), 9.

'Taylor's Folly,' 285
Terrington, St. Clement's, 238
Thetford, 239
Tobacco-smoking suppressed in 1695, in Methwold, 116
Tombland Fair, 210
Town houses, 159
Town life, the, 144
Towns, the chief, 205
Townshend pedigree, early part of, fabricated, 30
Trades, curious, 157
Trimmingham, 249
'True news from Norwich,' 188
Trotting horses, 132
Tumbler, a dog called, 116
Tyler's (Wat) rebellion, Litester's rebellion a branch of, 52

Viking's ship, 257
'Villani,' few in Norfolk, 21
Villeins, 107
'Virgin troop of Norwich,' 88

Walloon settlers at Norwich, 1565, 75; their surnames now traceable, 77-8
Walpole, Sir Robert, 100-1
Walpole St. Peter, 238
Walsingham Priory, 230
'Walsingham Way,' 173; our Lady of, 172
Walsoken, 237
Walton, W., 238
Wash, the, 237
'Watering-places and coast-line, 242
Waveney, the, 277
Wayside crosses, 178
Weather, folk-lore as to, 299
Wells, 229
Welsh, ran away at Kett's rebellion, 65
Westacre, Sir Thomas of, 176
West Wick, 223

Weybourne, 227-8
Weybourne Pits, 1
Wherries, the, 257
Wherrymen's tales, 260
Whitlingham, 285
'Whole' and 'Half' sisters of Norman's hospital, 179
Wiggenhall St. Germains, 238
Wiggenhall St. Magdalen, 238
'Wilby warning,' the, 300
Windham, William, 134
Wines, mediæval, 126
Winfarthing, the 'good sword' of, 177

Winterton, 243
Wolterton, 226
Women whipped in 1634, 116
Wool trade, said to be introduced into Norfolk in 1336, 75
Worstead, 222
Wretham Mere, 1
Wroxham, 222, 260; broad, 262

Yachts, 258
Yarmouth, 269; policemen at, carry walking-sticks, 274
Yarmouth Church, the largest parish church in England, 191

Elliot Stock, Printer, Paternoster Row, London.

www.ingramcontent.com/pod-product-compliance
Lightning Source LLC
Chambersburg PA
CBHW030740230426
43667CB00007B/786